The Kotler Legacy

Philip Kotler not only has been transforming the world of business but also humanity as we know it.

—José Salibi Neto
Founder of HSM and Author of Disruptive Leadership

Philip Kotler insists marketing must be driven by a deep concern for the Common Good. His work reminds us that marketing isn't just about markets—it's about people, communities, and the future we're building together.

—Christian Sarkar
The Regenerative Marketing Institute

The Kotler Legacy is an inspiring collection of Philip Kotler's most insightful essays. These reflections include the future of marketing, but go far beyond by addressing issues of the common good and democracy. The book offers inspiration for marketers, leaders and citizens alike.

—Prof. Dr. Dr. h.c. mult. Hermann Simon
Founder & Honorary Chairman, Simon-Kucher & Partners

I am glad that Kotler's excellent articles will now be available worldwide for readers seeking insight and clarity on world problems.

—Walter Vieira
Marketing Consultant, Author, Business Columnist,
Visiting Professor Chairman, Consumer Education
and Research Society, India

Kotler Legacy is an absolute must read for anyone interested in becoming a values based leader and doing their part to make the world a better place. Phil has a unique ability to combine business principles, the liberal arts and what it means to be a holistic human being.

—Harry M Jansen Kraemer, Jr.
Professor of Leadership, Northwestern University Kellogg
School of Management Former Chairman and CEO,
Baxter International

THE KOTLER LEGACY

Wisdom from the Father of Modern Marketing

PHILIP KOTLER

EDITOR: KHALID HASAN

Sutherland House Experts

TORONTO, 2026

Sutherland House Experts Corporation
260 Heath Street West
Suite 605
Toronto, Ontario
M5P 3L6

First edition, May 2026

Manufactured in Canada
Cover designed by Jordan Lunn

Library and Archives Canada Cataloguing in Publication
Title: The Kotler legacy : wisdom from the father of modern marketing / Philip Kotler ; edited by Khalid Hasan.
Names: Kotler, Philip, author. | Hasan, Khalid (CEO of ResInt Canada), editor.
Identifiers: Canadiana (print) 20260154024 | Canadiana (ebook) 20260154083 | ISBN 9781997739081 (softcover) | ISBN 9781997739098 (EPUB)
Subjects: LCSH: Social responsibility of business. | LCSH: Marketing. | LCSH: Leadership.
Classification: LCC HD60 .K68 2026 | DDC 658.4/08—dc23

ISBN 978-1-997739-08-1
eBook 978-1-997739-09-8

Dedications by Philip Kotler

This book is lovingly dedicated to my wife Nancy, whose partnership and support have sustained me through a lifetime of learning and teaching. I also give my heartfelt thanks to my three daughters, my nine grandchildren, and my great-grandchildren Isabelle and Levi, who continue to bring joy, meaning, and hope to my life.

CONTENTS

ACKNOWLEDGMENTS

I SINCERELY THANK *MEDIUM*, WHERE these essays were originally published over the years. I am grateful to its owner and editorial team for their support, which helped these essays reach readers across many disciplines, cultures, and countries.

I would also like to acknowledge Khalid Hasan—my good friend and coauthor of our recent book, *The New Sustainability Edge*—who suggested compiling these important *Medium* essays into a single curated volume for future generations. He generously volunteered to edit this book, and I am very grateful for his insight, initiative, and enthusiasm in supporting this project from start to finish.

I am also grateful to the team at Sutherland House Experts for their professionalism and care throughout the process. A special thanks to Neil Seeman, our publisher, for his tireless support in reviewing the manuscript, offering helpful suggestions under tight deadlines, and guiding this book from idea to finished product. I also want to thank Sydney Druckman and Sheila Penton for their careful work in copyediting, design, and quality checks at every stage.

Finally, I deeply thank all readers—past, present, and future—whose curiosity and love for learning give purpose to this work. Your engagement helps *The Kotler Legacy* continue to inspire, educate, and enlighten.

ACKNOWLEDGMENTS

ABOUT THE AUTHOR

PROFESSOR PHILIP KOTLER—widely regarded as the "Father of Modern Marketing"—is an acclaimed American marketing author, consultant, and professor emeritus. He served as the S.C. Johnson Distinguished Professor of International Marketing (Emeritus), Kellogg School of Management, Northwestern University. Known for popularizing the concept of the marketing mix, Kotler has authored or co-authored over 100 books, including *Marketing Management, Principles of Marketing, Marketing: An Introduction, Kotler on Marketing, Marketing Insights from A to Z, Marketing 4.0, Marketing Places, Marketing of Nations, Chaotics: The Business of Managing and Marketing in the Age of Turbulence, Market Your Way to Growth, Winning Global Markets, Strategic Marketing for Health Care Organizations, Social Marketing, Social Media Marketing, My Adventures in Marketing, Up and Out of Poverty, Entrepreneurial Marketing, Transformative Marketing,* and *Winning at Innovation.* His work has shaped the way marketing is taught and practiced globally.

Kotler's latest work focuses on economic justice and the shortcomings of capitalism. He published *Confronting Capitalism: Real Solutions for a Troubled Economic System* in 2015, *Democracy in Decline: Rebuilding its Future* in 2016, *Advancing the Common Good* in 2019, and *Brand Activism: From Purpose to Action* in 2018. In 2025, he coauthored three important books—*Regeneration, Wicked Problems,* both with Christian Sarkar, and *The New Sustainability Edge—Redefining Business from Startups to Industry Leaders* with Khalid Hasan.

A pioneer in the field, Kotler is credited with developing important concepts such as social marketing, which aims to influence behaviors for healthier and safer lifestyles. He also created the concept of "demarketing" to aid in the task of reducing the level of demand. He developed the concepts of "prosumers," "atmospherics," and "societal marketing."

ABOUT THE EDITOR

DR. KHALID HASAN recently co-authored *The New Sustainability Edge* with Professor Philip Kotler (September 2025). His other co-authored books include *Strategic Marketing Management in Asia* (Emerald Publishing, UK, 2017; second edition 2026) and *Marketing Practices in Developing Economies: Cases from South Asia* (PHI Learning, India). He also collaborated with Professor Kotler and other scholars on *Essentials of Modern Marketing* (2022), now published in more than 20 countries.

Hasan is the CEO of ResInt Canada, an international research and consulting organization. A seasoned marketer and researcher, he specializes in sustainability, global business strategy, market research, and marketing communication. He completed a specialization in Strategy at Harvard Business School, focusing on Sustainable Business Strategy and Global Business. He holds a PhD and MBA, along with advanced research diplomas from institutions in Asia, the United States, and Canada, and teaches Marketing and Human Resource Management at universities in Canada and South Asia.

With over 35 years of professional experience—including two decades with Nielsen in Canada and South Asia—Dr. Hasan has led major research initiatives on microfinance and poverty alleviation. His major clients include the US Government, Global Affairs Canada, World Bank, USAID, UKAID, UNICEF, WHO, UNDP, Cornell University, University of Toronto, CARE, BCG, Coca-Cola, and Unilever. He is a Paul Harris Fellow of Rotary International.

PREFACE

"We do not inherit the planet from our parents;
we borrow it from our children."

Behold *The Kotler Legacy*. Here lies far more than a collection of essays and reflections—it is a tribute to the extraordinary life's work of Professor Philip Kotler, the Father of Modern Marketing. Recognized by the American Marketing Association as the most influential marketer of all time, Professor Kotler is, to me, a mentor—a guru whose guidance has reached thousands, even millions, of knowledge seekers: from business students in America and Canada, to learners in a remote village in Bangladesh, a desert in Saudi Arabia, or a tech hub in China. This book is for you, for me, and for everyone—from a factory worker to a Nobel laureate, from the head of state to an Imam, from a parent to a military General, from a student to a professor—whose vision and ideas have profoundly shaped how we understand marketing, business, and society, always with a steadfast focus on the 3Ps: People, Planet, and Prosperity.

For decades, Professor Kotler has been a guiding light for generations of students, scholars, and practitioners. His writings challenge us to think beyond profit and embrace a broader vision—one that recognizes the responsibility of business to people, to the planet, and to the future. In classrooms and boardrooms around the world, his books have inspired critical thinking and kindled the desire to build organizations that serve society as much as shareholders.

I am fortunate to have been one of his disciples and coauthor. To learn under his guidance is to be challenged constantly: to question assumptions, link theory with practice, and aim always for the greater good. Beyond his brilliance as a thinker, I have witnessed his humility, warmth, and generosity—qualities that make his intellectual contributions even more enduring.

This book brings together 40 selected out of 108 writings, published in *Medium* magazine, spanning themes that touch on marketing, business, economics, sustainability, capitalism, democracy, inequality, and other matters germane to the evolving role of business in society. Each essay reflects not only Professor Kotler's intellectual rigor but also his moral clarity. Taken together, they remind us that marketing is not merely a discipline of exchange, but a discipline of meaning—of creating value that improves human lives.

The book is organized into five thoughtfully structured sections, reflecting a natural progression of ideas. **Section I: Humanism, Happiness, and the Common Good** explores philosophy and values. **Section II: Society, Peace, and Governance** examines social systems and civic responsibility. **Section III: Inequality, Capitalism, and Economic Justice** provides an incisive critique of economic structures. **Section IV: Business Transformation, Technology, and Sustainable Capitalism** focuses on practical corporate solutions for a sustainable future. Finally, **Section V: Leadership, Politics, and Democratic Reform** addresses political action and transformative leadership. This arrangement flows from philosophy → society → economic critique → business solutions → political action, offering readers a cohesive narrative arc: understanding ideas, analyzing society, examining the economy, exploring corporate solutions, and engaging with politics and leadership. The section titles are clear, professional, and forward-looking, enhancing both readability and thematic clarity.

While Professor Kotler has authored and coauthored more than 100 books and made many of his essays available online, *The Kotler Legacy* offers something uniquely valuable. This volume is carefully curated, organized, and thematically structured to provide a coherent journey through his ideas. Readers no longer need to search online or navigate multiple sources; here is a single, accessible volume, handy to carry in the boardroom, at home, or while traveling. It also makes an excellent gift for colleagues or sales and management teams, offering structured guidance and inspiration for practical application. The sections flow smoothly, like a stream, making it easy to connect insights across topics and reflect on their relevance today.

Most importantly, this book is empowering and refreshing for C-suite executives. It provides the insights needed to lead effectively, whether sharing ideas with teams at marketing or sales conferences, shaping discussions in the boardroom, or designing sustainable business strategies focused on the 3Ps—People, Planet, and Prosperity. It is equally valuable for teams across marketing, branding, PR, and sales, and for ambitious business students imagining fresh perspectives and innovative thinking. In this way, *The Kotler Legacy* offers a solid journey to the future, combining timeless principles with actionable wisdom. It is not just a book of essays; it is a practical guide and companion, prepared with care by the Father of Modern Marketing, to inspire, inform, and empower leaders, teams, and learners alike.

I am deeply honored to have worked alongside Professor Kotler in bringing this collection to life. My hope is that *The Kotler Legacy* serves as a source of wisdom, reflection, and guidance for all who care about building a more just, sustainable, and prosperous world. The challenges we face today—economic, social, and environmental—require bold ideas and principled leadership. In these pages, readers will find both.

With sincere respect and gratitude,

Khalid Hasan, PhD
Author and Researcher
Co-Author, *The New Sustainability Edge*, with Professor Philip Kotler
CEO, ResInt Canada
President, ResInt Sustainability Institute

SUSTAINING PASSION

PEOPLE DIFFER IN HOW THEY use their mind.

Consider, for example, how they handle "focusing". Some persons are happy to focus on one domain, such as money-making or bird watching. To their credit, they become an expert in that chosen domain.

Other persons do the opposite. They pay attention to everything of interest. To their credit, they become known as a person who knows a little about a lot.

Then there is the person who starts with an initial focus, later moves to another focus, still later to another focus, and so on. I happen to be that kind of person. My focus has moved to several different domains over time:

Inequality → Economics → Business → Marketing → Capitalism → Democracy → The Common Good → Essays

Inequality

One of the first issues puzzling me in growing up was the vast differences in the lives of the poor and the rich. Why were there so many poor people who went hungry, poorly clothed, and poorly housed? Why were there a few persons who were so rich that every human pleasure and object was available to them?

Economics

I thought I would find the answer by studying economics. At the University of Chicago, I studied economics under Nobel laureate Professor Milton

Friedman. Then I moved to M.I.T., and I studied under Nobel economists Paul Samuelson and Robert Solow. Frankly, I didn't feel that theoretical economics provided a satisfactory answer.

Business

I turned my mind over to how businesses actually work and how businesses decide how much to pay their Chief Executive Officers, all the way down to the lowest-paid worker. I could see how markets established normal pay levels. Today, CEOs of major companies get 300X the median worker's pay level in their company. And the lowest workers get barely enough to live on.

Marketing

At the heart of business is marketing. I agree with the late management expert, Peter Drucker, who said the two main functions of a business are (1) marketing and (2) innovation. A business makes its money by excelling in marketing and innovation.

Capitalism

In developing a deep understanding of how marketing and innovation create wealth, I needed to understand more deeply how capitalism works. Capitalism assumes that persons will work to the best of their ability and will be rewarded on their differing contributions. Those with lower ability will earn less; those with higher ability will earn more.

Democracy

My attention then turned to democracy, a system where each voter gets only one vote to decide who should govern the city, state, or nation. Yet my study showed that the rich in a democracy had much more power to influence who wins elections. The winners show their appreciation to their rich donors, and they are careful not to pass legislation that would burden their donors. Not surprisingly, the democracy ends up perpetuating the existing conditions of the poor and the rich.

Common Good

I became increasingly aware that the economic systems existed to preserve the poor class, to reduce the size of the middle class, and to augment the wealth of the wealthier class. Just growing the nation's Gross Domestic Product simply makes the rich richer. The nation needed a better objective, namely, to augment the Common Good. The society that allows so many of its citizens to be poorly fed, clothed, and housed is not a great society. America needs to adjust its laws and values to create a better sharing of the wealth of the nation.

Essays

At this stage, I am observing life and writing essays that might carry some degree of enlightenment. I have learned a great deal from reading other thoughtful essays.

My Sustaining Passion

My sustaining passion is to continue to pursue a more just distribution of income and wealth so that more people around the world can live more fulfilling lives.

EPILOGUE: A CALL TO ACTION

I DON'T EXPECT MY READERS to read all my essays in this book.

My hope is that among these essays, several give you new insights or ideas.

Please expand on these in conversations with friends and others.

If you are passionate about an idea or a cause, find others who have the same interests.

Search for existing organizations that promote the same idea or cause. Join them, meet new committed people. In numbers, there is power.

Think about the larger systems that make up your society. Is the economic system producing a fair distribution of incomes? Is the political system electing capable and creative legislators? Are social systems open, transparent, and inspiring?

Finally, ask yourself: What do you want to accomplish with your mind, time, energy, and resources? What makes you happy and fulfilled?

SECTION I

Humanism, Happiness, and the Common Good

CHAPTER ONE

Can Humanism Save Mankind and the Planet?

HUMANS HAVE A DEEP NEED to understand their individual lives and to understand the society in which they live. Why is there so much poverty? Why are there so many wars? Why can't people work together and pursue the Common Good?

Many doctrines and "isms" have been proposed as answers to these problems: Capitalism, Socialism, Communism, Fascism, and Libertarianism. Most of these isms have failed or made the problems worse.

I would assert that one "ism" would work better and should precede or be part of every other ism.

That "ism" is Humanism.

Humanism can be traced back to ancient Greek philosophers, ancient Indian thought, and Confucius. It represented an attempt to explain the world by focusing on human reason and natural law and abandoning reliance on myth or religion. Humanism's best articulation occurred during the Renaissance (14th–17th centuries), when Italian scholars started to study the earlier Greek writings of Plato and Aristotle, and schools started to teach the humanities of literature, poetry, and human history. Mankind transitioned from the Middle Ages to a period marked by advances in art (Michelangelo, Leonardo da Vinci), science (Galileo, Copernicus), technology (metal movable type for printing, banking, and accounting), and philosophy (rediscovery of classical Greek philosophy).

Humanism further bloomed in the age of the Enlightenment (1715–1789) with the spiraling growth of science and industrialism. New ideas flourished, such as the pursuit of happiness, sovereignty of reason, and the evidence of the senses as the primary sources of knowledge, and ideals such as liberty, progress, toleration, fraternity, constitutional government, and the separation of church and state. During this period, Jeremy Bentham and John Stuart Mill developed the moral philosophy of *utilitarianism* that centered its attention on human happiness and eliminating human and animal pain. Ethical societies were formed, paving the way for the contemporary humanist movement. The British Humanist Association (BHA) was formed. Humanist organizations flourished in the Netherlands, Norway, and other European countries. The American Humanist Association (AHA) was established in 1941. Humanism attracted prominent public figures such as Isaac Asimov, John Dewey, Erich Fromm, Paul Kurtz, and Carl Sagan. Humanist organizations from all continents formed the Humanists International to promote the humanist agenda, via the United Nations, UNESCO, and UNICEF.

Humanism never received the visibility and force of other isms such as Capitalism, Communism, or Fascism. Perhaps it suffered from appearing to be too "utopian," resting on principles of human compassion, collaboration, and peace.

Here I would like to answer three questions in the hope of spreading a broader interest in humanism and its potential to advance the Common Good. The questions are:

What is humanism?
How can humanism contribute to business and marketing?
How does humanism contribute to sustaining our Planet and humanity?

What Is Humanism?

Humanism is a doctrine, attitude, or way of life centered on human interests or values.

Humanism rejects supernaturalism. It prefers causal explanations to be born by reason and science, not myth and superstition. Humanists are mostly secular in their views. Humanists believe that people can achieve happiness and live well and morally without religion. Yet they may respect the great religions of the world for their positive aspects. Many humanists can live a religious life for the good and comfort and friendships that a religious community might add to their lives.

Humanists believe in the concept of human rights (free expression, right of assembly, self-determination, and other rights).

Humanists also strongly believe in the concept of human responsibilities (do not kill or maim another human being, do not lie, cheat, or spread hate). Follow the Golden Rule, "Do unto others as you would have them do unto you."

Humanists have a strong interest and concern for human well-being and happiness, human values, and human dignity. Humanists want to advance the Common Good.

How Can Humanism Contribute to Business and Marketing?

Mankind has established systems of markets and trades to produce and distribute goods and services to satisfy human needs and wants.

What would humanists think of the behavior of buyers and sellers? A humanist would want buyers to have good knowledge of goods and services (their features, performance, prices, and availability). Buyers would need to know how selling and advertising work so that they avoid being manipulated. As for sellers, a humanist would want sellers to make good products and services, communicate them accurately and price them fairly. The sellers should not spread disinformation about their products or competitors' products and services.

Humanists criticize the following marketing practices:

- Mass advertising that hits us with more ads than we care to see or hear
- Misinformation or lies about a product's performance
- Base appeals to our emotions (fear, passion, guilt, etc.) to sell more ("you will be more sexually attractive")

- Promoting unhealthy goods (cigarettes, guns, drugs) or excessive consumption
- Encouraging waste and pushing consumers to buy single-use products
- Introducing new styles and appliances aiming at planned obsolescence

As a humanist, I collaborated with others to write a book to give a new view of marketing called H2H Marketing (Human to Human Marketing). Marketing is about people dealing with other people humanely. The good marketer aims to create and deliver value for buyers. He or she describes carefully, honestly, and respectfully the value to prospective buyers. In return, the good consumer is honest and accurate in what he or she needs, wants, and expects.

How Can Humanism Contribute to Sustainability?

Humans are another species living on the earth. As a species, humans want to survive. Humans must develop a healthy ecological relation to the rest of nature made up of animals, plants, soil, water, and air. Humans must oppose actions that would pollute air, water, or soil.

Humans are now faced with a new problem, that of the earth's temperature getting warmer. The need to meet a growing population's needs for food, clothing, and shelter requires increasing amounts of energy. Modern industry depends on burning coal, oil, and gas. These fossil fuels emit carbon that is heating the planet. Can humans switch fast enough to natural sources like solar, wind, and hydroenergy to avoid temperatures rising to a level where humans cannot breathe? A huge number of people living near the equator will have to flee to cooler climates where they are not welcome. Wars and chaos will be the future of mankind.

Humanists are among the most ardent advocates of sustainability. Humanists support such policies as:

- Reduce the use of plastics in packaging
- Stop single-use packaging (such as throwaway bottles)
- Require products to be made more lasting

- Oppose superficial restyling of products
- Reduce city driving and air travel
- Replace fuel-driven cars with electric cars

These policies energize a new movement calling for slower economic growth or DeGrowth.

Being a humanist doesn't mean wanting to maximize the number of human beings in the world. Humanists wish for economic and social arrangements that maximize the number of people who are able to live good lives. Humanists favor a world where everyone can have enough food, clothing, and shelter to live healthy, joyful, and long lives.

Source: April 14, 2024; Can Humanism Save Mankind and the Planet? | by Philip Kotler | Medium

CHAPTER TWO

Being a Humanist

THE PHILOSOPHICAL CORE OF MY being is humanism. The movement called Humanism best describes my attitudes and beliefs.

Humanism affirms the freedom and dignity of each human being. Humanism affirms everyone's ability and responsibility to lead ethical lives of personal fulfillment that aspire to the greater common good. Humanism believes in human wellbeing (health and happiness), human autonomy, and human progress.

Humanism is a philosophy that moves away from religious and supernatural beliefs and is grounded in secularism. Humanism relies on science and reason rather than revelation to understand the world. Humanists are strong advocates for human rights, free speech, progressive policies, and democracy. Religion is not a precondition for morality. Humans can shape their own values, and live a moral, good, and meaningful life.

Humanists carry a set of human and nature values. They are against the imposition of one's culture or religion on another culture. They respect the laws of nature and avoid explanations involving myths or traditions. They are against violence. They seek to eliminate hunger and improve health, housing, and education. They favor improving the social conditions of humanity and improving the dignity of all humans.

Humanist traits are found in many countries. Confucius (551–479 BCE) placed a high value on human life and he discounted mysticism and superstition. Confucius emphasized respectfulness, reasonableness, kindness, and enthusiasm for learning. A person could achieve nobleness through education. Confucius advised people, "what you would not want for yourself, do not do to others," which is an early form of the Golden Rule.

Every philosophical movement is likely to draw critics. Religious people of a fundamentalist mindset might discriminate against non-believers. They may complain that humanists are agnostic or atheistic and place science over religion. They may complain that humanists emphasize the unity of brain and body in contrast to the belief that the mind is more important than the body. They may complain about humanists who promote gender equality and same sex marriages.

As a humanist, I am often asked questions. Here are some questions and my answers.

1. Can one be moral without accepting a religion? My answer is yes. Humanists accept the wisdom of the Ten Commandments even though they are unaffiliated with any religion. Humanist societies have published manifestos of human values. Dostoevsky's charge that "*If God does not exist, then everything is permitted,*" is not accepted by humanists. Evil does exist, and humanists would not want everything to be permitted.
2. Is there such a thing as Christian humanism? Humanists accept that Jesus preached a philosophy of love, which is essential humanism. They see Jesus as an extraordinary human being, prophet, and preacher.
3. Are socialism and communism compatible with humanistic thinking? The original impulse of Karl Marx and his followers was to create an economic and political system to improve the lives of people. Remember that most people were poor and at the mercy of the owners of land and capital, who benefitted from keeping people poor and using child labor and long hours of work. Marx wanted the poor to rise up and assert their human rights. Socialism was more of a cooperative vision of people working together to advance their conditions. Communism,

however, became an authoritarian movement completely contrary to all tenets of humanism.

4. Does humanism lead to moral relativism? If people have the right to autonomy, they have the right to decide and disagree on moral issues.
5. Do humanists have a definite answer to the question of the meaning of life? No. Humanists believe that individuals need to create their own meaning of what life is about.
6. Does humanism provide a definition of the Good Life? Humanism lets each person aim for a good life without hurting others.
7. Do humanists welcome all members, independent of race, religion, or sexual orientation? Yes. Humanists favor a pluralistic society.
8. Is there a difference between a libertarian and a humanist? Yes. A libertarian believes in full liberty for the individual. Libertarians generally favor small government, low taxes, and individualism. By contrast, a humanist believes in concerted social action to uplift lives and society so that more people have the means to lead a full life with health and happiness.
9. Are humanists of a liberal leaning? Yes. Humanism is at odds with conservatism that favors long-standing traditions and that tolerates xenophobia, bigotry, and ultra-nationalism.
10. Is empathy an important ingredient of humanism? Yes. Humanists have different opinions and persuasions. However, they carry empathy, a capacity to understand and respect persons with different views.
11. What are some other facets of humanism? Humanists celebrate self-actualization and creativity. They provide a constant voice supporting secularism, human and civil rights, personal autonomy, religious toleration, multiculturalism, cosmopolitism, and progressive policies.

Source: July 30, 2023; Philip Kotler, *My Life as a Humanist,* available from Amazon Books. Being a Humanist. The philosophical core of my being is … | by Philip Kotler | Medium

CHAPTER THREE

Human Rights and the Common Good

I SPENT MANY YEARS EXAMINING the idea of the Common Good (see Philip Kotler, *Advancing the Common Good: Strategies for Business, Governments, and NonProfits*, Praeger, 2019). Enlightened citizens, in voting on gun control, abortion, or environmental management, need to ask whether a proposed law would advance or hurt the Common Good. Is our society better with no gun control or strict gun control? Is our society better with permitting abortion as a woman's human right or with banning abortion? Is our society better off with no environmental laws or with rigorous environmental laws?

We first have to define what we mean by advancing the Common Good. The Common Good advances if more people in a society are happier, or improve their health and well-being, or are less ignorant and more educated. We can applaud the Nordic nations (Sweden, Norway, Denmark, Finland, and Iceland) because their social aim is to produce citizens who are happy, healthy, and educated. In all rankings of nations by these three measures, all the Nordic nations are in the top eight.

Consider two cases where new human rights advanced the Common Good.

- The US allowed human slavery to be practiced from 1619 until 1865. Slaves had no human rights. Their master could assign any tasks, punish them, and abuse them. Their family members could be sold to other landowners. Slaves led miserable lives. Abolitionists worked feverishly to free them and opposed letting new states establish slavery. Freeing slaves would allow these human beings to grow their potential and add to the Common Good.
- The US did not permit women voting rights until 1920. Men wanted women to be wives managing their children and the home. Women had jobs in the meantime earned only two-thirds of what men were paid for doing the same work. Men said that women knew little about commerce, governance, or politics and therefore couldn't vote intelligently. Clearly passing the women's right to vote produced over time a great increase in the Common Good.

Most social progress in industrial countries came from strengthening human rights. Americans refused to pay tea taxes to Great Britain on the grounds that "taxation without representation" is wrong and the American Revolution began.

Thomas Jefferson wrote the following words in the US Declaration of Independence:

> *"We hold these truths to be self-evident, that all men are created equal, that they are endowed by their Creator with certain unalienable Rights, that among these are **Life, Liberty and the Pursuit of Happiness**. That to secure these rights, Governments are instituted among Men, deriving their just powers from the consent of the governed."*

This majestic statement was inspired by Jefferson's reading about the European Enlightenment and its major thought leaders including Francis Bacon, Rene Descartes, John Locke, Voltaire, Denni Diderot, Jean-Jacques Rousseau, and David Hume. The Enlightenment period ran from 1637 (Descartes "I think, therefore I am") to 1815 (the end of Napoleon) and it produced a new consciousness of life and meaning. Disappearing were the feudal days of Kings, princes, and serfs. God and religion were losing some of their absolute power. Rapidly emerging was "freedom of thought, rational inquiry, critical thinking, religious tolerance, political liberty, scientific achievement, the pursuit of happiness, and hope for the future."

The Enlightenment period was followed by the invention of the steam engine and the Industrial Revolution. Major economic, social, and political changes were occurring. Population grew, the number of cities multiplied, economies expanded, new and cheaper consumer goods appeared, new production technologies emerged, and European nations expanded their colonial empires. Global expansion confronted Europeans with the recognition of new religions, cultures, and behaviors.

The Evolution of Human Rights

Let's recognize that most of humanity's time on earth was without a concept of human rights. The value of human life was slow in coming.

The earliest sign of reverence for human life can be traced back to Babylon's King Hammurabi drawing up the "Code of Hammurabi" (1760 BCE). The King promises to "make justice reign in the Kingdom and promote the good of the people." More than 1000 years later in India (528 BCE–486 BCE), Gautama Buddha spoke of morality, reverence for life, non-violence, and right conduct. At a similar time, the founder of the Jain sect, Lord Mahavira, talked about the right to life and "Live & Let Live." Finally the New Testament has Jesus preaching "Do unto others as you would have them do to you" (Luke 6:31). The "golden rule" could be seen as the beginning of the ultimate thinking about human rights.

Did the ancient Greeks believe in human rights? Ancient Greek writings do not carry the word "rights." Socrates, Plato, and Aristotle did posit the existence of natural justice. Aristotle was said to be the father of natural law. The major Greek philosophers were preoccupied with the themes of "justice," "virtue," "the good," and "the beautiful." Athens citizens had the "freedom" to discuss, debate, and vote on public issues. Once the public vote was taken, all citizens had to obey the vote. Greek society's needs had priority over individual needs. Greek citizens could be exiled, jailed, or executed if they violated Greek norms of behavior. Remember that much of the work in Greek society was done by slaves who had no rights. Greek society did not have the modern concept of man "as a free, autonomous agent who chooses his own ends, selects his own means to attain his desired ends, and in general lives for himself." Human and individual rights were an alien notion to the mind of the ancient Greeks. The right of an individual to live his own life as he or she desired with no interference or dictates by political interests was not present in Greek society.

Ancient Rome also lacked the modern idea of human rights. Up to a third of the Roman population was slaves. Free Roman citizens had to follow the norms of society.

The first historical light on human rights appeared in the Middle Ages on June 15, 1213, in the form of the Magna Carta. The Magna Carta was imposed on King John of England by rebellious barons to limit his power and prevent arbitrary royal acts like land confiscation and unreasonable taxes. The king would have to consult a defined body of laws and customs before initiating changes in land confiscation or unreasonable taxes. The Magna Carta advanced the rights of barons and official figures, not the rights of individual citizens.

The next step occurred in 1628 with the Petition of Right. The English Parliament sent this petition to King Charles, complaining of a series of breaches of law. Charles had tried to finance his war against Spain and imposed a forced loan compelling gifts from his subjects and imprisoning those who did not comply. Parliament found this to be a violation of the spirit of the Magna Carta and wanted to reclaim the rights of Parliament and of free men to observe the rule of law. The Petition of Right called for recognizing four principles: no taxation without the consent of Parliament, no imprisonment without cause, no quartering of soldiers on subjects, and no martial law in peacetime. The Petition of Right came to be regarded as a constitutional document of the United Kingdom.

In 1689, the Parliament of England passed the English Bill of Rights which created separation of powers, limited the powers of the king and queen, enhanced the democratic election and bolstered freedom of speech. The Bill of Rights established the doctrine of Parliamentary supremacy. The Parliament became the supreme source of law-making over the monarch and the courts. The crown may not create new taxes without approval of Parliament. No army may be kept during peace time without consent of Parliament. The people have the right to bear arms so long as they are allowed to by law. The United States Bill of Rights was mainly modeled after the English Bill of Rights.

In 1776, the new United States passed the Declaration of Independence—proclaiming the right to "life, liberty and the pursuit of happiness." This was the first utterance of this powerful phrase and it came from Thomas Jefferson.

Thirteen years later, in 1789, the French Revolution and the storming of the Bastille took place to secure "liberty, equality and fraternity." The French National Assembly released The Declaration of the Rights of Man and of the Citizen, stating that all citizens are equal under the law. The National Assembly believed that the ignorance, neglect, or contempt of the rights of man was the cause of public calamities and government corruption. The National Assembly determined to publish a solemn declaration of the natural, unalienable, and sacred rights of man.

The document listed 17 articles, including:

- Men are born and remain free and equal in rights.
- The natural and imprescriptible rights of man are the rights of liberty, property, security, and resistance to oppression.
- Liberty consists in the freedom to do everything which injures no one else. Law can only prohibit such actions as are hurtful to society.
- Every citizen has a right to participate personally, or through his representative, in its foundation. All citizens, being equal in the eyes of the law, are equally eligible to all dignities and to all public positions and occupations, according to their abilities, and without distinction except that of their virtues and talents.
- No person shall be accused, arrested, or imprisoned except in the cases and according to the forms prescribed by law. The law shall provide for such punishments only as are strictly and obviously necessary. All persons are held innocent until they shall have been declared guilty.
- No one shall be disquieted on account of his opinions, including his religious views. The free communication of ideas and opinions is one of the most precious of the rights of man. Every citizen may, accordingly, speak, write, and print with freedom, but shall be responsible for such abuses of this freedom as shall be defined by law.

- The security of the rights of man and of the citizen requires public military forces. These forces are, therefore, established for the good of all and not for the personal advantage of those to whom they shall be entrusted.
- A common contribution is essential for the maintenance of the public forces and for the cost of administration. This should be equitably distributed among all the citizens in proportion to their means. All the citizens have a right to decide, either personally or by their representatives, as to the necessity of the public contribution; to grant this freely; to know to what uses it is put; and to fix the proportion, the mode of assessment and of collection and the duration of the taxes.
- Society has the right to require of every public agent an account of his administration.
- Since property is an inviolable and sacred right, no one shall be deprived thereof except where public necessity, legally determined, shall clearly demand it, and then only on condition that the owner shall have been previously and equitably indemnified.

Finally, in 1948, the United Nations passed The Universal Declaration of Human Rights, the first document listing the thirty rights to which everyone is entitled. Driven by the desire to prevent another Holocaust, world leaders explicitly spelled out the rights everyone on the planet could expect and demand because they are human beings. Included in the thirty articles are:

- All human beings are born free and equal and should be treated the same way.
- Everyone can claim their rights regardless of sex, race, language, religion, social standing, etc.
- Everyone has the right to life and to live in freedom and safety.
- No one has the right to treat you as a slave nor should you enslave anyone.
- No one has the right to torture you.
- You should be legally protected in the same way everywhere like anyone else.
- The law is the same for everyone and should be applied in the same manner to all.

- You have the right to obtain legal help and access the justice system when your rights are not respected.
- No one can arrest or detain you arbitrarily, or send you away from your country unjustly.
- Trials should be public and tried in a fair manner by an impartial and independent tribunal.
- You are considered innocent until it can be proved you are guilty according to law. If accused of a crime you have the right to a defence.
- You have the right to protection if someone tried to harm your good name, enter your home without permission or interfere with your correspondence.
- You have the right to leave or move within your own country and you should be able to return.
- If you are persecuted at home, you have the right to seek protection in another country.
- You have the right to belong to a country and have a nationality.
- Men and women have the right to marry when they are legally able without limits due to race, nationality or religion. Families should be protected by the Government and the justice system. Men and women of full age, without any limitation due to race, nationality or religion, have the right to marry and to found a family. They are entitled to equal rights as to marriage, during marriage and at its dissolution. Marriage shall be entered into only with the free and full consent of the intending spouses.
- You have the right to own things. No one has the right to illegally take them from you.
- Everyone has the right to freely manifest their religion, to change it and to practice it alone or with others.
- Everyone can think and say what they like and no one should forbid it.
- You have the right to organize and participate in peaceful meetings.
- Everyone has the right to take part in their country's political affairs and equal access to public service. Governments should be voted for regularly.
- Society should help individuals to freely develop and make the most of all advantages offered in their country.

- Everyone has the right to work in just and favourable conditions and be free to choose your work with a salary that allows you to live and support family. Everyone should receive equal pay for equal work. Everyone has the right to form and to join trade unions for the protection of his interests.
- Each work day should not be too long and everyone has the right to rest and take regular paid holidays.
- You have the right to have what you need so that you and your family do not go hungry, homeless or fall ill.
- You have the right to go to school, continue your studies as far as you wish and learn regardless of race, religion or country of origin.
- You have the right to share the benefits of your community's culture, arts and sciences.
- To make sure your rights are respected, there must be an order that can protect them. This order should be global.
- You have duties toward the community within which your personality can fully develop. The law should guarantee human rights. It should allow everyone to respect others and to be respected.
- No one, institution nor individual, should act in any way to destroy the rights enshrined in the UN's Universal Declaration of Human Rights.

The United Nations Universal Declaration of Human Rights is distinctive in providing the most complete listing of human rights.

What Is Happening Now to Human Rights?

Human rights are far from universal. Human rights vary in every nation. Many "rights" issues arise with abortion, gun control, air and water pollution, crime and punishment, and immigration and refugees. Sovereign nations have the power to define citizen's rights and also to make changes in their rights. For example, consider how Ireland has handled the abortion issue.

In 1861, Ireland banned abortion. This ban remained in place until 1983 when Irish citizens voted and passed a referendum that acknowledges the right to life means the life of the woman and the unborn are seen as equal. In 1992, the Irish courts ruled against letting a 14-year-old suicidal rape victim travel to England to terminate her pregnancy. The ruling was later overturned by Ireland's Supreme Court, saying that the credible threat of suicide is grounds for an abortion in Ireland. Yet this left medical practitioners uncertain about how to handle tough abortion cases.

Over the next several years, the debate continued over whether a pregnant mother can flee to England for an abortion, or could abort a baby who has down syndrome, or a suicidal mother might abort, or a pregnant mother could abort a child resulting from rape or incest. In 2013, Ireland passed a new law legalizing abortion when doctors deem that a woman's life is at risk due to medical or suicidal complications. But the government also introduced a maximum penalty of 14 years imprisonment for having or assisting in an unlawful abortion. In 2016, the UN warned that Ireland's ban on abortion even when there is a fatal abnormality is a cruel and inhuman treatment.

In 2017, a Citizens' Assembly recommended the introduction of unrestricted access to abortion and won a 64 percent favorable vote. Finally, the Irish government said it will hold a referendum on whether to change the abortion laws. The vote was held in May 2018 and a 64.51 percent favorable vote led the government to introduce legislation allowing abortion in the first 12 weeks of pregnancy, and between 12 and 24 weeks in exceptional circumstances. All this took place in a country with a huge Catholic population, finally acknowledging the complications a pregnant mother faces in her pregnancy and the terrible uncertainties that medical personnel had faced.

Let's turn to the same abortion issue that has been bitterly fought in the US between the "right to choose" people and the "right to life" people. In 1973, the US Supreme Court finally decided the issue in the famous Roe vs. Wade Right to Privacy decision. The US Supreme Court ruled in a 7–2 decision that the US Constitution conferred the women's right to have an abortion. The court established a pregnancy trimester timetable to govern all abortion regulations in the US. The decision struck down many federal and state abortion laws and fueled a continuous debate on its legality, morality and religious implications.

On June 24, 2022, the US Supreme Court shocked the nation by overturning Roe v. Wade, ending the right to abortion which had lasted 47 years.

The US Supreme Court's majority in a 6–3 decision held that the earlier decision was "egregiously wrong" and the arguments "exceptionally weak" and "damaging." This decision meant that abortion was put in the hands of individual states to ban abortions for any reason. Several states are reinstating their old laws banning abortion. Many Republican states and their legislators and governors are busy adding criminal penalties to mothers and doctors who get involved in an abortion. The decision is producing legal chaos and unusual hardship on pregnant mothers and medical practitioners.

This reversal of Roe vs. Wade may affect other civil rights. Justice Clarence Thomas of the Supreme Court said that the legal rationale for the Roe-Wade decision overturn could be applied to overturn other major civil rights cases, including those that legalized gay marriage, barred the criminalization of consensual homosexual conduct, and protected the right of married people to have access to contraception. The Court may even approve of annulling single sex marriages.

Conclusion

My interest in civil and human rights arose in connection with hoping that the nation continues to favor decisions that advance the Common Good. Human rights are pillars that support the Common Good. In many cases, the majority of voters are strongly in favor of laws that protect and advance the Common Good. However, the legal maneuvers of minority opponents allow them to dismantle or weaken human rights. The majority of American citizens favor women's abortion rights, gun control, and environmental protection legislation. We need to worry about legislatures that get elected and don't represent majority opinion. Up to now, we assumed that the US Supreme Court will protect and advance human rights. Now this hope has faded.

Source: July 26, 2022. Human Rights and the Common Good | by Philip Kotler | Medium

CHAPTER FOUR

My Ruminations of Living a Happy Life

Most of my life, I have been too busy to reflect on my life. There were so many things that I wanted to do. I knew that life was too short. I remember reading a book with the title "The Hundred Things You Must See." I must see the Pyramids and Sphinx of Egypt, Machu Picchu in Peru, the Galapagos islands in Ecuador, the Taj Mahal in India, the Vatican and works of Michelangelo, and many others. I started to see these inspiring places. Sadly, I still have not seen most of them.

Life is about making choices. We have to decide what major activities to pursue and master. I now regret rejecting two major activities. First, I wish I had practiced and mastered a music instrument. Like many young persons, I was given piano lessons for a year. Making no progress, and finding better things to do, I gave up on piano lessons. My brother Milton took up the violin and he enjoyed learning to play and he developed a good understanding of music as a result. I never considered taking up another instrument. I now miss playing a clarinet or saxophone, joining or starting a band, and experience making music together. I look enviously at those who play chamber music or even who join a singing group.

The second choice would have been to get good at some sport. My father was a leading soccer player. He hoped that his three sons would play soccer. We enjoyed watching him play but we preferred to spend our time on other activities. I play a lot of tennis but I never hired a trainer. I was good enough. Looking back, I wish that I had become very good in tennis. At my age now, I should be playing golf which most of my friends play. I miss the camaraderie of sharing a game with others. Frankly, I decided that it was more important to develop my mind than my body. The thought of doing both never occurred to me.

What lessons can I give to others about growing older and not having too much regret?

Give and You Will Get

Persons can either behave as givers or takers. A giver will spend time with others, mentor them or invest in them, and get pleasure doing this. A taker spends time only with those who he can take something from, either by sharing in the person's reputation, circle of friends, or use as a reference. I realize that I am mostly a giver, going out of my way to help a student or friend. Yet in other cases, I have been a taker. In the end, the giver gets back more than the taker.

Favor the Common Good

When I view an issue, such as "Medicare for All," or raising taxes on the rich, I choose the side that will "create the greatest good for the greatest number." I favor "Medicare for All" because more American citizens would receive better health care. I favor taxes on the rich because the government could put this money to helping the poor and this would not limit the lifestyles of the rich. My new book, entitled *Strategies for Advancing the Common Good,* will go deeply into the issue of making decisions that will help the most people.

People Can Be Moral Without Being Religious

From an early age, I became aware that all religions are man-made. Religions are created to give comfort to people. Many people need to believe that their lives are in the hands of a superior being who knows everything about each of them, rewards good behavior and punishes bad behavior. I would need scientific proof to believe this, not inspired story telling. Too many religions, from Catholics who killed Jews during the Inquisition to Muslims who stone men and women and cut off their hands for a minor offense, end up doing as much harm as good. Most people will live a moral way, if not out of a strong sense of ethics, but just in wanting to be a trusted member of an ongoing community.

Persons Be Wise to Engage in Lifetime Learning and Hobbies

Alvin Toffler, the famous futurist, said, "The illiterate of the future will not be the person who cannot read. It will be the person who does not know how to learn." The world is changing at an accelerating rate. One cannot be sure that their present job, company or even industry will exist. College graduates will probably have three or four careers, not one. A willingness to unlearn and relearn is more important than a willingness to stay where you are. A person ought to take up a hobby that engages them fully into their retirement. In the future, the average person will live to 100. The person will work from age 20 to 60, namely 40 years. That leaves another 40 years without working. The person has to be prepared to enjoy leisure for 40 years by reading, learning and hobbying. I wrote a paper for retired persons listing over 50 activities to enjoy in the last 40 years of life.

Travel Is Mind Opening

The most narrow-minded people I know have never traveled. They live in the same community with the same friends saying the same boring things to each other. Let them go to India, China, or Africa. They would come back as very different and interesting people. On the other hand, let them enroll in a new course totally out of their interest and this can open their mind. I spent a few years with a movement call EST (Erhard Seminar Training) that opened my mind to new areas of human potential.

Develop Not Only a Purpose but Also a Higher Purpose

You will feel much better about yourself when you retire if you have put part of your life into creating happiness for others. Be able to list upon retiring all the good deeds that you have done. The longer the list, the more satisfied and enlightened you are.

Get Married or at Least Have Great Friends

I married my 18 year-old girlfriend when I was 24. Nancy was at Radcliffe and I was at M.I.T. We now have three beautiful daughters and nine beautiful grandchildren. I can't imagine not having my wonderful wife and extended family. Not marrying leaves one with parents, uncles and aunts, but not with a whole family of kids and grandchildren who care about each other and do everything possible to keep you happy in your old age.

Source: October 15, 2020; My Ruminations of Living a Happy Life | by Philip Kotler | Medium

CHAPTER FIVE

What Can We Learn from Intellectuals?

I HAVEN'T READ MUCH ABOUT intellectuals in America. In France, daily newspaper headlines talked about Jean-Paul Sartre, Simone de Beauvoir or Albert Camus. The French enjoy reading about their intellectuals and their radical ideas. "Existentialism" would be daily talk in outdoor French cafés.

America has its celebrities too, mostly Hollywood types, business leaders, politicians and athletes. American Intellectuals are less read about although they carry influence. Consider American intellectuals such as Ralph Waldo Emerson, Henry David Thoreau, John Dewey, Noam Chomsky, Susan Sontag, Gloria Steinem, and James Baldwin. Each has had strong influence on their followers but many Americans are not familiar with these names.

Why Are Americans Less Interested in Intellectuals?

My impression is that Americans grow up in a pragmatic culture where actions and utility carry more value. Americans more often ask "Does it work?" than "Is it just?" or "Is it beautiful?" These questions seem elitist and disconnected from everyday life.

Americans are more interested in "doers," namely **entertainers, entrepreneurs, and athletes.** They are less interested in philosophers or social theorists. Intellectual debates rarely make it into mainstream media. The US higher education system is more interested in job and market success than the life of the mind.

What Are Intellectuals?

Intellectuals have been described as individuals who use critical thinking, reflection, and reason to understand and interpret the world. They typically engage in cultural, moral, scientific, political, or philosophical discourse and help shape public consciousness.

We can distinguish between public intellectuals and private intellectuals. Noam Chomsky is a public intellectual who plans to comment frequently on public issues. A private intellectual is a person that we contact to get his or her opinion.

Many Intellectuals are on the left or on the right. They often operate in "think tanks." Rarer are intellectuals whose opinions are not left or right most of the time. Two recent intellectuals who can show two sides of an issue are Bill Maher and Scott Galloway.

What Can We Learn from Intellectuals?

I see intellectuals as contributing value in several ways. They often challenge assumptions and the status quo. They offer new frameworks for understanding society, economics, politics, and human nature. They often connect knowledge from multiple fields. They raise moral and ethical questions. They think more about the long run than the short run. They often propose ways to reform or improve society. Intellectuals are occasionally invited into public discourse and sometimes policymaking.

Besides France, What Other Countries Value and Respect Intellectuals?

I can list some countries that value and respect intellectuals.

- **Britain** has a large number of well-known intellectuals including Francis Bacon, Thomas Hobbes, John Locke, George Berkeley, David Hume,

Adam Smith, Jeremy Bentham, Bertrand Russell, and John Stuart Mill. More contemporary intellectuals include Isaiah Berlin and John Maynard Keynes.

- **Germany** has had its share of intellectuals such as Immanuel Kant, Friedrich Nietzsche, Georg Wilhelm Friedrich Hegel, Martin Heidegger and Karl Marx, all of whom are taught about in German universities. Their names often appeared in media and public debates.
- **Italy** was the birthplace of many Renaissance humanists (Leonardo da Vinci, Francis Petrarch, Giovanni Boccaccio) and 20th-century thinkers like Umberto Eco and Antonio Gramsci.
- **China** placed scholars at the top of the social hierarchy. Confucius and Lao-Tzu shaped philosophical thought and religion. Today China respects philosophers and intellectuals in science and engineering.
- **Japan** respects intellectuals for both cultural preservation and innovation such as Nishida Kitaro and Daisetz T. Suzuki. They frequently advised on policy and social change.
- **Russia** respects its scientists, philosophers (Ivan Ilyin), and its writers (Tolstoy and Dostoevsky) but currently suppresses intellectuals critical of their regime.
- **Iran** has deep traditions in poetry, philosophy and theology and many intellectuals were influential in its earlier times.
- **South Korea** has built a culture of education, scholarship and merit in which intellectuals and academics often are media commentators and policy advisors.
- **Argentina** has philosophers and sociologists such as Telma Luzzani who often influence national discourse and politics.

Conclusion

I have listed several countries that recognize and value intellectuals as public thinkers who help define national values, frequently critique those in power, and help solve complex problems.

Other countries may ignore intellectuals or suppress them. Authoritarian regimes often view intellectuals as a danger that might question their authority. They may use the few public intellectuals to justify the regime.

While the US may not revere intellectuals in the same way France and some other countries do, America has produced many of the world's most original and impactful minds. The American intellectual tradition is at its best when it defines American values, critiques those in power, and defines needed reforms that would contribute to the Common Good.

Source: July 10, 2025; What Can We Learn from Intellectuals? | by Philip Kotler | Jul, 2025 | Medium

CHAPTER SIX

My New Friend, Leo Tolstoy

IN THESE TROUBLING TIMES, MANY people are asking how to lead a good life. Is it enough to get a career, marry, have two children, earn a good income and be generous to others? Should the person take some responsibility for the problems in the world and contribute toward making a better world?

I keep hoping to find a role model who has dealt with difficult times and who undertook actions to make the world a better place.

This led me to spend time thinking about Leo Tolstoy (1828–1910). He led a most interesting life. Born into an aristocratic and wealthy family, he joins the military, fights as a brave soldier, writes one of the world's great novels, *War and Peace*, and ends up going through a profound change in his beliefs and behavior.

Tolstoy experienced a profound moral crisis in the 1870s, followed by a profound spiritual awakening. Instead of accepting the world as it was, he saw the need for a new humanistic consciousness. He saw that his family was blessed with a lot of wealth and property while so many other people were going hungry. He came to the view that the right thing to do is to help the poor by setting up schools and giving away his property.

Tolstoy described himself as a Christian but he did not belong to an institutional Church such as the Russian Orthodox Church. For his criticism he was excommunicated in 1901. By declaring himself as a Christian, Tolstoy meant that he believed in the Ten Commandments. He believed in the teachings of Jesus, but he did not comment on Jesus' miracles or divinity. Tolstoy believed in leading a simple ascetic life. He preferred to be vegetarian, non-smoking, a teetotaler and chaste. Having lived through the horrors of war, he became a Christian pacifist believing in nonresistance. He believed in love your enemy, don't be angry, don't lust.

Tolstoy also was critical of the State, including the police, law courts and army. He felt that agents of the state were capable of immoral, violent, and corrupt practices. He was appalled by slavery and the condition of the serfs. He would look favorably upon persons who criticized or fought against coercive state policies.

Tolstoy set up as many as thirteen schools to educate the children of serfs. He began to give away portions of his property. This made his wife Sophia angry because she felt that their wealth belonged to their children. She had fears of bankruptcy. Tolstoy finally decided to leave his wife and he traveled to another destination, only to get sick. He died shortly afterwards.

Tolstoy's life is one of reflection and transformation. His reading of the Sermon on the Mount triggered his interest in helping the helpless. Jesus provided a model of the simple but serving life. Tolstoy's transformation was an inspiration to Mahatma Gandhi and Martin Luther King, Jr. and their philosophy of nonresistance. Tolstoy remains an inspiration to those who want to reform Christianity to return it to its original values. He is an inspiration to those who criticize and oppose harsh, violent or corrupt behaviors of persons entrusted with government.

Source: July 20, 2023; My New Friend, Leo Tolstoy. Philip Kotler | by Philip Kotler | Medium

CHAPTER SEVEN

Step in Building a Better Future for Humanity

I HAVE SPENT A LOT of time thinking about humanity's future. I outlined how we need to improve capitalism in *Confronting Capitalism* (2015), how to enhance democracy in *Democracy in Decline* (2017), and how to improve the common good in *Advancing the Common Good* (2019).

I now realize that these meditations answer only pieces of the larger question: "What is the future of humanity?" Recent events are pointing to a dismal picture of humanity's future that go beyond the pain of inflation and recession. Here are three developments that present a bleak outlook of the future.

The persistence of deadly diseases. Covid-19 was first reported by the local government in Wuhan, China on December 27, 2019. It quickly spread around the world and millions of people died. The rapid development of vaccines reduced the death rate in the more advanced nations. But Covid-19 generated new variants of the disease that continued to spread among many citizens who refused vaccinations or wearing masks for protection. Many people thought the pandemic would be over by 2021 or 2022 but it is still showing recurrent impact on people's lives. Now we have the appearance of a new viral disease, monkeypox, a cousin of smallpox. Some virologists are predicting the continuation of various diseases for a number of years, with all of their calamitous economic, social and political dehumanization consequences.

The damage of climate change. The industrial revolution brought many benefits to mankind: new products, lower costs, widespread abundance, and global growth. It also brought disbenefits in poorer quality air and water and in the huge growth of cities and traffic problems. A debate occurred in the 1970s on whether governments should place limits on growth to keep down pollution and other risks. Increases in human activity and production release more carbon and greenhouse gas emissions into the atmosphere that cause the planet to retain heat. A hotter planet will produce adverse climate effects, including more fires, floods, storms, and hurricanes. Temperatures in equatorial areas will rise to make living and breathing difficult. Affected persons will flee in droves for cooler climates in Europe, North America, and Australia. These areas will refuse refugees and bitter conflict will occur. As more refugees settle in cities, the cities will lack the resources to feed, clothe and shelter so many new arrivals. Living standards will fall around the world.

The question of population size and food supply. The world's population grew from three billion people in 1960 to close to eight million people in 2022. The food supply grew during this period even with far fewer farm workers. At the same time, world soil has downgraded through desertification and insufficient soil renewal programs. Water for agriculture is increasingly scarce in many areas, reducing the productivity of agriculture. Population growth is slowing down in industrial areas where families have two, fewer or no children while developing countries often have large families receiving very poor or no education. This means that the people in developing countries will continue to lack the skills of modern economies and women will continue to work in agriculture and give birth to many children. Most governments in developing nations do little to reduce the high birth rates. Ironically, industrial countries like Japan, France, Germany, and Italy are busy setting incentives to raise their birthrates.

The Decline of Democracies

There is clear evidence that many democracies decline and transmute into authoritarian regimes. Turkey is now ruled with an iron hand by Toyyip Erdogan, Hungry by Victor Orban, and Brazil by Jair Bolsonaro. They have setback political rights and civil rights. Dictators aren't pretending anymore about obeying their Parliament or their courts. Orban won his fourth election and clearly could change Hungary's constitution at will. Citizens in Tunisia just voted to give their leader all the power that he wants. Other countries with authoritarian leaders include Cuba, Belarus, Eritrea, Syria, Saudi Arabia, United Arab Emirates, Oman, Azerbaijan, Iran, Turkmenistan, Uzbekistan, Kazakhstan, China, North Korea, Laos, Russia, China, North Korea, Pakistan, and Myanmar.

These dominant leaders can use their power to convince their people that their leader is working in the interests of the people. Russia is a prime example where Putin wages a war against Ukraine and convinces many Russian citizens that the war is justified to fight Nazis. Russian citizens cannot hear the foreign press and even Russians who are against this war are hesitating to speak out against Putin.

With so many autocratic leaders, how should democratic countries relate to them? The US cannot stop selling goods to these countries. US corporations have the right and the need to sell their products to all countries, except for certain defense and other specifically prohibited products and services. Also, the US wants to continue diplomatic relations with almost all of these countries, hopefully to make a case for restoring universal human rights.

Putin's invasion of Ukraine posed a challenging problem to Biden and Europeans. Putin had two things in mind. He wanted to prevent Ukraine from moving toward the West and NATO. Also Putin believes that Ukraine belongs to Russia historically and would aid Putin's aim to restore Russia's greatness. In response, the West adopted a new strategy to discipline a wayward country. The US negotiated with allies around the world to boycott Russia, to capture Russian funds and to go after superrich Russians assets. By pinching Russia's resources, the allies hope that Russia will come sooner to the bargaining table. Russia was shocked by the Ukrainian resistance and by learning of its own military weakness but still hasn't come to the bargaining table.

The Fragility of Humanity's Future

How can the weakening democracies get the leaders of many authoritarian countries to take seriously the possible collapse of human civilization?

Authoritarian leaders know about the raging diseases, the carnage of climate change, and the possible future food shortage. Yet these dictators will not give up their power and restore human rights.

One hope could come from a reinvigorated United Nations. The UN is the largest sounding board for the problems of the world. The UN has already published and committed to the 17 Sustainable Development Goals. UN members vote on many issues and are members of many committees. Could the countries in the UN agree that a future deadly crisis will affect all countries and greatly depress living standards throughout the world? Could these countries agree to specify changes in individual nations' behavior that will help mitigate this crisis? Can the UN set up working committees to define conditions that would help avert new crises?

Another hope is that major multinationals will recognize the financial crisis they will experience with persistent levels of disease, damaging climate conditions, and imminent food shortages. The CEOs of these companies can have a huge influence in spelling out the need for company and country collaboration in dealing with this crisis. They can harness their media resources to make citizens everywhere aware of these problems and the need for collaborative action.

Unfortunately, collaboration usually doesn't take place until visible damage occurs and deepens. Just like we had a peace movement throughout the 20th century to prevent war and yet had two terrible world wars, we need to worry that campaigning for a disease-free world without air or water pollution or food shortages will only get started when much damage has already occurred. Hopefully it will not be too late to pick up the pieces and start working together to build a better future for humanity.

Source: September 6, 2022; Step in Building a Better Future for Humanity | by Philip Kotler | Medium

CHAPTER EIGHT

How to Measure the Common Good?

IN 2019, I PUBLISHED *Advancing the Common Good.* My aim was to help citizens choose those decisions that advance the Common Good. I relied on Jeremy Bentham's measure of the Common Good: If a proposed policy makes more people happy than unhappy, that policy advances the Common Good. The whole idea is that a good society aims to maximize the number of happy citizens.

However, I am realizing now that more is needed to assess whether a proposed policy advances the Common Good.

Let's consider five policies that might impact the Common Good.

Would society be better if citizens could not own guns or be better if citizens could freely have guns?

Would the society be better if women were not allowed to have an abortion or if women have the right to an abortion?

Would society be better if private citizens could be banned from smoking or free to smoke?

Would the society be better if gambling was banned or gambling was allowed to everyone?

Would this country be better if it did not accept immigrants or is open to immigrants?

The Need to Consider Intermediate Solutions

Notice that each example requires choosing between two extremes, such as no guns or many guns, or no abortions or many abortions. Ex-President Bill Clinton would call these "false choices," We do not need to accept an either-or choice. We can imagine other alternatives to each extreme. Instead of choosing to completely ban something or completely permit it, why not prescribe the conditions under which a limited ban can be permitted.

As for guns, instead of a complete ban, give people the right to own a gun if certain condition are met. The conditions are:

1. Person has no criminal or behavioral problems.
2. The gun cannot be an assault weapon.
3. The person cannot own more than three guns.
4. Guns must be kept under lock and key.
5. Guns cannot be carried into public places. This intermediate solution will increase society's happiness. A small number of persons might be unhappy about these restrictions. But a huge number of persons will be happy because they can buy and own a gun. The total amount of happiness is increased.

As for abortion, it should not be totally banned. Pregnant women are free to choose an abortion under the following conditions:

1. The pregnancy is not more than 24 weeks.
2. If the pregnancy is more than 24 weeks, abortion is still allowed if the pregnancy would endanger the woman's life.
3. If the woman was raped, she can choose an abortion. This intermediate solution increases happiness because more women can choose abortion under the right conditions.

As for cigarette smoking, a person is allowed to smoke under the following conditions:

1. Cigarette packages clearly state the dangers to health.
2. Smoking won't be allowed in offices, factories, hospitals, public conveyances, airports, or airplanes.

3. Smokers must remove themselves if one more nearby persons object to the smoke. More people may benefit from this decision than are hurt by this decision.

As for gambling, people are allowed:

1. To gamble in their homes.
2. Gamble in casinos that are set up for gambling.
3. Casinos must agree to discourage excessive gambling by specific individuals.

As for admitting immigrants into a country, the following conditions must be met:

1. The country accepts immigrants who have no criminal record, who apply through the normal channels, and who have sufficient funds to not need public aid.
2. The country gives preference to those immigrants who bring a new needed skills or come with sufficient funds to open one or more new businesses.
3. The country gives preference to immigrants who have close relatives who are Americans citizens.

Other Considerations

Putting total bans on some activities appeals to some groups because it is simpler to legislate and enforce. Yet total bans are likely to make more people unhappy than happy. Moving from total bans to modified bans is likely to increase the total net happiness of that society.

The fundamental problem is that issues and debates involve more than just the choice's impact on total happiness. Many other issues arise. How do the different choices impact the person's feelings of identity and self-esteem. One's choices affect the quality of the person's relationships with his or her family, friends and acquaintances. Many issues spark moral questions of compassion, liberty, and privacy. All this makes measurement of an issue's impact on the Common Good difficult to measure.

Consider the issue of "climate change." One group says that there is no climate change, another that there is some minor climate change, and another that there will be disastrous climate change. What evidence can be gathered to support each positions' view of the Common Good?

Consider the issue of "taxing the rich." One group opposes taxing the rich with the argument that taxing the rich will slow down economic development and hurt the Common Good. Another group favors taxing the rich with the argument that the money will be used to increase the spending power of the poor and increase the Common Good.

Clearly groups will disagree on what is the Common Good. Yet it is important that debaters raise the question of the Common Good. Each side must answer how they see their choices' impacting not just on themselves or their group but also whether it elevates or diminishes the Common Good.

Source: July 18, 2024: How to Measure the Common Good. Philip Kotler | by Philip Kotler | Medium

SECTION II

Society, Peace, and Governance

CHAPTER NINE

Can People Live a Good Life in a Jobless World?

SEVERAL MAJOR COMPANIES HAVE RECENTLY reported large job cuts and layoffs in various industries.

- In May 2025, Microsoft announced the layoff of approximately 7,000 employees.
- Intel is planning to reduce its workforce by 15–20 percent, which could affect over 10,000 employees.
- Amazon CEO Andy Jassy indicated that AI advancements would lead to workforce reductions over time as part of the company's cost-cutting measures.
- Google in June 2025 extended buyout offers to more employees, signaling potential further job cuts across the tech sector.
- P&G announced plans to eliminate 7,000 nonmanufacturing jobs, accounting for approximately 15 percent of its global office workforce, over the next two years.
- Paramount in August 2024 announced it would lay off 15 percent of its US workforce, amounting to about 2,000 employees.

More layoffs will increase over time as companies implement more artificial intelligence and automation. At the same time, recent college graduates will be facing one of the most challenging job markets in over a decade. In May 2025, the unemployment rate for college graduates aged 22 to 27 climbed to 5.8 percent, the highest since 2012 (excluding the pandemic period). College graduates are busy submitting multiple applications for jobs at a time when companies are cutting down on their hiring plans. Many stories are heard about highly qualified college graduates spending weeks or months submitting applications and failing to get a job.

Several factors are at work:

- **Impact of Artificial Intelligence.** AI is reshaping the job landscape, especially in white-collar jobs in such roles as accounting, finance, legal services, and in coding and programming tasks.
- **Decline in Entry-Level Opportunities.** Jonathan, a 26-year-old software engineer, applied to hundreds of positions with minimal responses, highlighting the competitive and saturated job market.
- **Questioning the Value of a Degree.** Many graduates are questioning the return on investment of their college education. Some are accepting roles outside their field of study or pursuing additional education to enhance their employability.

Will Artificial Intelligence and Automation Kill Most Jobs?

All business firms will replace jobs that can be done better or cheaper with artificial intelligence and automation. This applies particularly to jobs based on repetitive work where the rules are clear. This describes many early-entry jobs.

One CEO made the following statement about AI: "I am of the opinion that AI can already do all of the jobs that we as humans do."

This CEO is clearly wrong. There will be many jobs that cannot be done by AI or machinery. Here are the characteristics of jobs needing a lot of human judgment or service:

- Jobs with a high level of complexity requiring experience and deep analysis.
- Jobs undergoing rapid changes in their work rules.

- Jobs involving personal service, care and empathy.
- Jobs involving decisions that will affect a huge number of people and require widespread approval beyond just cost savings.

If Most Jobs Disappear, How Can Jobless Persons Be Supported in a Post-Work Society?

One of the first people to raise this question is Jeremy Rifkin who published *The End of Work: The Decline of the Global Labor Force and the Dawn of the Post-Market Era* in 1995. Rifkin argued that advances in technology—especially automation, robotics, and information systems—were already reducing the demand for human labor in such areas as manufacturing, agriculture, services, and clerical jobs. Rifkin saw this happening years before AI, digitalization, machine learning, 3D printing, and several other new technologies existed. He predicted a polarized society and a shrinking middle class with a small elite of highly skilled professionals and millions of others facing precarious employment. To help the unemployed, Rifkin advocated a "third sector" of volunteer and community-based service organizations that would create new jobs with government support to rebuild decaying neighborhoods and provide social services. He advocated a value-added tax on nonessential goods and services and redirecting of federal and state funds to provide a "social wage" in lieu of welfare payments to third-sector workers.

Rivkin's solution is similar to normal policies applied when economies slide into a recession or a deep depression. Unemployed workers receive government payments while they remain unemployed. In the meantime, the government works hard to establish new jobs.

Here we are talking about something fundamentally different. We are talking about a situation of widespread permanent unemployment. The number of unemployed workers hugely exceeds the number of available jobs. The nation can produce all the goods and services that people need through automated work without needing their labor.

Of course there will be some jobs. Skilled people are needed to manage government agencies and companies. Service people are needed to do things that machines can't do, such as hair styling and taking care of older parents and younger children.

Most citizens will have no jobs and no income. How are they to be supported? What will government and business do to help?

The government will be much smaller in size because most government work will be run by AI. The government will raise money by taxing existing businesses. It will distribute the tax money to unemployed workers. Firms will call these taxes their "social responsibility" expenditures. The government will decide on how to distribute adequate payments to its jobless citizens. Large families will receive larger total payment. The government will set up a UBI system (Universal Basic Income). UBI provides all citizens with a regular unconditional cash payment to reduce poverty and improve financial stability. UBI was typically limited to low-income individuals. The system might start with every new baby receiving a $5,000 deposit in a bank that will earn a normal interest rate. The money cannot be withdrawn until the newborn reaches age 20.

The challenge is to maintain egalitarianism and meaning in the post-work society. Jobless citizens will receive UBI money and make cash payments for their purchases of goods and services.

We assume that a democratic government will take over in the post-work world. Otherwise, the government might be a dictatorship that controls and impoverishes the displaced workers. AI and automation can either liberate or enslave humanity.

How Will Jobless Citizens Spend Their Time?

Earlier, when jobs prevailed, the average employee worked eight hours a day Monday through Friday. Many gave more than 8 hours if we included transportation time to and from work and additional work carried on at home after the workday. By the time workers returned home and prepared and ate their meals, only a few hours we left for sundry activities such as talking to their children, watching TV or film, playing games, learning a new skill, or taking a walk. The Saturday-Sunday weekend was open to many sundry activities, including religious observance, driving to visit friends, traveling, attending entertainment venues, and so on.

What Would Happen if People Were Told That They Didn't Have to Work to Meet Their Needs for Food, Clothing, Housing and Healthcare?

This question was asked in a 2021 German study to test the effects of receiving a Universal Basic Income. The study found that choosing no work improved mental health, feelings of autonomy, and generosity. UBI studies across the world have shown that basic income benefits communities as a whole and does not cause everyone to quit their jobs.

Most people without work will adopt many different types of behavior.

- Some will put more time into raising their children and educating them.
- Some will spend time learning new skills such as painting, playing a musical instrument, learning a different language, or reading a lot of books.
- Some will spend more time doing local or foreign travel.
- Some will collect other jobless citizens to participate in projects such growing food, gardening, or joining a singing group.
- Some will form or join political or protest groups to change or improve government or business.
- Some will spend time playing card games, Mahjong, chess, or computer games.
- Some will turn to gaming where they play roulette, blackjack, or make bets on many events.
- Some will provide care services to others in need.
- Some will form or join gangs pursuing good or bad activities.
- Some will feel depressed and sit or lay around or sleep.
- Some will turn to hard drugs or alcoholism.

People will gain their identity and their status from the activities they engage in. Hopefully, society's output of goods and services will be more than adequate. New technology might produce a society of *abundance.* Otherwise, society will be one of *scarcity and hardship.*

Will Society Be Based on Individualism or Collaboration?

Americans developed a highly individualist culture. Each American individual and family have the freedom to pursue their own goals. Many will be successful in pursuing their goals and many others will flounder and fail. One could make the case that more happiness might be achieved by organizing and living in small self-governing communities that share resources collaboratively.

Conclusion

This essay seeks to understand a society in which most citizens are permanently jobless. Most jobs have been displaced by AI and automation. The existing firms manage to produce and distribute enough products and services to provide a livable life for most citizens. The firms are taxed and the tax money is distributed to these citizens using a Universal Basic Income system. Citizens will use their income as they see fit. The quality of their life will depend on whether their government is organized to deliver citizen well-being and happiness or citizen servitude and exploitation.

Source: June 30, 2025; Can People Live a Good Life in a Jobless World? | by Philip Kotler | Jun, 2025 | Medium

CHAPTER TEN

Can Peace Be Marketed?

Philip Kotler and Christian Sarkar

I have a Japanese friend, Mitsu Shibata, who contacts me regularly to help build more peace in the world. He refers to the time in 2016 when I was invited to visit Hiroshima to give a major address at a peace conference. The conference was well attended by businesspeople, academics and students. We featured a book containing a number of thought pieces on peace making.

My involvement in thinking about peace making occurred earlier. At a dinner in Jeddah, Saudi Arabia, in October 2010, the young son of a prominent Saudi Arabian family took me aside and posed a question. "Professor Kotler, you have marketed many products and ideas. You have run many marketing campaigns for causes. You are well-known for your work in social marketing and social responsibility. I wonder why you have not run a marketing campaign to bring more peace into the world. I hope that you will do that next."

I am still trying to figure out if a peacemaking marketing campaign is possible, and how it might look. The situation is as follows:

1. Several wars are going on, the most horrific has been Russia's invasion of Ukraine. Neither the world leaders of peaceful countries, nor the United Nations, seem to have a remedy to stop these wars.

2. Most citizens of the world want peace, including the citizens living in warring countries.
3. Peace groups abound in the world. Unfortunately, they work independently of each other rather than forming a sufficient force to influence public opinion.
4. Businesses are the great beneficiaries of a peaceful world. They are designed to meet human needs with effective solutions as long as supplies are readily available and affordable.

The Root Causes of Conflict. Hate is a major root cause of intense conflict. There are several levels of hate as shown by the "pyramid of hate"—initially developed by the Anti-Defamation League. Minor insults can escalate and turn into conflict and even genocide. Understanding the root causes of war is the first step to promoting peace.

The escalation process of hate can also be depicted as a systems-map [i] to better understand the connections between individual acts of violence and the escalation to institutional violence:

All conflicts start with separation—the exclusion of one set of people from the rest. This is the easy *trap of nationalism*—which begins as "patriotism" and "pride" and can be turned into exclusion and hate against the other—a group of people who are lumped together using a cultural dimension of difference like religion, beliefs, ideology, nationality, or other dimensions.

Major root causes of conflict include [ii]:

- Political, economic, and social inequalities
- Extreme poverty
- Economic stagnation
- Poor government services
- High unemployment
- Environmental degradation
- Individual (economic) incentives to fight

These root causes of conflict can be used to unite or divide people based on narratives promoted by the dominant factions in a society. When individual and institutional acts of violence are exploited for political gain, we must call it misleadership.

What is important to note is that the "cultural dimensions" of conflict are often artificial constructs. For example, many ethnic identities in the developing world today were "invented" by the colonial powers for administrative purposes and have only weak origins in precolonial times [iii].

An explanation [iv]:

> *Many groups of people who fight together perceive themselves as belonging to a common culture (ethnic or religious), and part of the reason that they are fighting may be to maintain their cultural autonomy. For this reason, there is a tendency to attribute wars to "primordial" ethnic passions, which makes them seem intractable. This view is not correct, however, and diverts attention from important underlying economic and political factors.*

In wars, political leaders may deliberately "rework historical memories" to engender or strengthen identity in the competition for power and resources. Examples include:

- Nazis in Germany
- Hutus in Rwanda
- Taliban in Afghanistan
- Ndebele in Zimbabwe

For two thousand years, anti-Semitism has been marketed by groups who either believed that Jews killed Jesus Christ or that Jews have too much power in the world. In the US, the white supremacy movement has continued from the nation's beginning.

Political parties in different countries often picture the other party in the most extreme way. The US Republican Party stylizes Democrats as being soft on crime, in love with socialism, and attacking family values. The Democrats see the Republicans as anti-choice, anti-labor, and anti-gay. The aim is to get citizens to hate the other party. Today the US is torn into two hate groups, the "reds" who are pro-Trump and the "blues" who are liberal or socialist. María José Carmona describes the difference between anger and hate:

> *Hate is not the same as anger. They look similar, but they are not the same. Anger is a simple, spontaneous emotion, a survival instinct that we share with the rest of the animal world. Hate, on the other hand, is a complex feeling that is built, nurtured, that needs time and intention.*

What elevates hate and conflict to war? In the US, the white supremacy movement has continued from the nation's beginning. Studies show that four economic *hypotheses* explain intra-state wars. We note that these hypotheses are *not* mutually exclusive [v]:

1. ***Group motivation hypothesis***—Since intra-state wars mainly consist of fighting between groups, group motives, resentments, and ambitions provide motivation for war. Groups may be divided along cultural or religious lines, by geography, or by class. Group differences only become worth fighting for, however, if there are other important differences between groups, particularly in the distribution and exercise of political and economic power.
2. ***Private motivation hypothesis***—War confers benefits on individuals as well as costs which can motivate people to fight. Young uneducated men, in particular, may gain employment as soldiers. War also generates opportunities to loot, profiteer from shortages and from aid, trade arms, and carry out illicit production and trade in drugs, diamonds, timber, and other commodities.
3. ***Failure of the social contract***—This derives from the view that social stability is based on a hypothetical social contract between the people and the government. People accept state authority so long as the state delivers services and provides reasonable economic conditions (employment and incomes). High and rising levels of poverty and a decline in state services would be expected to cause conflict.
4. ***Green war hypothesis***—This points to environmental degradation as a source of poverty and cause of conflict. For example, rising population pressure and falling agricultural productivity may lead to land disputes. Growing scarcity of water may provoke conflict.

5. Factors Affecting the Level of Peace in the World—We should ask ourselves a few questions about war to understand better what must be done to create the conditions for peace:
   - What can be done to stop the root causes of conflict and to mitigate their effects?
   - Who profits from war?
   - What is the role of governments in promoting conflict between people?
   - How does hate destroy social cohesion and escalate into war?
   - Who is promoting hate? Who profits from hate and division?
   - How do individual acts of violence become institutionalized?
   - What can be done to teach peace instead of hate?
   - Why are our politicians doing so little to stop this?

Peace is more likely to take place in a world of increasing prosperity. When companies grow and start selling their products and services abroad, they take an interest in other countries and the continued peace in other countries. These companies are likely to import more as well as export more. Trade produces more interdependencies among businesses and nations. Trade works best when nations minimize tariffs, quotas and other impediments to trade. It also works best when workers are not exploited, the environment is not degraded, and wealth building happens not just at the top, but also at the community level. Globalization failed because it was too extractive. We must act now to make the economy regenerative—protecting nature, people, and communities.

Peace also works better when various countries establish diplomatic relations with other countries so that their competing interests can be harmonized to the satisfaction of both parties. Countries must recruit the very best diplomats to carry forward their country's interests. Unfortunately, too many countries assign diplomatic posts to their largest donors who often accept the position while having little knowledge or skill.

Peace can be improved if nations better regulate the arms industry. We must end the license to profit from war. The public must be told what wars cost. They must also be told what we are giving up so that we can go to war—healthcare, education, renewable energy, and the shift to a regenerative economy.

In the US, Pentagon spending has totaled over $14 trillion since the start of the war in Afghanistan, with one-third to one-half of the total going to military contractors. A large portion of these contracts—one-quarter to one-third of all Pentagon contracts in recent years—have gone to just five major corporations: Lockheed Martin, Boeing, General Dynamics, Raytheon, and Northrop Grumman. The $75 billion in Pentagon contracts received by Lockheed Martin in fiscal year 2020 is well over one and one-half times the entire budget for the State Department and Agency for International Development for that year, which totaled $44 billion [vi].

When was the last time the Pentagon was audited? Shouldn't the public know how and where their tax dollars are being spent? To be clear: the Pentagon failed its comprehensive audit in fiscal 2020, the third year it has failed since the first audit was conducted in 2018, reflecting system and accounting problems across its vast bureaucracy that could persist until 2027 [vii].

In the business world, we often use zero-based budgeting—a budgeting method where all expenses must be justified and approved in each new budget period. Why can't the Pentagon do the same?

Armament makers and military contractors have a built-in-interest in pressuring countries to build up their military strength. Armament makers describe a nation's competitors as building plans to attack or hurt the nation. They continuously lobby for arming the nation better. The gun industry itself is a major enemy of peace. The industry profits when it gets all citizens to buy guns for self-protection. The gun industry profits further if they can get citizens to buy AK-47s.

The movie industry produces too many films involving guns, murder and wars, in some cases glorifying these battles. The movie industry produces few films featuring peace heroes and their work.

The media industry is to blame as well. We don't allow true voices of dissent to appear on national TV. In his latest book, *The Greatest Evil is War*, Chris Hedges tells us the story of Tomas Young [viii]—one of the first veterans to publicly oppose the war in Iraq. He fought as long and as hard as he could against the war that crippled him, until his physical deterioration caught up with him. His death and the death of millions go unnoticed.

Our politicians rely on donations from the arms contractors and their PACS to raise funds for their campaigns. Why would they voluntarily stop the arms contractors?

Toward Some Solutions

Every year, events take place that put peace temporarily in the minds of people. On September 21, the UN annually invites all nations and people to honor the International Day of Peace with a cessation that day of hostilities. The Day of Peace has been occurring for 41 years and was the reason the world established the United Nations in 1945.

Since 1901, the five member Norwegian Nobel Peace Committee announce in October the winners of the Nobel Peace Prize. Prizes are awarded to those who have "done the most or the best work for fraternity between nations, for the abolition or reduction of standing armies and for the holding and promotion of peace congresses." In 2022, the committee had to choose winners from a list of 343 candidates (252 individuals and 92 organizations) who might deserve 2022 Peace prizes. The final ceremony takes place on December 10 and gets the world's attention for the moment.

Hiroshima, the City of Peace, actively promotes each year the idea of peace. Hiroshima built a large space and memorial park to attract peace conferences and summits. Governor Yuzaki hosts a group of international diplomats, academics and policy makers as part of the "Hiroshima for Global Peace Plan." The city has trained more than 5,000 people from over 60 countries, who have come to experience Hiroshima's message of peace and learn from its post-conflict reconstruction. Hiroshima's peace plan is a set of concrete action plans that will free the world of nuclear weapons and promote sustainable peace in regions torn apart by violent conflicts.

In 2007, Norwegian businesses organized the Business for Peace Foundation in Oslo with the intention that all business leaders see improving society as their core purpose. Each year, the foundation names up to seven honorees who receive the Oslo Business for Peace Award in recognition of their individual and business-worthy contribution to the building of trust, stability and peace. A summit is held that includes keynote presentations, debates, and roundtable discussions featuring business leaders and experts from several fields. The event serves to accelerate the Foundation's vision to recognize, inspire and accelerate business worthy leadership.

Let us also note the peace roles played by great world leaders who we are reminded of several times each year. Jesus Christ symbolizes the message of love to be given to all friends and strangers. Mahatma Gandhi taught the world how to meet anger and hate with civil disobedience and peaceful resistance. We revere the wonderful messages of Martin Luther King who called for honoring all races of mankind and serving them with social justice.

The Need for More Active Intervention

Peace will not be won by words alone. Peace will be won by hard work to mediate and resolve areas of major conflict. These areas are easy to identify:

- Israel/Palestine
- Russia/the West
- China/United States
- India/Pakistan
- Iran/Saudi Arabia
- Syria
- Ethiopia
- Yemen

My strong feeling is that the United Nations, an organization established specifically for peacemaking, needs to redesign itself. The UN should set up responsible planning groups for each area of conflict. Each planning group would include affected nations, businesses, experts and others. Each group reports yearly on their progress in reducing conflict.

A further move is that the UN should contain a strong military force that is ready to oppose any nation that attacks another nation. The UN can rally other nations to add troops to stop the conflict.

How to pay for this UN force? UN member nations would contribute money to build this UN peacekeeping force and benefit by spending less on building their own military establishment. In addition, the UN would seek substantial donations from the richest individuals and businesses who believe in the importance of peace.

To promote peace further, we must:

- educate people of how money spent on war is public money not spent on the common good
- show the connections between our politicians, the arms lobby and war profits
- callout the unaccountability of the Pentagon (when was the last audit?)
- listen to the voices of dissent—the veterans who gave everything
- show the public the effects of war (much like the anti-tobacco campaigns showed us the effects of smoking on our lungs).

At an individual level we must escalate peace. Here is our "pyramid of peace"—one tool for building understanding:

We must create a pathway to peace:

The Larger Question

Achieving peace through developing a larger peacemaking force at the United Nations would only provide a partial solution. It might bring about peace but peace by itself is not enough. A dictator can take over a conflicted country and impose peace. The country might even gain prosperity. But it would be peace without two other ingredients, namely *freedom* and *social justice*. Just pursuing peace without freedom and social justice is not enough.

Social justice is a problem whenever a large group in the population go hungry and are ill-clothed and ill-housed, especially in the presence of great and growing wealth among the few. Many nations suffer from high—and growing—income disparity. Many problems in society stem from the injustice of over-concentrated wealth. Social problems are difficult to resolve because the rich are able to choose and manage the elected representatives. Social democracy dies under great income and wealth concentration.

Pursuing peace by itself omits too much from the full picture. What is needed is a richer model of the kind of society the world needs. Much of the debate is between conservatives who want minimum government and regulation and liberals who want an active government and regulation. I believe that economic prosperity can be achieved under both models. Consider Sweden and Switzerland. Both countries have a similar size population. Both countries have a long history of peace by being neutral. Both countries have profitable global companies. Citizens in both countries score high in happiness, health, and education. The two countries do differ in their attitude toward wealth distribution. Sweden historically has operated as a liberal democracy, making sure that everyone lives well. Switzerland has operated as a conservative democracy, putting more of a premium on safety and tradition. As two successful nations, they provide evidence that the issue isn't so much liberalism or conservatism as long as both can provide peace, freedom and social justice.

Now, more than ever, we must transform our economic system from an *extractive* to a *regenerative economy*—one that builds community wealth and creates a climate of trust in our institutions, in our leaders, and most of all in each other. To do this will require a new kind of ***regenerative politics.***

Other Possible Peacemaking Investments and Activities

Various institutions are capable to acting in the interests of peacemaking. Among them are religious institutions, educational institutions, businesses and government agencies.

Religious institutions by and large profess to value peace and love. Religious leaders deliver sermons calling for members to be good persons, giving and sharing with others. Many sermons talk against actions of bigotry, hate and anger. Hopefully, more religious leaders will sign up to support peace events and encourage their members to do the same.

Educational institutions aim to raise young people with positive attitudes toward others. Educational leaders and teachers should spot early signs of bullying or hate behavior and try to understand the sources underlying these negative behaviors. Families of these students should be alerted and urged to discourage these behaviors. Classroom material should highlight issues of bad behavior and propose remedies.

Businesses are adversely affected by bad behavior and intergroup conflict. Many businesses sign up and support campaigns to make a better world. The peace movement might develop a sign called "Companies for Peace" and urge companies to show this sign in their media work.

Government might undertake a more active role in rooting out hate behavior. Government can encourage citizens to report hate behavior and urge media to deny publication of racial or ethnic hate talk. Government might also develop a ***Peace Index*** to track the peace level for any city, state, or nation. When the Peace Index declines in a place, the government and citizens can undertake a set of actions to restore and improve the level of peace.

Final Thoughts

I worry sometimes that promoting world peace might be naïve. Most societies will continue to have people acting with anger, hate, greed, and jealousy. Christians have preached for 2,000 years about the importance of loving other human beings. Yet negative emotions and behaviors persist.

We need to believe that by pursuing the forces of good and trying to diminish the forces for bad that peacemaking activities can reduce the level of conflict. Mahatma Gandhi and Martin Luther King were never discouraged. The pursuit of peaceful coexistence is too important not to be pursued.

References

[i] See: www.wicked7.org (The Wicked7 Project)

[ii] Root, Stewart F. "Causes of Violent Conflict in Developing Countries." *BMJ*, 324, 7333, (2002 Feb 9): 342–345. Doi: 10.1136/bmj.324.7333.342. PMID: 11834564; PMCID: PMC1122271. https://www.ncbi.nlm.nih.gov/pmc/articles/PMC1122271/

[iii] Ranger T. The invention of tradition in colonial Africa. In: Hobsbawm E, Ranger T, editors. *The Invention of Tradition.* Cambridge: Canto; 1983. pp. 211–262. [Google Scholar]

[iv] Stewart F. Root *causes of violent conflict in developing countries.* BMJ. 2002 Feb 9;324(7333):342–5. Doi: 10.1136/bmj.324.7333.342. PMID: 11834564; PMCID: PMC1122271. https://www.ncbi.nlm.nih.gov/pmc/articles/PMC1122271/

[v] Stewart F. Root *causes of violent conflict in developing countries.* BMJ. 2002 Feb 9;324(7333):342–5. Doi: 10.1136/bmj.324.7333.342. PMID: 11834564; PMCID: PMC1122271. https://www.ncbi.nlm.nih.gov/pmc/articles/PMC1122271/

[vi] https://watson.brown.edu/costsofwar/papers/2021/ProfitsOfWar

[vii] https://www.reuters.com/article/us-usa-pentagon-auditor/pentagon-fails-audit-yet-again-could-pass-around-2027-comptroller-says-idUSKBN27X03P

[viii] https://consortiumnews.com/2022/10/04/chris-hedges-the-greatest-evil-is-war/

Source: October 12, 2023; Can Peace be Marketed?. Can Peace be Marketed? | by Philip Kotler | Medium

CHAPTER ELEVEN

Should There Be Any Limits on Free Speech?

ELON MUSK SURPRISED EVERYONE IN October 2022 when he bought Twitter, the free speech platform, for $44 billion dollars. Why did he buy Twitter? "I invested in Twitter as I believe in its potential to be the platform for free speech around the globe, and I believe free speech is a societal imperative for a functioning democracy." But Twitter was always seen as a platform for free speech. People of all kinds published their opinions on Twitter.

Musk had something else in mind. He felt that Twitter was largely showing the interests of liberals and was underrepresenting conservatives. Musk bought Twitter to make Twitter more evenly balanced about free speech. Musk pledged to broaden Twitter's definition of acceptable speech and he was heavily applauded for this by conservatives.

In reaction, the liberal and progressive community expressed pain to see Twitter change from a public company to a private company run by one man. Before Musk, Twitter had guard rails and suspended accounts posting harmful content like hate speech, harassment, and misinformation. Liberals worried that Musk would allow free speech to include hate speech, foul language, lies and misinformation.

After purchasing Twitter, Musk changed its name to X. Initially, he wanted to allow all speech without limit. This could include accepting racist speech, terrorist speech, hate speech, and pornographic speech. Musk's associates pleaded with him to reinstate constraints or otherwise X would lose major advertisers. Activist groups pressured advertisers to stay away from X; X's revenue plummeted. Musk finally agreed to ban some types of speech where harm was likely to happen to X or to specific groups in society. Musk adopted a more aggressive position, almost shutting down free speech. Musk gave up being a free speech absolutist.

In the 2024 election race, Musk announced that he would join Donald Trump and donate $75 million to Trump's campaign. He also implied that joining Trump was to extend free speech. The irony is that Trump increasingly talks like a dictator who would take away free speech if elected. Trump now talks about fighting "the enemy within," namely the Democratic Party, candidate Kamala Harris, liberal politicians and journalists, and others who have attacked him. He threatens that if he wins the 2024 Presidential election, he will jail enemies. This would clearly be an attack on free speech. How can Musk have so strong a desire for political power that he would willingly abandon truthful free speech and back Trump who is notorious for his lying, misinformation and disinformation?

The Case for Free Speech

Most supporters of free speech go back to John Stuart Mill and his book *On Liberty* (1859). Mill stated that without human freedom, there could be no progress in science, law, or politics. He argued that "… there ought to exist the fullest liberty of professing and discussing, as a matter of ethical conviction, any doctrine, however immoral it may be considered." Mill believed that the fullest liberty of expression is required to push arguments to their logical limits. He argued that truth drives out falsity and should not be feared. Truth is not fixed but evolves over time. Much of what we once considered true has turned out false. People thought that earth was the center of the universe. Mill argued that free discussion is necessary to prevent the "deep slumber of a decided opinion." Mill argued that silencing the expression of an opinion is an injustice to a basic human right. For Mill, the only instance in which speech can be justifiably suppressed is to prevent harm from a clear and direct threat. Shouting "fire" in a theater when there is no fire can cause panic and great harm. However, offending someone, as opposed to deeply harming someone, should be tolerated.

Harm can be thought of taking place in cases of slander, libel, obscenity, pornography, hate speech, fighting words, sedition, incitement, blasphemy, perjury, copyright violation, trade secrets, or food labeling. Some nations forbid journalists to write with disrespect or disapproval of the royal family, religion, or the government. By placing these limits, democracy might be hurt. Democracy can't work in a country if those in power can stifle criticism.

Today, the freedom of speech includes any medium, whether orally, in writing, in print, through the internet or art forms. Freedom of speech can be viewed as a negative right. A nation cannot stop a person from free speech but is under no obligation to help any speakers publish their views, and no one is required to listen to, agree with, or acknowledge the speaker or the speaker's views.

Specific cases involving free speech continue to occur:

- Should people be permitted to deny that Germany perpetrated a Holocaust. Many European countries outlaw speech that might be interpreted as Holocaust denial.
- Should people be permitted to commit blasphemy such a disparaging Muhammad? Austria sees disparaging Muhammad as not protected free speech whereas France protects this blasphemy under its free speech law.
- Should US citizens be able to speak openly for violent action and revolution in broad terms? The US Supreme Court in the case of Brandenburg v. Ohio (1969), allowed it to be a right even to speak openly of violent action and revolution in broad terms. The exception is where such advocacy directly incites or causes imminent lawless action.
- Should hate speech be permitted? The Supreme Court ruled that hate speech is permissible except in the case of stimulating imminent violence.
- Should Americans have the right to hold a peaceful protest? This is a fundamental right in a democracy.
- Should the US Congress have the right to regulate pornographic material on the Internet? The Communications Decency Act (CDA) of 1996 attempted to regulate pornography. But this would reduce the speech

available for adults on the internet. The real need was to protect against child sexual abuse material.

- Should city or state governments have the right to ban books? It appears that book banning has increased and that credible laws have not appeared to stop it.
- Should people be allowed to lie, misinform and disinform without being sued and fined? Again, the legal course is to demonstrate the great harm that dishonest acts cause to specific groups.

All these knotty problems keep coming up.

Conclusion

"Should there be any limits to Free Speech?" The answer clearly depends upon whether the country is a dictatorship or a democracy. In a dictatorship, the dictator of a "closed society" cannot permit "ill-informed or malevolent speech." Suppressive states like Russia, China, Iran, North Korea, and Saudi Arabia have rigorous limits governing what people in these countries can talk about. They will quickly jail dissidents to send a message to the rest of the population regarding taboo topics.

Democratic societies, on the other hand, favor the freedom to say publicly whatever you want to say. George Orwell said in his book *Animal Farm* "If liberty means anything at all, it means the right to tell people what they do not want to hear." Noam Chomsky went further, "If you believe in freedom of speech, you believe in freedom of speech for views you don't like … That means you're in favor of freedom of speech precisely for views you despise." Voltaire went further, "I disapprove of what you say, but will defend to the death your right to say it."

The right to speak freely is the essential right in a democracy. Democracy is based on the idea of self-government and the right of citizens to freely get information and to form and express their opinions publicly. Every democracy needs to support Free Speech. However, when free speech directly incites violence or physical harm to a particular group, there need to be constraints in a democracy.

Source: October 23, 2024. Should There Be Any Limits on Free … | by Philip Kotler | Medium

CHAPTER TWELVE

De-Gunning: Strategies for Increasing Gun Safety

AMERICA PRIDES ITSELF FOR ITS belief and practice of individual freedom. Almost anyone can go into a gun shop and buy a gun. Here are some facts:

- Today there are more guns in the US than people. In 2018, there were approximately 390 million civilian-held firearms in the US, or 120.5 firearms per 100 residents. Yemen, which has the world's second-highest level of gun ownership, has only 53 guns per 100 residents; in Iceland, it's 32.
- There are super owners of guns who average seventeen guns each.
- About 42 percent of American households owned guns in 2021.
- Many states are now pressing to permit persons to carry their guns wherever they are.

Many countries have stricter laws on gun ownership than the US. Why is it legal for almost anyone to buy a gun in the US? There are two answers to this.

One is that a gun culture is part of US history. As Americans moved West, they had to confront hostile natives or bandit gangs. They would settle in small towns lacking legal institutions or law enforcement. Guns were one way to settle disputes or carry out robberies. The American Civil War taught citizens both in the North and South about owning and handling guns. America's engagement in two World Wars further deepened normal families with gun knowledge and ownership.

The other answer is that the Second Amendment of the US Constitution states: "A well-regulated Militia, being necessary to the security of a free State, the right of the people to keep and bear Arms, shall not be infringed." Later the 14th Amendment to the US Constitution was passed: "No state shall make or enforce any law which shall abridge the privileges or immunities of citizens of the United States; nor shall any state deprive any person of life, liberty, or property, without due process of law; nor deny to any person within its jurisdiction the equal protection of the laws." In earlier years, the Supreme Court placed its emphasis on "militias." More recently, the Supreme Court has moved the emphasis to "individuals." Today, a large portion of the American public holds that all individuals have the right to own a gun.

America has a gun culture. When a US mass shooting occurs (defined as an episode of killing four or more persons), more Americans immediately act to buy more guns. When other countries experience a mass shooting, the country's government immediately works to tighten up gun control.

How Extensive are Gun Killings in the US?

In 2020, 45,222 people died from gun-related injuries in the US Slightly more than 54 percent were suicides and 43 percent, or 19,445, were murders. Every day, 120 Americans die at the end of a gun, including suicides and homicides. The overwhelming number of murders occur in streets or in home and normally the public hears little about them. The US has a much higher gun homicide rate and suicide rate than other countries. The number of persons murdered in mass shootings account for a small percentage. Yet the mass shootings are so upsetting that the media gives them extensive long term coverage and it raises the public's interest in passing more legislation to regulate gun ownership.

Consider the following mass shootings that occurred in 2022:

- Walmart in Chesapeake, Virginia
- LGBTQ nightclub in Colorado Springs, Colorado, at a gay nightclub killing ten people and wounding seventeen

- University of Virginia football team
- Highland Park, Illinois, Fourth of July parade, largely Jewish neighborhood
- A hospital in Tulsa, Oklahoma
- Uvalde, Texas, an elementary school
- Buffalo, New York, at a supermarket, killing ten people and targeting Black people

Note that some of the mass shootings aimed at particular groups such as gays, Blacks, and Jews. Some experts say that shooters seem to be moving more to semiautomatic handguns and rifles, especially in hate and dispute cases.

Mass shootings in the US steadily increased from 2018 (336), 2019 (417), 2020 (610), and 2021 (690). Then in 2022, there were 617. Hopefully, this may mark the beginning of a downward trend.

After decades of inaction, in June 2022, Congress passed new national gun legislation. Firearms can be denied to anyone deemed a threat to public safety. New mental health programs are funded and enhanced background checks are required on gun buyers aged 18 to 21. Many Democrats tried to ban semi-automatic weapons but this was opposed by many Republican lawmakers who warned that "Democrats are coming after law-abiding American citizens' Second Amendment liberties."

What Measures can Congress, States or Cities Take to Reduce Gun Violence?

In spite of mass shootings, Congress remains slow in passing new gun safety legislation. The slow response is due to the opposing attitudes of the two major political parties. Also the National Rifle Association (NRA) plays a significant role. NRA makes major donations to politicians who will resist further legislation or regulation. The Republican Party (GOP) is a large opponent of gun control. Any Republican who favors gun control legislation will immediately lose the largess and the respect of Republican colleagues. The Democrats are more liberal and concerned with gun violence and only a few of them accept money from the NRA.

How Has the Supreme Court Affected Gun Safety in the US

The Supreme Court in a 5–4 decision in ***District of Columbia v. Heller*** (2008) held that the Second Amendment protects an individual right to possess a firearm. It reasoned that "good guys with a gun" could stop "bad guys with a gun."

Justice Antonin Scalia in this case claimed that an "inherent right of self-defense has been central to the Second Amendment right." He completely ignored that the Second Amendment's purpose is to preserve "a well-regulated Militia," not to allow individuals to use their weapons for personal self-defense. In a latter case, ***New York State Rifle & Pistol Association v. Bruen,*** the Supreme Court further expanded the Second Amendment, providing that persons can carry guns *outside of the home*. This made it possible for the overwhelming majority of gun murders to proliferate on American streets rather than within family homes.

What Has to Be Done?

US President Joe Biden, after a deadly US school shooting that killed 19 children and two adults at Robb Elementary School in Uvalde, Texas, cried out: "For God's sake, how much more carnage are we willing to accept? How many more innocent American lives must be taken before we say enough is enough?"

No other high-income country has suffered such a high death toll from gun violence. The US has lots of guns, and more guns mean more gun deaths. Countries such as South Korea, the UK, and Australia have few guns per 100 people and few gun-related deaths per 100,000 people. Consider the following:

- In Australia, the federal government banned rapid-fire rifles and shotguns, and passed unifying gun owner licensing and registrations across the country. The government's 1997 buyback program of 650,000 firearms led to an average drop in firearm suicide rates of 74 percent in the five years that followed.

- South Africa. The Firearms Control Act of 2000, went into force in July 2004. The new laws made it much more difficult to obtain a firearm. Gun-related deaths almost halved over a 10-year-period after new gun legislation.
- New Zealand. Just 24 hours after the 2019 Christchurch Mosque shootings in which fifty-one people were killed, Prime Minister Jacinda Ardern's government banned all military-style semi-automatic weapons and passed a buyback scheme as well a restricting semi-automatic weapons and they later established a firearms registry.
- Britain. The government banned most private handgun ownership after a mass shooting in 1996, that was followed by a drop of murders by almost a quarter over a decade.
- Canada banned military-style assault weapons two weeks after a 2020 mass shooting in Nova Scotia.

To reduce shootings in the US, experts see ten key actions that would reduce shootings and increase public safety:

1. Carry out more thorough background checks, especially of gun buyers under 21 and ex-convicts and those with domestic violence convictions.
2. Earlier confiscation of guns from people who display warning signs of violence.
3. Banning assault weapons would mass shootings less deadly.
4. Building a national data base of information collected on every gun owner and how many guns they have under license.
5. Strengthening the gun laws in every state and city with weaker gun laws and higher rates of gun deaths.
6. Passing a law placing a maximum number of guns that a private household could possess.
7. Increase the punishments to end the thriving black market in ghost gun trades.
8. Start "buy back guns" programs.
9. Survey the super collectors of guns. Watch out for pro-Nazi groups, Proud Boys, who collect and possessed many guns.
10. Prohibit the carrying of guns near or in schools and churches and government agencies.

Will Anything Be Done?

The reality of a divided Congress makes it highly unlikely that anything will pass over the next two years. Many Democrat-led states are busy trying to enhance gun laws while Republican-led states are seeking to challenge or eliminate existing gun restrictions. Democrats believe that more guns will lead to more deaths and many Republicans believe that more guns will lead to less deaths.

Republicans argue that if robbers knew that every household has a gun, robberies would stop. If every public meeting included some citizens with their guns, mass murders would decline. They point to three countries—Switzerland, Israel and Singapore—where many persons have guns and the crime rate is low.

Democrats point out that the murder rates per 100,000 populations are highest in heavy gun states such as Mississippi, Wyoming, New Mexico, Alabama and lowest is low gun states such as New York, Hawaii, Massachusetts, and Rhode Island. This seems to support the idea that the more guns in a place, the more gun deaths. Clearly, more research is needed on whether more guns in a place reduces or increases the number of murders.

The problem is that the two political parties have adopted opposite positions and demand that all party member accept their position. This freezes open discussions and compromises. Hopefully, more talk will take place if the term "gun safety" is used rather than "gun control."

The basic problem is that America has built a gun culture. As the country undergoes more social isolation, mental instability, and pressing economic and health problems, the situation can easily worsen. We have to hope that some wise persons in Congress, the Supreme Court, gun reform groups, and among law abiding citizens in the states and cities put pressure to examine and pass gun-enabling legislation that increases public safety.

Source: March 6, 2023. De-Gunning: Strategies for Increasing … | by Philip Kotler | Medium

CHAPTER THIRTEEN

Saving Democracy: Six Broad Areas of Improvement

NEWS HEADLINES ABOUND WITH THE theme that American democracy isn't working. Our states are described as red or blue. The red and blue sides won't talk to each other or work together. Fewer than 60 percent of Americans vote in our major elections. Elected officials tend to get reelected repeatedly as a result of gerrymandering. Many Americans distrust voting outcomes, saying that the election was stolen. Much legislation is designed to satisfy special interests rather than the broad interests of citizens.

We admit that democracy is even worse in other countries. Many former democracies—such as Hungary, Brazil, Philippines and Turkey—have been overtaken by autocrats. Had Donald Trump been reelected, our democracy would have succumbed to an autocratic leader. Autocratic leaders are a stark reminder of what can happen in America.

We need to improve the working of American democracy. In my book, Democracy in Decline I described fourteen shortcomings of American democracy (Sage, 2016). Here I have condensed them into six broad areas needing reform:

1. Improve the Citizen Voting Process. All citizens should feel free and motivated to vote on election days.
2. Improve the Quality of Candidates and Elected Officials. The political candidates and elected officials should be of high quality.
3. Improve the Power of the Big States in the Senate. States with small populations have too much weight in the Senate in relation to states with large populations.
4. Improve the Election Winning Process. Eliminate winner-take-all-votes and eliminate the Electoral College.
5. Improve the Congressional Legislative Voting Process. Remove the filibuster and other delaying processes of getting legislation passed.
6. Improve the Supreme Court's representativeness. The SC members are overrepresented by political or religious groups.

The challenge is to propose specific improvements in each of the six broad areas that will improve the functioning of American democracy. Here I list the main reforms needed in each of the broad areas.

1. **Improve the Citizen Voting Process.** All citizens should feel free and motivated to vote on election days.
    - Move voting days on weekends or holidays
    - Allow voting by mail
    - Expand the hours of voting
    - Prevent voter suppression
    - Prevent gerrymandering
    - Promote rank order voting
2. **Improve the Quality of Candidates and Elected Officials.** Political candidates and elected officials should be of high quality.
    - Improve the primary or caucus voting system in the selecting of candidates
    - Use rank order voting when several candidates are competing
    - Set term limits for Congress members (set up to five terms for representatives and three terms for Senators)

3. **Improve the Power of Big States in the Senate.** States with small populations have too much weight in the Senate in relation to states with large populations.
    - The big states should have (say) three Senators instead of only two Senators
4. **Improve the Election Winning Process.** Replace winner-take-all-votes with a proportional system
    - Eliminate winner-take-all-votes
    - Improve or eliminate the Electoral College
5. **Improve the Congressional Legislative Voting Process.** Remove the filibuster and other delaying processes of getting legislation passed.
    - Limit the use of the filibuster (60 percent vote required)
    - Limit the talking filibuster to 1 hour and only allow five talking filibusters
    - Bring up voting proposals sooner
    - Put limits on lobbying influence
6. **Improve the Supreme Court's representativeness.** The SC members are overrepresented by political, educational, or religious groups.
    - Find a better method of choosing Supreme Court members
    - Put term limits on Supreme Court members

These six broad areas are offered as a starting point for moving to consider more specific democratic reforms. A Democracy Reform Committee needs to be appointed. The Committee sets up six broad area groups. Each group gathers evidence and opinions, debates alternatives, and develops specific proposals. The Democracy Reform Committee decides on the timetable for offering the different proposals to Congress from consideration and voting.

It is my impression that average citizens will know some of these democracy shortcomings but not know the full array. I present the full array so that citizens can put critical questions to political candidates about their opinions. Citizens can form groups with others to work on specific democracy shortcomings.

Source: October 12, 2023; Saving Democracy: Six Broad Areas of Improvement | by Philip Kotler | Medium

SECTION III

Inequality, Capitalism, and Economic Justice

CHAPTER FOURTEEN

Social Justice vs. Meritocracy

I AM A FAN OF Social Justice and a fan of Meritocracy. Until now, I saw no inconsistency. Then the case occurred when Harvard decided to ask its new President, Claudine Gay, to resign.

Having attended Harvard, I was pleased to hear in 2023 of the appointment of Claudine Gay, a Black scholar, to run Harvard. In appointing her, Harvard showed that it was color-blind. Her race made no difference to her merit. The appointment scored a home run for both social justice and merit.

Slowly we began to hear questions about her scholarly stature. Had she published any scholarly books? Did any of her articles show originality or unique impact? Had she shown unusual management skills? The answers to these questions was "no."

Then we learned that Claudine plagiarized in some parts of her doctoral dissertation.

Claudine had also appeared before a Congressional Committee following the October 7 attack on Israel. The Committee wanted to assess how three presidents of major colleges felt about possible anti-semitism in their university. GOP Representative Elise Stefanik quizzed Gay on whether "calling for the genocide of Jews" would violate Harvard's rules against bullying and harassment. Gay responded: "It can be, depending on the context." Stefanik immediately reproached Gay for that answer. How could Gay permit calls for the genocide of Jews be acceptable at Harvard, of all places?

All these findings raised the question: "Is Claudine Gay one of the strongest candidates that Harvard could have hired to run Harvard? Couldn't Harvard have nominated many superior candidates, Black and white, to be Harvard's president? Did Harvard thoroughly review her background, writings and teachings or did Harvard make the choice to show that Harvard is liberal-minded?"

When major corporations search for a new CEO, they hire a leading recruiting firm to find and propose several candidates who have considerable merit and experience. A major university should do the same. The university should define the mix of scholarship, skills, temperament, and experience its next president should have. Scholarly merit should at least be present in addition to other attributes.

But is it really fair to always decide in favor of meritocracy? Isn't meritocracy an unfair standard given that people grow up with different parents, education, and income? Wouldn't meritocracy perpetuate the same ruling class who grew up with the same special benefits? How can those who didn't grow up with these benefits ever rise to positions of leadership in major institutions?

What can be done to help members of marginal groups rise to the top?

Is Affirmative Action the Answer?

Most companies in the past hired workers without any interference from government. They either hired workers on their ability or on their cost, or on both criteria. Companies avoided hiring Black workers or women. Black segregation was in full operation after the end of the Civil War.

To help the freed slaves, General William Sherman proposed in 1865 to divide the land in the former slave states and give Black families "Forty acres and a mule." This humane proposal drew sharp opposition and was revoked by President Andrew Johnson. For the next century, little was done to help Black Americans until the 1950s and 1960s when the Civil Rights Movement gathered strength under President Lyndon Johnson. Civil rights guarantees occurred with interpreting the Equal Protection Clause of the 14th Amendment affirming the civil rights of Americans.

Companies pleaded that they would apply a nondiscrimination approach in hiring workers. Pressure groups dismissed this and insisted that companies put into practice affirmative action. Companies should establish a goal of hiring a certain number of minority workers. They should give preference to Black Americans in filling their job requirements.

Many states adopted affirmative action as their policy. The argument was that a diversified workforce is better for a company than a homogenous workforce. This led later to explicit DEI policy, namely practicing diversity, equity, and inclusion.

But this fell hard on the white workers who were better qualified but not hired. These white workers complained that they were victims of reverse discrimination. A number of states dropped their policy of affirmative action.

Many things happened to affirmative action under the subsequent Presidencies of Ford, Reagan, Obama, and Biden. In 2022, the Supreme Court in a case related to admissions practices at the University of North Carolina, rejected affirmative action at US colleges and universities on June 29, 2023. President Biden strongly disagreed with this decision on the grounds that "discrimination still exists in America. The hiring rights and responsibilities of colleges and companies are still to be settled."

Imposing affirmative action on organizations is not really the best answer to creating more jobs for Black Americans. Affirmative action is a band-aid and often hurts Black Americans. In one law school study, 23 percent of Blacks failed the bar exam as opposed to only 3 percent of whites failing. The failing Black students lacked the needed background to pass the bar exams. They were not up to law school standards. The problem is that most of them never received a good public education growing up. I am convinced that if Black Americas were given good public schools with good teachers, more Black Americans would pass the bar exam. By law schools required to admit a certain percent of students, many of these students will not pass the bar exam. Imposed admission standards in law schools ends up screwing poorly prepared Black students and depriving qualified white students of attending law school.

Are Organizations Likely to Drop DEI?

The accusation has been made, mainly by anti-woke Republicans, that universities have become too political. Instead of confining themselves to the pursuit of knowledge, they have moved politically toward embracing diversity, equity and inclusion (DEI). Colleges argued that if they didn't practice DEI, the student body would be more homogenous and lose the benefit of wider knowledge and ideas. And companies too would lose out to more homogenous group-think and dogma. This debate about diversity is likely to go on a long time. Should diversity rule or should meritocracy rule?

Can Betting on Meritocracy Be a Trap?

Americans have long believed that economic and social rewards should go to those with ability, talent and hard work. I believe that Claudine Gay met that test in managing to rise to high and responsible positions on Harvard's faculty. She had merit. The complaint might be that Harvard should have found a person with more merit instead of settling slightly in favor of a dose of social justice.

Daniel Markovits raised excellent questions about meritocracy in his excellent book *The Meritocracy Trap* (2019). He postulated three harms to a nation that confines its rewards to meritocracy:

- Those at the top of organizations usually have great ability and education. They are among the hardest workers with little time for idleness and often neglect their families in their pursuit of winning. They are paid very high incomes which deeply increases the nation's level of income inequality. Ironically, these elite leaders are generally unhappy people, have problems with their children or spouse and have no time to enjoy a measure of idleness.
- Members of the middle class are frustrated. They can't rise to the top because they didn't graduate from top schools. They end up not enjoying their work and work less hard than those at the top. The members of the middle class face stagnating incomes, increasing debt and rising despair, especially those in the lower end of the middle class.
- Those in the working class work hard but with experience rising costs and debt. They have little chance to enter the middle class. They can't afford to give their children a college education. They are always struggling to pay their weekly bills and often need to apply for expensive loans.

The picture in a nation that over-relies on meritocracy is one of a widely saddened nation. In such a nation, there is great need for therapy and for social justice.

So a nation suffers when there is too much focus on merit. Somehow a balance must be found in the weight given to merit and the weight given to social justice. Maybe Claudine Gay's appointment to the Harvard Presidency was precisely the search for a needed balance.

Source: January 15, 2024; Social Justice vs. Meritocracy. Philip Kotler | by Philip Kotler | Medium

CHAPTER FIFTEEN

Is American Capitalism Serving or Hurting the Working Class?

THE LATEST GALLUP POLL (AUGUST 1–20, 2025) shows a real downward shift in American attitudes toward capitalism. In 2021, 60 percent of Americans viewed capitalism positively. Four years later, in 2025, only 54 percent view capitalism positively. This is the lowest recorded level since Gallup began tracking American attitudes toward capitalism in 2010.

Nevertheless, 54 percent still means that the majority of Americans still favor capitalism.

Let's look further into the current Gallup numbers.

1. Among **Democrats,** only **42 percent** view capitalism favorably, while **66 percent** view socialism positively.
2. For Americans aged **under 50,** only **31 percent of Democrats** favor capitalism.
3. 37 percent of Americans view **big business** negatively.
4. Small business and free enterprise, in contrast to big business, remain immensely popular.

What Is Behind the Growing Skepticism Toward Capitalism?

In 2015, I published *Confronting Capitalism.* I pointed out fourteen weaknesses in current American capitalism, adding that each weakness could be overcome and lead to a better capitalism.

1. Proposes only a weak solution to poverty.
2. Fails to charge businesses with the social costs of their activities.
3. Capable of exploiting workers in the absence of collective bargaining.
4. Capable of exploiting natural resources in the absence of regulation.
5. Sees citizens as mainly consumers who are to be persuaded to buy more goods and services beyond their means.
6. Exhibits a growing high level of income and wealth inequality.
7. Emphasizes individualism over community.
8. Encourages greed, financial creativity, and materialism.
9. Produces periodic business cycles and economic instability.

The major accusation against capitalism is that the rich continue to get richer while the middle class is getting smaller and the poor are remaining poor, living distressed from paycheck to paycheck. Let's add that 28 percent of retired Americans have $0 savings when they retire; they rely primarily on Social Security. The occurrence of one new medical problem not fully covered by Medicare can destroy them financially.

Also consider that the working class has little or no voice in our political system. Unions are extremely weak and they are bitterly opposed by our corporations, Unions that lobby for worker rights are grossly underfunded compared to the big corporate lobbyists.

In the past, as the nation's productivity increased, worker pay increased at roughly the same rate. Since the 1970s, worker pay failed to increase at the productivity rate, leaving most of the productivity gain to go to the owners of capital, namely the rich.

American workers have been fed a string of lies about what American capitalism offers to them.

First, that the wealth gains of the rich will trickle down to the middle class and the poor. Clearly this hasn't happened, given the increased indebtedness of American workers and their inability to find and afford decent housing.

Second, that America is the land of opportunity and that anyone who works hard will achieve a growing income. And that Americans who get a college education will most probably achieve a growing income. Yet 65 percent of the US labor force does not have a four-year college degree. Even those who have a college degree often find that jobs are scarce in their chosen field.

Third, that rich Americans are very generous in their philanthropy and give workers and the poor a lot of charitable support. Yet the majority of charity goes to other causes such as medical research and education that do not uplift low paid workers or the poor.

Fourth, that the poor are much better off today than the poor of the past. The poor have cellphones, television sets, modern kitchen appliances and can do their shopping using the internet without traveling to specific stores. Yes, today's poor live a "richer" existence than the past poor but their lives are saddled with money worries and illnesses leaving them with despair.

Is Socialism the Solution?

If you asked conservatives, they see socialism as a terrible solution. They say that under socialism, Americans will lose free speech and the rights to protest. US President Donald Trump said, "We are alarmed by the new calls to adopt socialism in our country." Earlier former Vice President Michael Pence added more. "Under the guise of Medicare for All and a Green New Deal, Democrats are embracing the same tired economic theories that have impoverished nations and stifled the liberties of millions over the last century. That system is socialism," he said.

Clearly these two leaders are indulging in the classic Red Scare. Their job is not to serve the citizens as much as to protect the wealthy and the powerful. Pence doesn't mention the successful Nordic countries and Canada that have a social democratic system, not a Socialist system where government runs industry. The Nordic countries enjoy a higher level of happiness and well-being than found in Laissez Faire, Financial Capitalist or Welfare Capitalist economies.

We can't answer this question unless we carefully define what socialism is. In a previous article, I distinguished among six different economic systems stretching from highly individualistic to highly collectivistic systems.[i]

1. Laissez Faire Capitalism
2. Financial Capitalism
3. Welfare Capitalism
4. Social Democracy
5. Socialism
6. Communism

The first four are different forms of capitalism. Let's examine each in turn.

Laissez Faire Capitalism (also called Free Market Capitalism) leaves all decisions on product development, production, marketing, finance and distribution in private hands. Private property and ownership is paramount and are protected by the legal system. Persons possessing or borrowing sufficient capital can start legitimate businesses with the aim of profit-making. The most salient current manifestations include (1) avoidance of government action to regulate negative externalities such as air and water pollution, (2) avoidance of antitrust and other regulatory measures to prevent competitive capitalism degenerating into monopoly capitalism, (3) avoidance of progressive taxation and a preference for minimal taxation and minimal public services, (4) privatization of even the most popular social services such as social security, and (5) all avoidance of redistributive programs. This version also favors privatization of otherwise public functions such as prisons, schools, and the army (and its immense current reliance on private contractors). The government runs no industries and keeps regulations to a minimum. The government's role is kept to what is necessary for Laissez Faire Capitalism to function. Government provides police, firefighters, defense, and courts. The government takes responsibility for roads, public transport, airline safety and public education. The government provides regulations regarding health, fair business practice and other issues. In a Laissez Faire economy, there is a tendency toward Monopoly Capitalism in the absence of strong government countermeasures. When led by a strong winning political party and a cultist leader, Capitalism could turn into Fascism, as it did in Hitler's Germany.

The argument offered for laissez faire capitalism is that it maximizes individual liberty and the individual's pursuit of happiness.

Financial Capitalism (sometimes called Casino Capitalism) is the next evolution stage of capitalism. Financial institutions—banks, private lenders, insurance firms, a stock market—assume a growing role in the economy. Financial firms make money charging interest on their loans, rent on owned property, and on speculative investments. Financial firms and individuals search for opportunities to enhance the value of their assets. They buy and sell stocks hoping to make a big gain. They lend money to ambitious entrepreneurs hoping for a big win. They hope for substantial gains that will cover the risks that they are taking. The major problem is over-speculation leading to periodic recessions. The public loses but the banks will gain because the government cannot let banks fail and many are saved through massive government intervention.

Welfare Capitalism is a third evolution of capitalism in which government plays some role in mitigating the tendencies of Capitalism to produce growing income inequality and some negative externalities in the realms of public health and safety. Capitalism produces both winners and loser and the government has to do something to help the losers who are paid low wages or who lose their jobs as industry fortunes change.

In Welfare Capitalism, the government builds a social cushion to help those who lose through no fault of their own or through poor personal decisions. The cushion consists of unemployment insurance, food stamps, food kitchens for the homeless, poverty assistance and grants, health care assistance, housing assistance and work projects initiated by the government. Welfare Capitalism adds "heart and humanity" into the lives of those who have been hurt by Capitalism's shifting sands. The aim is to preserve the benefits of Capitalism by reforming and softening some of its features. One additional action is passing higher income taxes and/or wealth taxes on the rich to pay for the social cushion. Another additional action is to encourage more trade unions or workers' councils to give a voice and power to labor to counter the dominance of capital.

Welfare Capitalism gives rise to the concept of Mixed Economy Capitalism—the idea that successful societies need both strong public and private sectors, and that the public sector often needs to have a larger role than just welfare and the regulation of major externalities. Often the government is the financier of most basic science and supports important technological advances such as the internet and space research. The government finances most education and health care which would otherwise be neglected by corporate interests.

Private enterprise is still in control of economic development. But the government might encourage businesses to invest in new industries that have a promising future (such as solar and wind energy). Japan's government pushed its business community to develop the automobile industry and the electronics industry. The governments of France, Germany and Spain developed the Airbus to provide Europe with more transportation alternatives. Yet the US is normally highly averse to government guidance, and conservatives are quick to point to past failures.

Social Democracy is a more advanced stage of Capitalism where private enterprise runs most businesses but the State reserves the right to regulate business so that it is competitive and serves the public interest. The State also may participate or operate in a few industries that greatly impact the public's welfare, such as health care or public education. The State might also provide universal health insurance. It might regulate prescription drug prices to balance the aims of affordability and of incentivizing innovation. The State might control prices on pharmaceutical drugs to be sure that citizens can afford the drugs that they need. The State also makes sure that the system provides a social cushion to help those who experience hardships beyond their control. The State also favors labor unions and work councils so that workers have a say in how business is conducted. In large German companies, about 40 percent of the directors are nominated by the trade union.

The Nordic countries—Sweden, Norway, Denmark, Finland, and Iceland—are the prime practitioners of Social democracy. These countries have less income inequality than other countries, higher livable wages for the working class, and less extreme pay for CEOs and top managers. The citizens in these countries score higher in national happiness and well-being.

Socialism involves the Marxian concept of public ownership of all major industries. This system came out of Marxist-Leninist theory about class conflict and the oppression and exploitation of the working class by capitalists. Marx and Lenin called for a revolution where the proletariat would take over the government, expropriate the wealth of capitalists, and run industry to meet the needs of the people, instead of profits for the capitalists. The aim was to produce eventually a classless and stateless society. All people would be equal and enjoy all the same rights and benefits. The system would run on the rule "From each according to his ability, to each according to his needs." Marx explained his belief that each person would be motivated to work for the good of society because work would have become a pleasurable and creative activity.

Each major industry is run by a ministry devoted to that industry. A huge State bureaucracy determines what to produce, in what quantities, at what prices, and how the goods and services are to be allocated to different buying groups in the society. The aim is to make the goods and services that serve the Common Good.

Democracy is less likely to last in a Socialist economy. Management decisions tend to be highly politicized. There is a strong tendency to protect old industries and its many workers at the expense of emerging ones. Often it is hard to produce good consistent quality and quantity. Goods are often scarce or shoddy. Innovation is likely to be weak.

Communism is a system where all enterprise is owned and run by the State that itself is run by a powerful clique and leader. The self-selected group eliminates all opposition. The dictatorship of the proletariat becomes a tyrannical dictatorship run by a strong leader for whom total obedience and deference is expected and demanded. The leader may not be charismatic but nevertheless will be portrayed that way. If elections are held, the purpose is to select the leaders, officials and bureaucrats of the one party system of the State. Under Communism, individual liberties and rights are severely repressed or non-existent.

The state runs a propaganda system internally and externally to present a picture of a happy creative society. The educational system glorifies the state, its leaders and its history and produces an exaggerated official view of its accomplishments and its enemies. The State invests in a health care system and in science and technology. It also builds a strong defense force to protect the State from internal or external opposition.

The two strongest current examples of a Communist system are Russia under Vladimir Putin and China under Xi Jinping. The irony is that these two nations claim to be communist but they now operate large capitalist sectors. It seems that their system passed through the stage of full blown communism to a successor stage with capitalistic features. In the case of Russia, several large companies are operated and partially owned by capitalists. What is common in China and Russia is that they are single party systems with totalitarian characteristics. There is a dictatorship component politically but the economy includes a substantial amount of capitalism subject to very close government oversight or supervision.

Which of These Six Types of Economic Systems Are Favored By Young Left-Leaning Americans Who Say They Leaning Toward Socialism?

I would conclude that those Americans who may vote socialist mean that they favor what we call Social Democracy (often called Democratic Socialism). They want more than the Welfare state which they have now. They want more of the benefits found in Nordic countries. They favor the ideas of the "progressive" wing of the Democratic Party represented by such a figure as Senator Bernie Sanders.

Here are the main reform proposals that Senator Bernie Sanders supports, based on his longstanding platform.

1. **Healthcare/Medicare for All**
   Sanders is a major proponent of a single-payer national health insurance system ("Medicare for All"), which would treat healthcare as a human right. It aims to replace most private insurance with a public system providing universal coverage, including preventive care, prescription drugs, long-term care, mental health, dental, and vision.
2. **Minimum Wage Increase**
   He supports raising the federal minimum wage to $15/hour, to help tens of millions of workers who are currently under supported.
3. **Taxation/Fair Share**
   Sanders argues for taxing the wealthy and large corporations more heavily, in order to fund public services, reduce inequality, and ensure those with greater means pay a fairer share. He also supports taxing financial speculation and limiting credit card interest rates.
4. **Social Security & Retirement Security**
   He supports expanding Social Security benefits (particularly for low earners) and ensuring the program remains solvent via increased taxes on

high-income and investment income, so that no one in the US is forced into poverty in old age.

5. **Education Reform**
   Among his proposals are making public higher education tuition-free (or greatly reduced) for many students and reducing or eliminating student debt burden.
6. **Labor & Workplace Democracy**
   He supports strengthening unions and workers' rights, expanding collective bargaining, modifying labor laws to give more power to workers (e.g., through the *Workplace Democracy Act*), and reducing or eliminating "right to work" laws.
7. **Campaign Finance Reform**
   Sanders favors stronger transparency and limits in campaign financing, public financing of elections, reducing the influence of corporate money and special interests in politics.
8. **Regulation of Financial Sector/Wall Street**
   He has pushed for stricter regulation of banks, taxing financial speculation, curbing practices seen as exploitative (like high interest credit card fees), and making sure large financial institutions do not get bailouts or benefit unfairly.
9. **Climate Change/Environment**
   Sanders supports aggressive action to curb carbon emissions, shift to renewable energy, fund clean energy infrastructure, and enact laws to reduce pollution from vehicles and power generation.
10. **Workweek/Labor Time**
    He has promoted reducing the standard workweek to 32 hours (four-day workweek) without loss of pay or benefits, especially in light of increasing productivity aided by technology and AI.

As an American citizen trying to define your preferred economic system, which of the ten reforms would you favor? If you publicly favor all 10 reforms, you are definitely a Social Democrat. Even if you favor fewer, but more of the ten, you are still mainly a Social Democrat.

All ten reforms need debate. Questions of cost and feasibility need to be addressed. In the end, some of Bernie's reforms will hopefully gain the highest support and need to get enough Congressional votes to be enacted into law.

Note that Bernie's reforms are still relatively modest compared to what Europeans, and especially the Nordic countries of Sweden, Norway, Denmark, Finland and Iceland would prefer. They would favor longer maternal care for both parents of the new child and longer paid vacations for the working class.

Conclusion

Recent polling by Gallup indicates that only 54 percent of Americans view capitalism favorably. If this number falls further to say 49 percent, than we can say that most Americans favor a different system than capitalism.

I distinguished between six different economic systems:

1. Laissez Faire Capitalism
2. Financial Capitalism
3. Welfare Capitalism
4. Social Democracy
5. Socialism
6. Communism

I pointed out the main characteristics of each system. I defined socialism as a system where most industry is run by the government. I concluded that most Americans reject classic socialism. What some are leaning toward is Social Democracy (sometimes called Democratic Socialism). Social Democrats reject laissez faire capitalism, financial capitalism, and in many cases even welfare capitalism. They think that welfare capitalism doesn't go far enough in improving American lives. Welfare capitalism softens the pain of inadequate income but doesn't lift income and family well-being. Most Americans are living under Welfare Capitalism but the next political battle will be whether more Americans organize to press for Social Democracy.

Reference

[i] Philip Kotler, "Which Economic/Political System Do You Favor?"

Source: September 17, 2025; Is American Capitalism Serving or Hurting the Working Class? | by Philip Kotler | Sep, 2025 | Medium

CHAPTER SIXTEEN

Should You Aim for Financial Success or Contentment in an Unstable World?

MOST AMERICANS HAVE BEEN RAISED on the creed of Financial Success. "Find a great job, work hard, and you will have great financial success." "You will be able to buy a big home, have lots of family and friends, and travel the world." "Happiness will be yours."

To improve your odds of financial success, be sure to go to college. You can't miss if you choose the right profession, such as a doctor, lawyer or engineer. You will experience "the good life."

This advice worked well when the flow of life was steadier and more predictable. But much has changed. The biggest changes came from technology. Technology has given us better cars, refrigerators and aircraft. Technology has given us computers, the Internet and online ordering. Technology also recently gave us artificial intelligence (AI) and robotization. AI contributed to great efficiency improvements in productivity. Now much of the world's knowledge is available to everyone on their cell phone. ChatGPT enables people to do tasks in minutes that normally took hours. The result: companies found themselves with too many workers. One newspaper item mentioned that Amazon laid off 14,000 corporate employees in October 2025 and might lay off as many as 30,000 in total.

Corporate layoffs deliver a scary message to young people. Young people have to decide whether they can afford to go to college. If they went, what career can they confidently choose where many jobs will remain available. For example, becoming a computer software expert appeared to be a safe choice. However, today a person can could ask ChatGPT on their computer to design a particular software program without needing to pay a computer software expert to design it.

Choosing to go to college means not only having no earnings for four years but also piling up much debt to pay for college. In the end, most college students graduate with high indebtedness that keeps them from getting married or buying a home. Many end up having to live in their parent's home.

Instead of college, students need to consider enrolling in a vocational school to learn a trade such as carpentry, plumbing, electricity or welding. Or they might seek training to give care to the elderly, sick and disabled. These choices will lead to a lower amount of indebtedness and a steadier but lower income. Plumbers today have better job security than product managers who have to worry about his or her job. A growing number of high school graduates are favoring blue-collar hands-on-work than white collar desk jobs. However, blue collar workers have to be satisfied with achieving a lower level of financial success.

What Coping Strategies Are Available?

Modern times have led to many unhappy lives. Often social mobility leads to moving away from family and community support. The challenge for an unhappy person is how to feel better about not having achieved the life and happiness they hoped for. I remember a talented friend who primarily wanted to be a concert pianist but his family pushed him into a law career. My friend became a financially successful unhappy lawyer.

There are several coping strategies for unhappy people to get to feel better about their disappointment. These strategies can work for people who are employed, but less so for the young who are asking what kind of work they can do to support themselves and a family.

1. I know that many financially successful people are unhappy.

People who climb the financial ladder and arrive at a top job must spend most of their time setting goals, attending meetings, pressuring best efforts from their employees, and traveling to meet suppliers and distributors. They have little time for their wife and children and no time for other interests they may have. They might like the good praise said about their success but privately they feel locked into an inescapable routine. Young people might want to assess carefully whether this is the job and life that they want.

2. Adopt a stoic attitude toward their situation.
A person with a stoic attitude accepts the endurance of pain or hardship without complaining. The person tries to live in harmony with the forces that govern nature and the vicissitudes of fortune. Some might turn to Buddhism that accepts the inevitability of pain and suffering as part of life. Buddhism sees the cause of pain and suffering to lie in attachment and desire. This can be overcome through the Noble Eightfold Path. Key solutions include cultivating meditation, mindfulness and awareness, accepting the impermanence of all things, and developing compassion for oneself and others by letting go of attachments and expectations.

3. Adopt a positive view about well-being.
Professor Martin Seligman developed a positive psychology based on cultivating positive emotions and deep engagement and strong relationships with others. A more cheerful attitude can come from calmness, energy, restfulness and daily interest. Try to reach a balance of physical and mental health, family, spirituality, fun, and personal growth. Many more studies of happiness have led to the development of happiness coaches and courses. The question remains: how to make a living?

4. Adopt a contentment attitude.
Research has revealed a lot about contented or life-satisfied people. Contented people seem to exhibit a consistent set of characteristics:

- They have strong, supportive relationships. They have one or two reliable close relationships. They feel they "belong" to a community of family, friends, clubs, religious or cultural groups.
- They have a sense of purpose or meaning. They wake up with a purpose in mind. They feel that their actions matter to others.

- They are optimistic—but realistically. They expect difficulties that they can handle. They see these difficulties as temporary.
- They practice emotional regulation. They recover from negative emotions fast. They use strategies like reframing and acceptance.
- They show gratitude and appreciation. They notice and savor small pleasures. They spend more time focusing on what they have than on what they lack.
- They have modest but adequate material conditions. They do not tie their self-worth to wealth or consumption. They spend their time on experiences and relationships, not status goods.
- They maintain autonomy. They make their own choices. They have some control over their schedules and work style. They resist making social comparisons.
- They stay in the present and distract themselves less.
- They contribute to others. They help others, volunteer frequently, and enjoy the "warm glow" of altruism.
- They accept imperfection—in themselves and others. They don't chase perfection.

Conclusion

We started with the question of whether a person operating in an unstable and unpredictable world should aim for financial success or aim for contentment.

Achieving financial success and power typically comes with great responsibilities that must be met at a high cost to their family and their friends. There is hardly any free time to enjoy their own personal interests and pleasures.

Unhappy people can resort to coping strategies. They can adopt a stoic attitude or adopt a positive cheerful attitude. I would make the case that the best coping strategy is to search and find contentment. Contented people see themselves as leading satisfying lives and helping others to seek a satisfying life.

Source: November 22, 2025: Should You Aim for Financial Success or Contentment in an Unstable World? | by Philip Kotler | Nov, 2025 | Medium

CHAPTER SEVENTEEN

Are Capitalism and Democracy Compatible?

AMERICA PRIDES ITSELF ON BEING able to run two great systems—the economic system of Capitalism—and the political system of Democracy. Americans believe that these two great systems are highly compatible. If not, we may have to live with either strong Capitalism and weak democracy or strong Democracy with weak Capitalism.)

Thomas Piketty, the noted French economist on economic inequality, worried that strong Capitalism might weaken our democracy.

> *Market forces and capitalism by themselves aren't sufficient to ensure the common good and to limit the concentration of wealth at levels that are compatible with democratic ideals.*

Martin Wolf, the highly regarded financial commentator raised the same question in his new 2023 book, *The Crisis of Democracy Capitalism.* Wolf argues that market capitalism and liberal democracy must continually safeguard one another from the perils of autocracy, tyranny and civilizational decline.

Yanis Varoufakis, former Finance Minister of Greece, claimed in 2016 that "Capitalism is 'Eating' Our Democracy." He asserted the current version of our Capitalism, financial Capitalism, is definitely stabbing our democracy.

Let's look at two questions. Here is the first.

Does Capitalism Weaken Democracy?

The aim of Capitalism is to perform many needed economic activities that satisfy customers and produce profits. In this pursuit, capitalists want full freedom in determining their activities. They favor minimum regulations and minimum taxes, full property control, and minimum interference from government or labor unions.

Capitalism has unquestionably produced the highest level of economic growth and efficiency that the world has ever seen. Yet the growth came with a questionable sharing of the new wealth. The largest share of the economic gain went to those who invested, took risks, and who organized and executed wealth producing projects. The wealth of the rich grew year after year. Today the richest 0.1 percent of Americans owns 20 percent of the national wealth while the bottom 50 percent of Americans own just 1.3 percent.

Wage workers have not experienced much financial improvement since the 1980s. Many worker paychecks do not provide a livable income for a family of four or more. Fortunately, workers are able to acquire sufficient goods and services, thanks to the credit system. Workers borrow money to pay for their home, car, and many other needed goods and services. As a result, workers manage the appearance of having a livable income. However, they are burdened with increasing debt and their interest payments take a significant share of their income.

American capitalism on its own has not managed to produce enough common prosperity. Great wealth did not "trickle down" to the working class. Instead, government had to create a huge number of bandages and transfer payments to prop up the living standards of the working class.

As for American democracy, we celebrate the idea of one vote per citizen. In practice, the wealthy have considerably more influence and power in determining who gets elected. Candidates running for office need mass support to cover their expenses during the months of electioneering. They use their own means, solicit their family and friends, and hope to find a few wealthy donors. To the extent that they get much support from wealthy donors, this affects how they vote. Successful candidates with major donors favor conservative policies that won't alienate their donors. Candidates who have liberal donors or who have won broad support from their constituent voters have more freedom to vote their views. Ultimately, candidates must gauge and respect the wishes of the majority of voters in their district.

Much legislation in Congress is influenced by the activities of well-financed lobbyists pursuing the interests of large companies. The governing boards of large companies consist of wealthy citizens, former politicians, ex-government executives, retired military people, academic professors and administrators, industry experts, many of whom *prefer* the least number of regulations or taxation. Many board members prefer that workers are without unions or voice in shaping their company's policies. Companies are not designed to be democracies. Policies of most companies reflect the interests of the owner and investor class.

American Capitalism largely dictates which policies will be passed by Congress. Citizen polls may show that most Americans favor a national ban on assault rifles. Yet Congress fails to propose or pass such a ban. Citizen polls may show that most Americans believe women have a right to choose an abortion, especially if she was raped or bearing a deformed embryo. For many years, Congress treated this as a women's right. Yet the Supreme Court says this is not a right guaranteed in the Constitution. So, it is a matter for the States to decide.

Legislation often fails to reflect majority opinion. Real democracies always carry some imperfections. Furthermore, democracy is often threatened with economic crises such as recession, depression or inflation. The presiding President in these circumstances is often driven to take more control to "save the nation." Several former democracies—Hungary, Turkey, Malaysia, Venezuela, Kazakhstan, Philippines—morphed into dictatorships. When it comes to saving an economy or a democracy, often the preference is to save the economy.

Now to the second question.

Does Democracy Weaken Capitalism?

The essence of democracy is to make sure that the majority opinion of American citizens on various issues runs the country. In ancient Greece, the birthplace of democracy, free citizens voted on various issues and the majority opinion prevailed.

American democracy does not use direct issue voting by its citizens. Our political system is designed to be a republic. American citizens vote for which representatives in their district should represent them in the legislature. Two-thirds of American voters are split fairly evenly between being Democrats (liberals) and Republicans (conservatives). The remaining one-third of citizens are independent or favor smaller political parties.

Let's imagine a democracy where citizens have power, where labor is unionized, where voting laws are respected. Assume that citizens want to end poverty, improve the quality of public education, and have affordable colleges, healthcare and childcare. Further assume that citizens have livable minimum wages, social security, and needed social services for those persons who are hungry, needy or disabled.

This sounds like an ideal democracy. However, all of these "goods" costs money. The costs would have to be borne by someone.

Here is where tax policy has to operate. The most logical answer is to pass higher taxes on the rich. They are the only group for whom higher taxes would not diminish their standard of living. During the period 1930–1980, the top income tax rate on high earners was 82 percent. This high tax rate did not stop economic growth or innovation. In fact, this period created the largest middle class.

Starting in 1980, conservatives pushed for deep reductions in the maximum income tax rate. The top tax rate now stands at 37 percent. This has contributed to the outstanding growth of wealth in the rich class. Today's Chief Executive Officers of corporations earn about 350 times what they pay the average workers in their companies. The original "fair" ratio was CEOs receiving 20 times the average worker rate.

The rich put most of their wealth into property, stocks and bonds and deposits abroad where it is hard to tax. The wealth is passed on to family members at relatively low inheritance tax rates. Expert tax advisors help rich families to pay the least taxes over time. The average tax rate of wealthy families is 8 percent, much less than the rate tax rate paid by teachers, plumbers, and nurses.

Recently, President Biden said that there would be no tax increases on any citizen earning less than $400,000. Senators Bernie Sanders and Elizabeth

Warren aim to go further. They are pressing for raising the tax rate on the rich and adding a wealth tax for the first time. Thomas Piketty, the economist, called for "Tax[ing] the super-rich at 90 per cent."

The available money exists to fulfill the dream of a better democracy marked by increased spending on education, health, and childcare. Conservative critics counter that higher taxes would reduce investment in the economy and result in slower economic growth. We would have a stronger democracy but a weaker economy.

Liberals counter that businesses would continue to invest and workers would receive a better income, have more money to spend, and the economy would be strengthened further. Liberals claim that the country would have both a stronger democracy and a stronger economy. The two great systems are seen as compatible in the minds of liberals.

Conclusion

The pressing need is to encourage more public discussion and debate on these issues. We need to redefine the proper rate of economic growth as well as the proper percentages in its distribution. We must also take into account the growing impact of climate change. The more economic growth, the more carbon, the more heating of the ocean, the worse the climate problems, and the likelihood of more mass migration fleeing the hottest areas of the earth. The need today is to add sustainability to profitability as the objectives of companies. The times call for reinventing our views of capitalism and democracy. Can they both work better together to serve the common good?

Source: July 3, 2023. Are Capitalism and Democracy… | by Philip Kotler | Medium

CHAPTER EIGHTEEN

Billionaires Can Save the World

Most People Never Met a Billionaire

I met someone who I thought was a billionaire, the late Jack Welch, former head of GE. We were both on a panel and we carried on an energetic conversation about capitalism. I found out later that he was only a multimillionaire, with a net worth of only $720 million.

Recently I did meet a billionaire. Not one of the Silicon Valley giants. A billionaire who is virtually unknown to everyone, even other billionaires.

In attending a recent party, I was impressed with one of the guests, a man in his mid-thirties. He talked about supporting environmental and social causes. I learned that he had inventions and patents of interest to Silicon Valley companies. He mentioned in passing that one of the high-tech companies recently bought his main company for $6 billion. He plans to give away a lot of his money as soon as he could find trustworthy causes. He is not interested in just sitting on his fortune and letting it grow. He doesn't see accumulating more money as defining his life's purpose or making him happier.

How Can an Ernest Billionaire Choose Worthy Social Causes?

I wondered how wealthy people decide on which social causes to support. They don't respond to every cause that comes their way. Most proactively search for the best social causes to support.

Consider the case of MacKenzie Scott who divorced the multibillionaire Amazon founder Jeff Bezos in 2019. MacKenzie left this marriage with a fortune worth $37 billion. She chose to join the Giving Pledge organization (started by Bill Gates and Warren Buffett) and she committed to give at least half of her wealth to charity. She made an extremely large gift of $5.8 billion in 2020; and in 2021, she gave another $2.7 billion. By mid-December 2022, Scott had given $14 billion to over 1600 charitable organizations. Her gifts focused on racial equality, LGBTQ, democracy, climate change, Covid, and college grants. Her focus was on "identifying organizations with strong leadership teams and results, with special attention to those operating in communities facing high projected food insecurity, high measures of racial inequity, high local poverty rates, and low access to philanthropic capital."

I was curious how Melinda French Gates used the money she received in her 2021 divorce from Bill Gates. I was shocked to learn that Melinda only received $2 billion as a settlement. My guess is that Melinda chose to leave Bill with virtually all his billions because Bill would continue the Gates Foundation and put money into improving the world.

An Austrian woman, Marlene Engelhon, received an inheritance of $27 million from her family. She chose to send emails to approximately 10,000 randomly selected Austrians and she ended up choosing 50 people who represented Austria's demographic makeup in terms of gender, ethnicity and income. The 50 chosen persons formed the ***Good Council for Redistribution*** and they ended up choosing 77 social organizations to invest in. Instead of Marlene Engelhon deciding who should be gifted, she left it to a group of 50 Austrian citizens to decide who should get the money. The chosen social causes included nature conservation, aid to homeless people, climate charities, a left wing think tank and religious organizations. Marlene Engelhorn was a longtime critic of Austria's policy of not placing any taxes on inheritance. She said, "A large part of my inherited wealth, which elevated me to a position of power simply by virtue of my birth, contradicting every democratic principle, has now been redistributed in accordance with democratic values." She went further and displayed a sign "Tax the rich!" outside the World Economic Forum (WEF) in Davos on January 15, 2004, knowing that many superrich persons would pass and see the sign. As a rich woman, she is an active advocate for higher taxes on the ultrawealthy.

Getting to Make Choices

Wealthy persons with an urge to help others to live a better life need guidance given the millions of social cause organizations. The most comprehensive classification of meaningful social causes is found in the United Nation's 17 Sustainable Development Goals. Here are the seventeen social causes:

1. No poverty
2. Zero hunger
3. Good health and well being
4. Quality education
5. Gender equality
6. Clean water and sanitation
7. Affordable and clean energy
8. Recent work and economic growth
9. Industry innovation and infrastructure
10. Reduced inequalities
11. Sustainable cities and communities
12. Responsible consumption and production
13. Climate action
14. Life below water
15. Life on land
16. Peace, justice and strong institutions
17. Partnerships for the goals

This list serves as a starting point. No billionaire will want to distribute his or her fortune to support all seventeen social causes. Most billionaires will want to invest in one or two arenas. A wealthy woman such as Melinda

French Gates may choose #6 clean water and sanitation because of her previous work with ex-husband Bill Gates in this arena. Elon Musk would clearly favor investing in #9 industry innovation and infrastructure. Bill Gates might continue to focus on #4 quality education.

In choosing even one of these 17 sustainable development causes, a whole world of challenges and opportunities open up. A billionaire hoping to impact on #16, "peace, justice and strong institutions" would find a huge number of peace-seeking organizations, including Anti-conscription organizations, Carnegie Endowment for International Peace, Quaker organizations, Buddhist Peace Fellowship, Center for Global Nonviolence, Feminist Peace Network, International Confederation for Disarmament and Peace, International Peace Research Association, UNESCO, World Congress of Imams and Rabbis for Peace, and World Peace Congress. The task is to learn the leading "do-good" organizations and the leading "do-good" experts working in the area.

The key is to support the organizations that have the lowest administrative costs. Ideally, one wants 90 percent of the money to go to the people needing help and only 10 percent spent on administration and fundraising. The philanthropist needs to watch the supported organizations through time. There is always the danger that recipient organizations will expect the grants to continue through time even if their performance starts slipping.

Conclusion

Most billionaires are fairly generous in making gifts to needy organizations and causes. Some of their gifts normally go to their religious organizations and colleges where they were trained. Much less goes to really meeting the needs of hungry and starving poor people. That's why one of the most impressive events has been Bill Gates and Warren Buffett's creation of The Giving Pledge. The Giving Pledge created an arena where billionaires could talk with each other and compete in showing their generosity. By May 2024, the Giving Pledge had enlisted 245 pledgers from 30 countries. Their pledges are estimated to total $600 billion. This is impressive. The pledgers promise to give away at least 50 percent of their fortune to philanthropic causes either in their lifetime or in their will. Warren Buffett goes further and pledges to donate roughly 99 percent of his nearly $120 billion fortune to charity. In 2014, the Giving Pledge created the Next Pledge for the children of the super-rich to become involved in thinking ahead to their obligations.

At the same time, it is disconcerting that the world has over 2,755 billionaires and only 245 (less than 9 percent) have joined the Giving Pledge. Among the world's richest persons who have not joined the Giving Pledge are Bernard Arnault ($157 billion net worth), Gautam Adani ($130 billion net worth), Jeff Bezos ($116 billion net worth), Larry Page ($88.7 billion net worth), and Steve Ballmer ($86.3 billion net worth). All of them have been approached but often say either they are giving away a lot of their wealth without joining the pledge or that they are not ready to pledge giving away more than 50 percent of their wealth to philanthropy. Signing the pledge involves only a moral commitment and is not legally binding.

All said, today's world mostly relies on governments to raise enough money to help lift the poor out of poverty and to improve the lives of people. But let's not forget the huge riches of the wealthy class in the hope that more billionaires will want to join The Giving Pledge to make the world a better place for all people.

Source: June 30, 2024; Billionaires Can Save the World. Philip Kotler | by Philip Kotler | Medium

CHAPTER NINETEEN

Why Can't Billionaires Advance the Common Good?

Philip Kotler and Christian Sarkar

The cover of the May 20, 2020 issue of *Forbes* magazine carries a picture of Larry Ellison, billionaire founder of Oracle Corporation. On page 114, there's a Billionaires Index that runs six more pages in very small print. The following becomes clear:

1. Almost every country has billionaires. Even Venezuela and Zimbabwe each has one billionaire.
2. The US has the largest number of billionaires, around 624 (in 2020).
3. China has the second largest number of billionaires, 390. Not bad for a country professing communism. In fact, the number of Chinese billionaires is even higher, because Hong Kong is listed separately with 66 billionaires, and independent Taiwan adds additional 40 Chinese billionaires.
4. Germany has 110 billionaires, Russia has 102 billionaires, followed by India with 94 billionaires.
5. Each of the remaining countries has fewer than 100 billionaires, with many in Australia, Canada, France, Switzerland.

6. I would guess that there are more billionaires who were not known by *Forbes* or not counted because their wealth couldn't be estimated. This would include royals, dictators, and criminals. I would venture that the world has somewhere between 2,000 and 2,200 billionaires. The estimated total net wealth of the world's billionaires is over $8 trillion.

Our thesis is that billionaires could become a force for good—especially if their resources were used for the Common Good. There are three way this can happen:

1. The billionaires suddenly realize that the Common Good of the planet is an important goal for them, so they join forces to save humanity and Nature,
2. Our governments make billionaires pay their "fair share" of taxes, or
3. Society decides that billionaires shouldn't exist, and our governments simply tax them out of existence.

Will the billionaires agree to higher taxes? In the recent US elections, we recall that Bernie Sanders suggested billionaires should be taxed out of existence, while Joe Biden warned us against demonizing the wealthy.

There's a common myth that there will always be billionaires. And the media worships billionaires like Bill Gates and Warren Buffett who illustrate that some billionaires can work for causes that are beyond their own selfish interests. MacKenzie Scott, Jeff Bezos's ex-wife and the world's 18th richest person, recently donated more than $4 billion to 380 charities.

Where Do Billionaires Come From?

We should start by asking where do billionaires come from? Do they just spring out of the fertile digital soil of Silicon Valley? Can anyone—with enough hard work—become a billionaire?

So how do you become a billionaire? Robert Reich, former US Secretary of Labor, explains four sources of wealth:

- Inherited Wealth: around *60 percent of wealth* in the US is inherited. The best chance you have of becoming a billionaire is to marry or be born into intergenerational riches.

- Monopolies: Jeff Bezos' Amazon accounts for nearly 50 percent of all e-commerce retail sales in America. Our patent and trademark systems, which have been extended in duration, create billionaire like George Lucas and Oprah Winfrey.
- Insider Information: Hedge fund billionaire Steven A. Cohen made "hundreds of millions of dollars of illegal profits"—through his expertise in insider trading. This is not an isolated incident.
- Politics: You can invest in politicians—or even bet on them, like racehorses—through your timely campaign contributions. Americans for Tax Fairness estimates that Charles Koch and David Koch and/or Koch Industries could save between $1 billion and $1.4 billion combined in income taxes each year from the Trump tax law—and that doesn't include how much the Koch Industries save in taxes on offshore profits or how much their heirs will benefit from weakening the estate tax.

Good luck with these four strategies.

Without them, the average US worker would have to work for ***25 thousand years*** to become a billionaire.

How has the number of billionaires grown over the past few decades? In 1996 there were 423 billionaires spotted in the wild. In 2019, that number rose to 2,153. Billionaires constitute just 0.00003 percent of the world population, but they currently own the equivalent of 12 percent of the GWP (gross world product) and a much larger percentage of the total wealth of the world.

Interestingly, even as Covid destroyed the economy, billionaires got richer– to the tune of $10.2 trillion.

The Billionaire's Defense

Arguments used to defend billionaires are often based on the story that *without billionaires, society would not progress*—innovation and philanthropy would diminish—making life even worse. Facebook CEO Mark Zuckerberg, worth $70bn, explains this in an appearance on Fox News. Billionaires should not exist in a "cosmic sense," but in reality most of them are simply "people who do really good things and kind of help a lot of other people. And you get well compensated for that." He warned about the dangers of ceding too much control over their wealth to the government, allegedly bound to stifle innovation and competition and "deprive the market" of his fellow billionaires' funding for philanthropy and scientific research.

"Some people think that, okay, well the issue or the way to deal with this sort of accumulation of wealth is, 'Let's just have the government take it all,'" Zuckerberg said. "And now the government can basically decide, you know, all of the medical research that gets done."

So who decides what research gets done? The drug companies? The billionaires themselves? There is a serious argument to be made that allowing billionaires to decide societal priorities is profoundly undemocratic. Should mega-rich donors like Bill Gates drive philanthropy, usurping the role of democratic governments to decide what social ills to tackle and how?

Even in terms of innovation, Zuckerberg is wrong. The Information Technology and Innovation Foundation (ITIF) reports that while in the 1970s almost all innovation winners came from corporations acting on their own, more recently over two-thirds of the winners have come from partnerships involving business and government, including federal labs and federally funded university research. Moreover, in 2006, 77 of the 88 US entities that produced award-winning innovations were beneficiaries of federal funding.

Facebook, for all Zuckerberg's talk about innovation, makes the bulk of its profits from selling access to customer data via advertising. It's certainly *not* a fountain of societal innovation.

Unfortunately, the record of billionaire activism is not always a stellar example upholding human values or even democracy, for that matter. The John Birch society, for example, was principally backed by Fred Koch, the father of the infamous Koch brothers. The society famously attacked Martin Luther King and the Civil Rights movement, as well as JFK—with a campaign to spread hate just two weeks before his assassination in Dallas. This thread of regressive billionaire activism continues to this day. The John Birch society's tired slogan—"this is a republic, not a democracy" is now being amplified by the Trumpists.

These are billionaires who are *not* interested in the Common Good. In fact, it is their actions that have driven our society to a level of public insecurity and mistrust, not seen since the 60s, or the Civil War, as some have argued. Clearly, not all billionaires are interested in saving the world.

Will Billionaires Solve the World's Biggest Problems?

Our world is plagued with wicked problems. Recently, we started a project studying what we can do to mitigate the seven most Wicked Problems in the world. Covid-19, for example, would be classified under "health and livelihood" and hopefully the new vaccines will get the coronavirus problem under control within a few years.

Note that one of the Wicked7 problems is inequality. As a problem, it also contributes to other problems such as war and health and livelihood. Inequality is an insidious and growing problem and it is intrinsically related to the growing number of billionaires in the world. As the number of billionaires increase, and average incomes remain the same, income inequality grows as a problem.

Given that these wicked problems are an existential threat to our future as a civilization, why is it that the smartest minds in the world are still busy working on algorithms to maximize advertising efficiency or building financial instruments for hedge-fund profits?

What would happen if the world drafted Bill Gates, Elon Musk, Tim Cook, Jamie Dimon, and Jeff Bezos—gave them a mission to find solutions to "save the planet in the interest of the common good" and then presented their "solutions" to the governments of the world—put them to a global vote? The Big 5 CEOs could afford to be paid *nothing* for this challenge. Well, isn't that what they should be working on? Paul Polman, former CEO of Unilever, could also be drafted as the project manager of this *Manhattan Project to save humanity*. Let's lock them in a "zoom-room" for the next six months and see what they come up with—we're pretty sure their businesses will continue doing well without batting an eyelid.

Narrowing the Distance Between the Rich and the Poor?

We also must ask: what would happen if our governments started working for the Common Good?

What would it mean to the world if we (1) got rid of *monopolies*, (2) stopped the use of *insider information*, (3) prevented billionaires from *buying off politicians*, and (4) made it harder for the billionaires and their corporations to *avoid paying taxes*?

You can't—as the late Paul Polak used to say—"donate your way out of poverty." Billionaires know that just giving money to the poor is not a lasting solution. The statement is often made "don't give fish to the hungry, just teach them how to fish." The task is how to create a better education and better skills in people so that they can create value for others and get paid for the value they create.

A quick review of the history of taxation in the US shows us what's been going on: for too long, too many wealthy persons have paid taxes on their wealth at a lower rate than their secretaries! Today's top US marginal income tax rate is 37 percent. This is the rate paid on the last bracket of income, not on the whole income. The rich person pays substantially less that 37 percent on his or her total income. The 37 percent bracket only affects persons earning an annual income of $518,400 or more.

Look at how high the top bracket income tax has been historically. The rate was almost 80 percent in World War 1, over 90 percent in World War 2, and pushed down over time by Republicans to a low of 37 percent.

This 37 percent top tax rate seems ridiculously lower compared to Scandinavian countries that pay a top income tax rate of 70 percent. What do Scandinavians get back for this very high marginal tax rate? They get back "freedom from insecurity." Scandinavians don't have to pay for medicines, surgeries, college education, maternity leave, longer vacations, and so on. The evidence is clear that many Americans might prefer to live in a country with higher taxes on the rich, than in today's America where at least 15–20 percent of US citizens can't meet their basic needs without help. Yes, most of us have plenty to eat but the important things we need like health care and a college education are priced as luxury goods.

Isn't it interesting that US citizens have to pay US taxes no matter where in the world they earn their money, but our US corporations don't have to do the same. And we thought *corporations were people too*!

Americans for Tax Fairness points out the loopholes:

- Tax avoidance through offshore tax loopholes is a significant reason why corporations, which paid one-third of federal revenues 60 years ago, now pay one-tenth of federal revenues.
- US corporations dodge $90 billion a year in income taxes by shifting profits to subsidiaries—often no more than a post office box—in tax havens.

- US corporations hold $2.1 trillion in profits offshore—much in tax havens—that have not been taxed in the US.
- General Electric, which uses a loophole for offshore financial profits, earned $27.5 billion in profits from 2008 to 2012 but claimed tax refunds of $3.1 billion.
- Apple made $74 billion from 2009–2012 on worldwide sales (excluding the Americas) and paid almost nothing in taxes to any country.
- 26 profitable Fortune 500 firms paid no federal income taxes from 2008–2012. 111 large, profitable corporations paid zero federal income taxes in at least one of those five years.

The simplest solution is to end tax "deferral." Corporations would pay taxes on offshore income the year it is earned, rather than indefinitely avoid paying US income taxes. This would also remove incentives to shift US profits to tax havens, and it would raise $600 billion over 10 years.

Why isn't this happening? Ask your local Senator or Congressperson.

Chances are they are too busy raising campaign funds for their re-election.

Passing a higher tax on the rich only slows down the growth of their wealth. Senators Elizabeth Warren and Bernie Sanders have called for a wealth tax. Elizabeth Warren proposed that households should pay an annual 2 percent tax on their net worth above $50 million, and a 3 percent tax on every dollar of net worth above $1 billion. She recently added possibly raising the billionaire wealth tax rate to 6 percent instead of 3 percent to help pay for "Medicare for All." Note that the working poor and the middle class do not pay higher taxes. The wealth tax is only paid by very rich.

Another solution is to raise the estate tax. Wealthy persons need a plan describing how their wealth should be divided upon their death. They cannot be allowed to avoid paying estate taxes on their wealth. Married couples won't pay any inheritance tax on the first $22.36 million in exemptions. The tax on the remaining wealth after exemption is 40 percent.

The estate tax could yield more if two changes occurred:

1. lower the tax-exempt amount to a much lower number, and
2. increase the tax rate on the remaining amount from 40 percent to a much higher number—say 70 percent.

The government should increase the estate tax rate in a further effort to reduce the growing concentration of wealth in the US. Yet Republicans argue that higher estate taxes will lead to more avoidance and also lead talented people to work less hard or threaten to leave the country. I would counterargue that there are a great many civic-minded talented people waiting to move up the wealth ladder and take their place. The tough issue is what the government will do with the higher estate taxes? Will it be used by government to increase wages and jobs? Or will it go into more defense spending and more bureaucracies? Why don't we ask citizens to decide?

Convincing Billionaires to Consider the Future of the Planet

Let's return to how to encourage the super-rich to give back more of their wealth to society. Bill and Melinda Gates and Warren Buffett carried out an excellent approach to this problem, with their giving pledge. They recruited billionaires to make a commitment to distribute half of their wealth to philanthropic causes within the next 10 years. Today 211 billionaires have made this pledge. Furthermore, each billionaire describes the cause(s) that might get his or her "give-back." There is an argument to be made that if the rich have to "give back" to society, they took too much from society to begin with.

The recruiting effort is continuing. Imagine how many low income persons would benefit if 2,000 billionaires, not just 211 would implement a giving pledge.

Billionaires face the problem of identifying which giving causes would do the most good. This problem faces all the billionaires, including the largest ones: Jeff Bezos ($200B), Bill Gates ($98B), Bernard Arnault and family ($76B), Warren Buffett ($67.5B), Larry Ellison ($59B), Amancio Ortega ($55.1B), Mark Zuckerberg ($54.7B), Jim Wolcott ($54.6B), Alice Wolcott ($54.4B), and S. Robson Walton ($54B).

Billionaires prefer giving away their money to their favorite causes rather than giving their money as taxes to the US Treasury. They want to control who gets the money. They might not want to see the money go to make or buy more weapons of war.

This problem has been dubbed "gilded giving" by the Institute for Policy Studies. Here is their description of the problem:

- *The charitable sector is currently experiencing a transition from broad-based support across a wide range of donors to top-heavy philanthropy increasingly dominated by a small number of very wealthy individuals and foundations. This has significant implications for the practice of fundraising, the role of the independent nonprofit sector, and the health of our larger democratic civil society.*
- *Risks to charitable independent sector organizations include increased volatility and unpredictability in funding, making it more difficult to budget and forecast income into the future; an increased need to shift toward major donor cultivation; and an increased bias toward funding heavily major-donor-directed boutique organizations and projects. The increasing power of a small number of donors also greatly increases the potential for mission distortion.*
- *Risks to the public include an increasingly unaccountable and undemocratic philanthropic sector; the rise of tax avoidance philanthropy; the warehousing of wealth in the face of urgent needs; self-dealing philanthropy; and the increasing use of philanthropy as an extension of power and privilege protection.*

This privatization of charity and the job of government does not bode well for democracy *or* the common good. Yet there are exceptions. When Andrew Carnegie, the richest man at the time, decided to start giving back money to good causes, he landed on a brilliant idea. He wanted to raise the educational level of average Americans. Instead of giving money to colleges, he decided to build public libraries, first in America and later around the world. With public libraries, persons would have access to books and be able to build their knowledge in whatever field of interest. Young students could sit quietly in a library, do their homework and chance on seeing a book that might change their life.

Lessons from the Gilded Age

The US simply needs to look back at history, to our Gilded Age, to see what can be done to curb wealth growth.

President Theodore Roosevelt, elected in 1901, moved to break up the monopolies. John D Rockefeller's Standard Oil was split into 34 separate companies, including the predecessors of Exxon, BP and Chevron.

What's stopping us from doing this today?

We need to convince billionaires that contributing to an equitable and harmonious society is as pleasurable as earning a lot of money.

The Danger to Democracy

Finally, are billionaires a threat to democracy?

Both Trump and Biden raised a substantial part of their campaign contributions from billionaires. Apparently the total cost of the 2020 election was close to $14 billion, making it the most expensive election in history and twice as expensive as the previous presidential election cycle! The Institute for Political Innovation points out: although people tend to think of the American political system as a public institution based on high-minded principles, it's not. Politics behaves according to the same kinds of incentives and forces that shape competition in any private industry. Katherine Gehl and Michael Porter sound the alarm, and make suggestions on what can be done to unrig our political system.

Rebecca Henderson points out that in the US and the UK, only around 30 percent of the youngest voters feel that it is "essential" to live in a democracy, compared with upwards of three-quarters of voters born before WWII.

She explains:

> *If government is the counterweight to the free market, democracy is the force that ensures that governments do not devolve into tyranny, seizing control of the markets in the process. I believe that strengthening democracy is the only way to ensure the widespread survival of free-market capitalism, and with it the prosperity and opportunity that has changed the lives of billions of people. It's also the only way to tackle the world's biggest threats, from global warming to inequality. Business has the resources, political power, incentives, and responsibility to make significant progress in this endeavor. Indeed, it has widespread support. People today report trusting their employer more than the government or the media, and a recent global survey finds that 71 percent of respondents believe that "it is critically important for my CEO to respond to these challenging times."*

So, the final outcome of this debate is political. And that is not always, as history has taught us, a pleasant outcome.

Studies show that as income inequality grows, so does social unrest and populism. The threat of fascism increases exponentially.

It's time to come to our senses as a society, and put a stop to this unbalanced economic system. Times of crises call out for public leadership in service of the Common Good. Absent that leadership, businesses have a responsibility to not be silent, and more importantly, to act.

In a Democracy, that means all of us, billionaires, businesses, and citizens, must act in a transparent way to:

1. ensure the public is given access to the truth, and protected from misinformation and "alternative facts,"
2. ensure elections will be fair and free (without the imposition of poll taxes, and other suppression techniques),
3. promote policies for the Common Good, instead of tax-breaks that serve narrow, special interests.

In short, businesses should support Democracy, and protect society from corruption. Without this basic understanding, we will see a government, institutions, and markets that are no longer trusted by the consumer or the citizen. We will be unable to react to other, more difficult, challenges, and the government of the people, by the people, and for the people will perish from this Earth.

If you're a billionaire, ask yourself: what kind of world do I want to leave to my children?

The rest of us should ask ourselves this question as well. Our time as humans on this planet is almost up. Who will lead us?

Initially published on FIXCapitalism.com, December 6, 2020

Source: January 13, 2021; Why Can't Billionaires Advance the Common Good | by Philip Kotler | Medium

CHAPTER TWENTY

Making the World Better: Higher Taxes or Higher Philanthropy

THE WORLD IS IN PAIN. The world's people are immersed in a deep psychological depression. Having been infected with Covid 19, warned that planet earth is warming, living with product shortages and rising inflation, and witnessing power "wars" (China, Russia, Iran and North Korea), people yearn to go back to the relative peaceful economic and social conditions of 1945–1980.

The world's nations are struggling with infinite problems in the face of very limited resources. Most of the world's wealth is concentrated in very few hands. In America, 750 billionaires have 50 percent more wealth than the entire bottom half of American society. Worldwide, Oxfam reports that the world's 2,153 billionaires have more wealth than the 4.6 billion people who make up 60 percent of the planet's population (Oxfam, Time to Care 2020).

What is wrong with this incredible concentration of wealth? For one thing, billionaires exercise too much control over our elections. They support the most conservative candidates who want minimum government, minimum taxes and minimum regulations. Their candidates will favor trimming or abolishing Social Security and Medicare and other programs. America can no longer be called a democracy when so few people have so much influence on our country's policies.

To protect democracy, one answer is for the government to raise taxes on the wealthy and use the additional revenue to fix our economic and social problems. However is this fair to wealthy people? Many—such as Bill Gates, Warren Buffett, Michael Dell, Mark Zuckerberg and others—have earned their wealth by creating new successful product and service businesses providing many jobs to people. On the other hand, a great number of multi-millionaires and billionaires inherited their money and did not create new products or businesses. They had the luck of being born into a rich family. True, many inherited-wealthy persons are active in philanthropy. By raising their taxes, their philanthropy might decline and hurt museums, universities, churches, and other worthwhile institutions and causes.

The Case for Relying on Philanthropy Rather Than Higher Taxes

Does it make more sense to rely on philanthropy rather than higher taxes to solve our formidable social problems? Most wealthy individuals and families practice some level of giving to others in need. They might donate money to homeless people or contribute cans of food to a local food pantry. These acts of charity are short term responses at the moment. Philanthropy is a much broader effort to commit money and/or time to a few basic causes that will improve the well-being of people. The gift of money may go to improve the conditions and services of museums, hospitals, universities, libraries, religious organizations and other qualified nonprofit organizations. As an example, MacKenzie Scott, Jeff Bezos' ex-wife, donated nearly $3.9 billion to 465 nonprofits over the last nine months, including Planned Parenthood, climate action, reproductive rights, youth outreach, support for military veterans and refugees.

The Internal Revenue Code (IRC) defines the list of "qualified charitable organizations" whose purpose might be religious, charitable, scientific, literary, educational, testing for public safety, the prevention of cruelty to animals or children, or the development of amateur sports. In

the US, a qualified charitable organization is known as a 501(c)(3) organization and its role is to help society or groups in the community flourish over a long-term period.

A qualified charitable organization enjoys tax privileges. Donations that these organizations receive are not subject to taxation. At the same time, the qualified charitable organization is prohibited from engaging in any political advocacy, including supporting specific candidates or trying to influence legislation. Also, If the charitable organization receives a large amount of money from commercial activities, it can lose its standing as a qualified charitable organization.

Wealthy philanthropists typically make commitments of their money and time to selected 501(c)(3) organizations. They often establish a foundation to handle the gift giving. The foundation might be managed by an experienced foundation manager or entrusted to a relative of the giving family.

How do wealthy persons view their gift-giving? We assume that they feel good about giving gifts to worthwhile causes and institutions. It takes the edge off of thinking that they have earned or received too much. They are not misers or living just to accumulate money. Furthermore, this money goes to good causes. They think that they do a better job than the government would do with the same money. The government would just give more to the defense department and lots of the money would be spent on wasteful projects. They see their philanthropy as a form of efficient altruism using "private initiatives for the public good."

This probably describes the 223 families who signed the Bill Gates/Warren Buffet "giving pledge." The pledge says that they will give away half of their wealth to good causes within 10 years of the pledge. We have to admire these pledgers more than the thousands of billionaires who did not sign the pledge.

Who are the top givers? For five years running, Berkshire Hathaway chairman Warren Buffett tops the list at №1, while Bill and Melinda Gates, Michael Bloomberg, the Walton family and George Soros round out the top five. In total, America's 50 most generous philanthropists gave out $14.1 billion in 2018. A positive finding about the high-givers: some studies show that high-giver philanthropists have less depression, higher self-esteem, lower blood pressure, and may even live longer than those who don't give.

Giving USA publishes an annual report on giving levels. In 2021,

- $471.44 billion in total giving by individuals, foundations, bequests, and corporations
- 28 percent Religion ($131.08 billion)
- 15 percent Education ($71.34 billion)
- 14 percent Human Services ($65.14 billion)
- 12 percent Grantmaking foundations ($58.17 billion)
- 9 percent Health ($42.12 billion)
- 10 percent Public-society benefit ($48 billion)
- 6 percent International affairs ($28.89 billion)

Since a Lot of Philanthropic Giving Goes to Good Causes, Why Do Pro-Tax Critics Complain?

Here is the list of complaints:

1. The philanthropic money goes in a scattershot way to causes. There is little or no coordination by gift givers. As a result, a lot of highly important causes are under resourced and too many less important causes are over resourced.
2. Wealthy families carry a disproportionate influence in determining who is chosen to run for political office and who votes for policies favoring the rich. A new report from Americans for Tax Fairness shows that 465 billionaires spent nearly $900 million to influence the 2022 US election.
3. Philanthropy may be done for tax breaks. Some very wealthy individuals use charitable giving to shield themselves from large tax bills. They dodge paying their fair share of taxes under the guise of charitable giving to the needy.
4. The wealthy should continue their charitable giving but also be required to pay much higher taxes in order to prevent the wealth gap from worsening.

The Case for Relying on Higher Taxes to Address Major Social Problems

Here we examine the case for raising taxes on the rich. Among the advanced industrial nations, the US has one of the lowest income tax rates on wealth. The federal income tax system use seven income brackets, For the 2021 tax year, the tax rates are 10 percent, 12 percent, 22 percent, 24 percent, 32 percent, 35 percent, and 37 percent.

Let's examine the tax brackets more closely. For married couples filing jointly, here are the results depending on their income.

A family whose total income is just less than $19,000 pays an income tax of 10 percent, that is $1900. If instead, the family has an income of $80,000, their taxes would be $9,202, or approximately 11.5 percent of their income.

If the family instead has an income of $628,301, their income tax would be $168,993, or 37 percent.

The good news is that the tax system is progressive. The higher the income, the higher the tax rate. The bad news is that the progressive character immediately stops at an income over $168,993. The person who earns $5 million will actually pay a tax of 32 percent, not 37 percent on his income of $5 million.

The progressivity of the income tax system stops and slightly reverses for those with much higher incomes than $168, 993! Super rich individuals and families never pay more than 37 percent, however high their income is. This has a simple solution. To build further progressivity into the income tax system calls for creating several more brackets for upper income families, with each successive bracket carrying a higher income tax rate reaching at least (say) 50 percent for very high income earners. A large number of tax experts say that the tax system needs to create more brackets with the tax rate going higher in higher brackets.

Add that high income people employ the best tax advisors who find a way to get the average tax rate maybe at 30 percent of his income that year or even zero. These tax experts and tax loopholes have led to the following mischief:

- Jeff Bezos's company Amazon in a given year paid nothing in federal income taxes after making billions in profits. Bezos himself paid nothing in federal income taxes despite being worth nearly $200 billion.

- FedEx paid $0 percent on $8.2 billion in profits from 2018 to 2020.
- Nike, 3.3 percent on $9 billion in profits between 2018 and 2020.

We need a new tax bracket system and a better closing of tax loopholes. This way the government would raise considerably more revenue. The legislators would be in a better position to identify big potential solutions to big economic and social problems. In the past, some elected political party would declare a war on drugs or war on alcohol (prohibition). However, how about the government finally declaring a war on hunger or a war on homelessness!

Yet the opposition to setting higher taxes on the rich remains unabated. In 2021, Democrat Elizabeth Warren proposed an annual tax of 2 percent, or 2 cents, on every dollar of people's wealth worth above $50 million. Individuals with fortunes worth more than $1 billion would face an annual tax of 3 percent, or 3 cents, on every dollar above that threshold. This was never passed.

More recently, Democrats unveiled another plan for a billionaire tax. Billionaires would be taxed on the unrealized gains in the value of their liquid assets (stocks, bonds and cash). Billionaires normally don't cash in on their stock and bond profits. Their value continues to grow endlessly and the billionaires can borrow any needed money virtually income tax free.

Yet Joe Manchin, a Democrat, told reporters "I don't like the connotation that we're targeting different people … who contributed to society and create a lot of jobs and invest a lot of money and give a lot to philanthropic pursuits. It's rime that we all pull together and row together." It should come as no surprise that the billionaire tax proposal went nowhere.

Which Solution is Better, Higher Taxes or Philanthropy?

In theory, the best solution would be higher taxes on the rich, in the form of higher income taxes, wealth taxes, and estate taxes. Otherwise, income disparity would continue to rise to an obscene level, enough to possibly cause an armed insurrection. The billionaire Nick Hanauer warns "Beware, Fellow Plutocrats, the Pitchforks are Coming." In Brazil and many other countries, members of the upper classes have to employ armed guards and worry about their children being kidnapped.

With low tax rates continuing, the rich will enjoy ever growing wealth ("money produces more money") until a point might be reached where most people are serfs working for a pittance to serve the rich.

There is, however, a lingering question. If the government substantially increases income and wealth taxes, how will the rich react? Will many philanthropists sharply cut their gifts to museums, hospitals and religious organizations? We don't know the answer. Certainly nonprofit organizations will oppose the passage of new taxes on the rich if they believed that their donations would drastically fall.

My purpose in writing the article is not to say that I have the answer. My purpose is to encourage more discussion of a thorny issue that is too often buried or avoided.

Source: November 13, 2023; Making the World Better: Higher Taxes or Higher Philanthropy | by Philip Kotler | Medium

CHAPTER TWENTY ONE

Should CEO Executive Pay Be Capped?

SUPPOSE YOU WORK FOR AMAZON and you are at the median pay level of $33,000. You just learned that Andy Jassy, Amazon's CEO, had a take home pay in 2021 of $212 million that he can cash in over the next decade.[i] This CEO pay ratio is 6,424:1(212,000/33,000). How do you feel?

Is Amazon paying it's CEO too much? You may remember reading that Peter Drucker, the "father of modern management," stated in 1965 that a reasonable CEO pay ratio is 20:1. In this case, Andy Jassy, Amazon's chief executive, is vastly overpaid. It is even worse if we calculated the CEO pay ratio to the lowest full-time paid worker in Amazon. The CEO pay ratio to the lowest paid Amazon worker would be considerably higher than 6,424:1.

Consider that the CEO has a free apartment, the company pays for his golf games, and he has a chauffeur who drives him to work. The Amazon CEO pay ratio is even much higher than 6,424:1.

Also consider that when the CEO gets a very high pay, the other senior officers also receive high pay. The Financial Vice President might be paid at the level of 2/3 of the CEO's pay. The other Vice Presidents are also paid handsomely. This places a huge burden on US firms competing with foreign firms in that the foreign firms have much lower executive costs and can compete with a lower price.

What Is the Normal CEO Pay Ratio?

In 2010, Congress passed the Dodd-Frank bill requiring companies to publish in their annual report the ratio between the pay of their CEO and the median pay of the company's workers. Dodd and Frank wanted the American public to be reminded annually of the high pay going to top management. The public could see which companies and industries pay the most to their CEOs.

Many Republican members of Congress were unhappy with the passage of Dodd-Frank legislation. They fought to delay its implementation. Finally, in 2018, US companies begin to report their CEO pay ratios. On average, US companies were paying about 300:1 to their CEO.[ii] Some CEOs took home less than 300 times the median worker pay in their firm. On the other hand, other CEOs took home a much higher pay ratio than 300:1. Fran Horowitz, CEO of Abercrombie & Fitch, had a CEO pay ratio of 3283:1.

American Opinion on CEO Pay

In 2009, a study reported that 59 percent of the American public said they would support a bill that capped CEO pay [iii]. Then in April 5, 2018, the Gallup Poll reported that 47 percent of Americans favored having the government limit executive pay. So support of capping CEO pay dropped to 47 percent but is still significant [iv]. In both cases, a large block of Americans believe that the government should take steps to limit the pay of executives at major companies. Here are the questions companies need to ask:

- How do our customers feel about high CEO pay? Do they know about it or care? Are some of our customers leaving us because of our high CEO pay?
- How do our employees feel about high CEO pay? Are they complaining or working less hard? Are they favoring organizing a union as a result? If they have a union, is the union actively pressing to keep CEO pay down during contract negotiations?

- How do our stockholders feel about high CEO pay? Do they know or care? Do they think that our high pay has produced our superior competitive performance?
- How does the Federal Government feel about high CEO pay? Are some government agencies discriminating against companies who have a high CEO pay ratio?

How Is CEO Pay Determined

Let's start with the Board of Directors who must decide on the pay to offer a new CEO. The Board spells out what skills and responsibilities it wants in its new CEO. The Board then chooses a search firm that will identify leading experienced candidates for this job. The search firm finds a few candidates for the Board to consider. Some Board members arrange to meet a few of the best candidates to see how they would answer important questions. By this time, the Board pretty much knows who it wants to hire. The question is: What pay terms to offer the preferred candidate?

The preferred candidate knows what the company paid to its previous CEOs in terms of cash, stock, and options. He or she doesn't want less and will actually want more. The search company will explain to the Board that CEO pay has been rising steadily and that this isn't the time to lose a promising candidate. The Board members want the search to be over and often agree to what the candidate wants. In this way, CEO pay rates are moving up an escalator with no limit in sight.

Is the High Pay of CEOs Producing the Intended Results?

Companies need to rethink their pay level and components as to whether they produce the desired results. There are two concerns.

The **first** concern is whether the companies that pay the higher CEO pay ratios are outperforming their competitors. The shareholder advocacy group, *As You Sow,* has produced an annual list since 2015 of "The 100 Most Overpaid CEOs" by correlating data on CEO pay with figures on total shareholder returns. Their finding: "According to this correlation, companies with the most overpaid CEOs have consistently fared worse financially than the average S&P 500 company. The cumulative underperformance was 20 percentage points."[v]

The **second** concern is whether tying CEO pay largely to stock price improvements results in largely short term performance. The CEO will do everything to get the stock price higher (including reducing R&D, ignore climate change, etc.) and hope to make up for it later. But this behavior can seriously hurt long term performance. Some critics think that stock price performance should not be included or given less weight in judging the CEO's performance.

The **third** concern is whether the compensation plan is sufficiently tied to rewarding CEOs for practicing sustainability and meeting ESG (Economic, Social and Governance) goals. There is evidence that some pay packages pay little or no attention to social issues and other pay packages may overdo it and end us hurting current performance.

What Can Be Done to Lower the High CEO Pay Ratio?

Different proposals have been made for stopping this rising pay escalator.

- Congress could pass a new law that the CEO pay ratio cannot be higher than 100:1 median worker pay in their company. Congress would describe why a pay of 100:1 is generous, adequate and reasonable in relation to CEO pay levels of other industrial countries.
- Congress could ask US government agencies not to buy products and services from companies whose CEO pay ratio exceeds the 100:1. In the past, the Department of the Treasury limited executive pay at companies that were receiving federal stimulus money. The Obama administration also sought more oversight of pay for top executives at publicly traded companies. The United Kingdom, Switzerland and a few other nations have considered this approach.
- Congress could make it easier for workers to organize a union. Unions have substantially declined since the 1960s as businesses keep opposing

their organizing. Today bitter unionization campaigns are fought at Starbucks, Amazon, Apple, Lowe, and elsewhere. A key union message to rally union support is to complain about the company's overly high CEO pay ratio. If the union gets established, one of union's pressures will be to reduce the CEO pay ratio.

- Congress can encourage more widespread public knowledge of high CEO pay ratios and encourage consumers to buy less or avoid buying from companies with high CEO pay ratios. If enough customers switch away from high paying CEO companies, this will bring down the CEO pay levels.
- Congress can encourage more companies to issue stock to their employees so that the employees also gain when the stock price improves.
- Congress might fight high CEO pay by raising its tax rates on income and wealth. Today the maximum income tax bracket rate is 37 percent, Congress needs to add several more brackets with a rising progressive tax rate. Someone earning $1 million a year and someone earning $5 million a year should not both pay a tax rate of 37 percent. The person who takes home $5 million instead of $1 million should be paying a higher tax rate than 37 percent.

Will There Be Enough Qualified CEOs if the CEO Pay Ratio Is Lowered?

If Congress passes the 100:1 CEO cap on pay, many experienced CEO's will quit CEO positions. This cap means that these companies can't hire their first choices. The good news is that this will open up CEO positions to younger men and women who are eager to achieve company sales and profit goals without needing an extreme level of pay. One can expect more fresh thinking to occur about the future of the company and its fairness in sharing productivity gains equitably with all the stakeholders.

Conclusion

Many Americans believe that CEOs are overpaid. The percentage tends to increase during down periods in the economy or when Democrats are in power. As the gap between the earnings of CEOs and other rich Americans and the average pay of workers widens, the issue of pay equity will grow more intense. When the nation's productivity grows, why should most of the gain go to the rich rather than be shared with the working class. Shouldn't companies encourage their workers to buy stock in their company on special terms so that the workers get rewarded in good times not only in higher wages but also in stock price improvement? We listed several possible solutions to bringing down the high CEO pay ratio. It is time for more companies to reexamine their assumptions about what makes a generous and acceptable pay package for their CEOs.

References

[i] See Sarah Murray, "How to pay executives in the age of stakeholders," Financial Times, December 15, 2002.

[ii] The CEO pay ratio is probably more than 300:1. According to the Economic Policy Institute, whose calculations include estimates of the worth of granted shares when cashed in, the average CEO in the top 350 US public companies by revenue earned 399 times more than a median employee,

[iii] See Frank Newport, "Americans Split on Government Action to Limit Executive Pay," April 5, 2018, *Politics.*

[iv] Ibid.

[v] Op.cit, Sarah Murray.

Source: February 3, 2023; Should CEO Executive Pay be Capped? | by Philip Kotler | Medium

CHAPTER TWENTY TWO

What Would Happen if Credit Cards Were Terminated?

THE VAST MAJORITY OF AMERICANS use a credit card to pay for their groceries, new clothing, doctor bills, and sundry other items. We no longer need to carry a wallet full of cash to pay for our purchases. We just insert our credit card and the merchandise is ours.

I would go further and say that the credit card has been the key of our economic growth. If we did not have credit cards, our economic growth would be limited to our actual incomes. Persons would buy far fewer cars, appliances, and vacations.

The credit card is a miracle in that it makes it possible to live a good life beyond one's actual means. Every purchasable thing and experience is available. The major cost is financing the good life at an annual interest rate of 5–10 percent. The car you purchased on credit cost you substantially more than the price of the car over time.

Who profits from the omnipresence of credit cards and credit in general? Certainly the banks and finance companies benefit. The business community as a whole benefits by achieving much higher sales. But the business community benefits in quite another way. Businesses can continue to pay unlivable wages! The availability of easy credit was set up to prevent a worker uprising.

To really appreciate this trick of capitalism where we make it possible for people to have cake while we pay them little, imagine what would happen if a law is passed that prevents banks from issuing credit to consumers. Suddenly, consumers find that they have to live on their income. They will have to cut down on their food and clothing purchases, buy a cheaper car, forego a college education, give up travel and vacations. They can no longer live a better life because the artificial prop, the credit card, is no longer available.

As life gets poorer and workers see the growing gap between their lives and the lives of the rich, they will start organizing and demanding higher pay. They will strike for high wages. They will rally against the high pay of CEOs and top managers.

In the past, businesses would use legislation and the police to stop workers from organizing or striking. But today the citizens and employees would press the legislators to protect the organizing of unions. If the workers organize and win higher wages, companies will make lower profits. They will have less money to invest in R&D and growing their business. Some companies will close down and unemployment might increase.

So we are faced with a Hobson' choice. We can either keep credit flowing easily to consumers so that they can access the good life by bearing the burden of debt, or end the credit flow and face a declining economy that will be marked by strikes and conflict. Most people, I would guess, would want to continue easy credit rather than fight for a living wage and see the economy slide down.

Hopefully, there is a middle way. The basic remedy lies in tax policy. The taxes on the rich are too low. The rich in the US pay 39 percent on the top bracket of their income. The rich in the Nordic countries pay 60–70 percent on the top bracket of their income. The Nordic countries use the higher tax revenue to make health care free, higher education free, and child and parent benefits higher, along with substantially longer vacations than the two week vacations in the US. The remedy is straightforward: raise the income tax rate on the rich, pass a wealth tax and raise the estate tax. These measures would hardly affect the lives of the rich while at the same time bring livable wages to the vast majority of citizens.

Source: September 2, 2022; What Would Happen if Credit Cards were Terminated | by Philip Kotler | Medium

CHAPTER TWENTY THREE

Should the US Pursue "Common Prosperity"?

MOST NATIONS EXHIBIT A HIGH level of income inequality. Virtually every nation has a small rich, elite class and a large destitute class. The rich continue to grow richer. If there is a middle class, this class provides some stability to the economy. The middle class includes government functionaries, professionals (e.g., doctors, lawyers, health care specialists, educators), expatriates living in the country, and managers in small businesses.

This highly skewed income distribution can lead to political instability and citizen protests under certain conditions. Such conditions might be a natural or man-made disaster, a climate event that diminishes food supply, a government move to reduce or eliminate government subsidies for fuel, or butter, causing high inflation.

In a democratic country, there are likely to be liberal leaning and conservative leaning groups. Liberals favor candidates and policies that propose a fairer distribution of income. Conservatives generally favor smaller government, lower government spending, lower taxes, and protecting the interests of the rich. Liberal groups also have a class of elite and wealthy citizens who generally espouse more liberal policies.

What should be done to deliver a fairer distribution of income? The US, the 3rd most populated nation, is one of the richest countries in the world and still has a large number of its citizens earning less than an adequate wage. Many citizens are resorting to more and more debt to finance their minimal daily needs. This solution is unsustainable. The debt creates additional need for income to pay the interest on the growing burden. But if there was adequate income to begin with, the debt would have been unnecessary.

So why don't we have an organized movement in the US pressing for a fairer distribution of income and wealth. Smaller Socialist Democratic countries, to some extent, accomplish this with their broad safety net of social services to their relatively homogeneous ethnic and cultural populations.

What Is China's Solution to the Lopsided Distribution of Income?

China has high income and wealth inequality similar to the US High income inequality is one of several problems that China is beginning to deal with. In 1953, the *People's Daily* defined two alternative paths for China, either *capitalism* "a road of a few getting rich, while the vast majority are poor and destitute," or *socialism* "the path of common prosperity." A previous Chinese Communist Party (CCP) chairman, Deng Xiaoping, said "our policy is to let some people and some regions get rich first, in order to drive and help the backward regions, and it is an obligation for the advanced regions to help the backward regions." That was 70 years ago, prior to China's opening to the modern world in the late 20th century. Now that they have achieved a prosperous market economy, under their continued Communist government, they are pivoting to include "Common Prosperity" into their future goals.

China chose to adopt the best capitalist practices of the West. They used their vast unskilled labor to offer lower consumer prices to the West, while developing their own growing middle class through this economic system. After succeeding in manufacturing more and more complex forms, and building a competent class of engineers, managers, and technocrats, China moved to heavy manufacturing and invited technology transfer and foreign investment. For several years, their GDP grew at a rate of 10 percent, significantly higher than other nations. The Chinese economy was run by a one-party autocratic system. In China's long history, the people were always ruled by an Emperor from dynasties that lasted centuries. This ruling mode is part of their culture, and is expected and accepted by their people. It should be kept in mind that other ethnicities and cultures around the world are comfortable with this very system too.

China managed in the last 25 years to bring millions of Chinese out of poverty. In the process, it also produced 607 billionaires, putting China second in the world, after the US with 735 billionaires. China successfully transmuted into a full blown Market/Capitalist economy, in certain industries, and up to a certain size with high national growth rates. Certain industries vital for the safety, security, and technical advancement of the nation, however, remain government controlled.

Xi Jinping, the current Chairman of the Chinese Communist Party (CCP), observed that "the wealth gap and middle-class stagnation have aggravated social divisions, political polarization and populism." In a meeting in August 2021, Xi announced that China should promote "common prosperity" to guard against this fate. He saw common prosperity as "an essential requirement of socialism and a key feature of Chinese-style modernization" in contrast to Western modernization.

Xi defined "common prosperity" as prosperity for all, rather than the few. Yet he cautioned that common prosperity is not "uniform egalitarianism." He emphasized that "not everyone will be wealthy at the same time." He hoped that by 2035, China would make "substantial progress" in the realization of common prosperity. There will be "equitable access to basic public services." By the middle of the 21st century, common prosperity will be "basically achieved," in which the urban-rural income gap will be shrunk "to a reasonable range." He vowed to "adjust excessive incomes," but he also spoke out against "welfarism," saying that too much welfare "encourages laziness."

Xi's hope was that people "who get rich first" would help others. It would be a mistake to "kill the rich to help the poor." The aim is to avoid making everyone poor. The aim is to create an "olive-shaped" society with a large middle-class and fewer people in extreme wealth or poverty.

China used common prosperity in 2021 to pass large-scale regulations and crackdowns against perceived "excesses" of private industries, specifically the tech, property and the tutoring sectors. Several tech companies and billionaires obliged the new mission by pledging large investments and donations in common prosperity. The government got the large property sector to pledge to build 6.5 million low-cost rental houses from 2021 to 2025. The government also ordered large pay cuts for investment bankers. The CCP, during its 20th Congress, amended its constitution to include a goal of "gradually achieving common prosperity."

Will China's pursuing of "common prosperity" slow down economic development as measured by the Gross Domestic Product (GDP)? One group in China argues that everything should be done to "make the cake bigger" and then debate over how to share the benefits. Another group argues for first deciding how the benefits will be divided, even if this results in a smaller cake.

The main point is that China wants to reduce the income and wealth gap so that more Chinese citizens can lead a good life. This mission of "common prosperity" has the potential to make China admired by citizens in many underdeveloped nations. The poor in these nations will press their leaders for "common prosperity."

China and the US are the two strongest world powers. Instead of working together to make the world better, each country is trying to prove that their system, American capitalism or Chinese socialism, is the best for most countries. *Will the Chinese manage to convince the citizens of other counties, that China is more serious than the US in improving the well-being of more people around the world?*

What Is the US Message to Other Countries about Why American Capitalism Is the Better System?

The US does not pursue a mission of "common prosperity." In American capitalism, the rich continue to get richer, the middle class continues to get smaller, and the huge number of poor people remain poor with huge debt. The US government does provide assistance in the form of social security, food stamps, health insurance, aid to the poor and a large number of other social programs. In addition, many of the rich donate money to good causes to improve education, health and other services to the middle class and poor. At the same time, it can be argued that the great need is to get more money to flow into the hands of the working class. Today the rich only pay 37 percent of their top bracket income to the government's needed revenue. Proposals include establishing a more progressive income tax system, adding a wealth tax, closing tax loopholes, and taxing capital gains income at the normal income tax rate.

The US offers to the rest of the world a different message than China. **The US is the land of freedom and opportunity.** For people living in countries with poor opportunities or with little freedom, the US remains a hope for such people. They would rather move to the US than move to China. They could hope to live a better life in the US and even have a chance to become a millionaire. Many immigrants come to the US and they, or at least their children, will end up living a better life and with more freedom. Migrants come for more opportunities and freedom that are not available in their countries.

Should the US Strive to Make Everyone Prosperous?

Historically, the US favors making the cake bigger and worries less about how the cake is sliced. Capitalists argue that the benefits of a bigger cake flow down to the working class gradually in the form of more jobs and possibly higher wages. More wealth will "trickle down" and "All boats will rise." But the wealth never really "trickled down to the poor." If anything, the wealth trickled up to the rich. The rich used their lobbyists in Congress to write rules that create tax loopholes that benefit the already affluent. The rich put their money in stocks and bonds and they live on capital gains earnings that are taxed at a lower rate than labor earnings.

American Capitalism provides jobs but many are not receiving livable wages. The vast majority of Americans must use credit to achieve a livable standard of living. The ordinary credit card pays for their groceries, new clothing, doctor bills, college education and sundry other items. **Credit has been the key to America's economic growth!** If we did not have credit, our economic growth would be limited to our actual incomes. People would buy far fewer cars, appliances, and vacations. Some people would be more likely to protest or rebel.

Credit is the miracle that allows Americans to live a good life beyond their actual income. The major cost is spending a significant part of their income to pay interest on the debt. If they fail to pay interest, they must give up their car or home or declare bankruptcy.

The business community benefits by achieving a much higher level of sales by extending credit. The business community benefits in another way. **Businesses can continue to pay unlivable wages!** If citizens couldn't get credit, they would either live without the good things in life or protest or rebel. The availability of easy credit prevents a worker uprising. Credit makes it possible for poor people to have cake and eat it too. People can live a better life because the credit card is available. Credit makes it possible for consumers to have more than their income allows but at the cost of high indebtedness and high interest charges.

Americans today are living with 24.5 trillion dollars of debt. They won't ever be able to liquidate this debt. Nor does business want the debt to go away. Businesses and banks depend on the steady flow of interest to keep moving into their accounts.

As workers see the growing debt and the gap between their lives and the lives of the rich, some might press for organizing unions and demanding higher pay. Some unions will strike for high wages. They will oppose CEOs being paid 320 times more than the average worker.

In the past, businesses would use legislation and the police to stop workers from organizing or striking. But today's citizens and employees will press legislators to protect unionization. If workers organize and win higher wages, some companies will make lower profits unless their productivity increases or they move to lower cost areas. Some companies will have less money to invest in R&D and grow their business. Some companies will close down and unemployment might increase.

Hopefully, there might be a middle way. The basic remedy lies in tax policy. The taxes on the rich are too low. The rich in the US pay 37 percent on the top bracket of their income. The rich in the Nordic countries pay 60–70 percent on the top bracket of their income. The Nordic countries use the higher tax revenue to make healthcare free, higher education free, and child and parent benefits freer, along with substantially longer vacations than the two-week vacations in the US. **The remedy is straightforward: raise the income tax rate on the rich, pass a wealth tax and raise the estate tax.** These measures would hardly affect the lives of the rich while at the same time would bring more education, healthcare and childcare to the vast majority of citizens.

Critics say that the Nordic countries are smaller and more homogenous and agree to these higher taxes because they can see the benefits that it brings to their countries. They argue that the US is too multi-cultural and divided politically to pass Nordic level taxes.

The question is whether the Democratic party might want to embrace the goal of "common prosperity." Clearly the left wing of the party with leaders such as Senators Bernie Sanders and Elizabeth Warren would be happy to announce the cause of "common prosperity." Ray Dalio, an American billionaire and long-time supporter of the Chinese government, praised the common prosperity campaign and said that the US "needs more common prosperity" along with many other countries.

It is a fitting time to have a national discussion of the issues raised by pursuing "common prosperity." **Should the US pursue common prosperity? What plan would it use? Would it slow down economic growth or would it increase economic growth? How would other nations view the US if the US had a plan to pursue common prosperity?**

Source: June 10, 2023. Should the US Pursue "Common… | by Philip Kotler | Medium

CHAPTER TWENTY FOUR

Degrowth: The Case for Constraining Consumption

EVER SINCE THE START OF the Industrial Revolution, the economic goal has been to grow profits by growing consumption. Every country wants to report that its Gross Domestic Product (GDP) rose. It didn't matter if the workers exhausted their health or if many products were harmful (guns, cigarettes).

Marketers played a critical role in pumping up the economic growth engine. It was not enough just to produce an endless stream of sold products and services. Marketers made their best use of advertising, salesmen, promotion, and pricing to get all the product sold.

A number of critics have emerged to challenge the endless push toward more consumption. The economist Kenneth Boulding pointed out that "Companies not only produce goods but bads!" Economies produce cigarettes, fattening foods, poorly made cars and housing, and some other bads. Other critics see non-stop Capitalism as harming or depleting our natural resources and causing poorer soil and the loss of important minerals. Other critics worry that industrial activity is producing pollution that hurts our air and water. Some critics accuse endless production and consumption as threatening the survival of our Planet.

The emergence of *sustainability* raised this question of the Planet's survival. Sustainability is the hope that our economic activity today would leave the next generation with as good or even a better life than our generation.

The sad truth is that sustainability is now less likely to be achieved. We have learned that industrial and consumer activity generate so much carbon and greenhouse gas emissions that the earth will inevitably heat up. People living near the equator will find it difficult to breathe. They will flee to cooler climates and overwhelm urban areas with growing shortages of food, clothing and shelter. As the planet warms, the climate worsens with more intense hurricanes, floods, wildfires and soil blanching, all of which contribute further to the growing deficit of food, clothing and shelter.

The Limits to Growth Study

The problem of endless economic growth was highly debated in the 1970s under the name *Limits to Growth* (LTG). ***The Limits to Growth*** is a 1972 report studying the consequences of interactions between the earth and human systems. The report used computer simulation to project the impact of exponential economic and population growth on the earth's finite supply of resources. The findings were reported by Donella H. Meadows, Dennis L. Meadows, Jørgen Randers, and William W. Behrens III. The report warned that, without substantial changes in resource consumption, "the most probable result will be a rather sudden and uncontrollable decline in both population and industrial capacity."

The simulation model used five variables: population, food production, industrialization, pollution, and consumption of nonrenewable natural resources. All these variables were increasing and were assumed to continue growing exponentially, while the ability of technology to increase resources grew only linearly. The authors examined three scenarios. Two of the scenarios saw "overshoot and collapse" of the global system by the mid- to latter-part of the 21st century, while a third scenario resulted in a "stabilized world". A subsequent review held that if the present growth trends in world population, industrialization, pollution, food production, and resource depletion continued unchanged, the limits to growth on this planet will be reached sometime within the next one hundred years.

Critics complained that the entire endeavor behind Limits to Growth (LTG) was to get economies to slow down their growth rate. Many critics rejected the idea of limiting consumption and held that technological advances will solve all the so-called problems of resource depletion. As a precious resource runs down, its price would rise and humans would use less and be motivated to find substitute materials. Critics warned that intervention and restraint of growth would be bad moves and "consign billions to permanent poverty."

Four groups saw the LTG findings to be a threat: businesses, professional economists, the Catholic Church that promoted high population growth, and the political left who worried that workers would no longer believe that a proletarian paradise would be possible.

Yet others saw LTG as a rigorous and creditable study that sadly lost 30 years of necessary action. They held that endless economic growth on a finite planet will ultimately lead to an overshoot of the Earth's support capacity or a societal collapse.

What Can Be Done?

Marketers were specifically blamed for the endless growth of consumption. Marketers used their art and scientific tools to nudge consumers into endless buying. Marketers were in no position to tell their companies to slow down consumption. For their livelihood, commercial marketers must push for endless consumption.

Will some companies willingly slow down their production and consumption to protect the planet from overwarming. This is unlikely. Most companies want to pursue strong profits. Companies need profits to satisfy their investors if they are to obtain needed capital. They need profits to provide jobs and money for workers and consumers.

This leaves primarily government as the force that might restrain endless economic growth. Governments could propose policies to slow down population growth by persuading families to have fewer children. Government might put limits on car production on the grounds that not everyone needs to have a car. Government might discourage the introduction of new models of products that really don't make the product much better.

Some consumers may also join the movement to slow down consumption. These consumers would reject the mantra "More is Better." These consumers acknowledge that they buy more clothes than they need, eat more food than they need, and many have more housing than they need. Some consumers might escape from this Capitalist plot by buying less on the mantra "Less is More." They might keep their car longer and wear their clothes longer before replacing them.. They might eat less and choose to diet more and exercise more. They may grow to a new consciousness that "less is more."

This new consciousness of "less is more" won't come from commercial marketers, it might come from social marketers. Many social marketers work for nonprofit organizations that use marketing to change behavior and lifestyles. Social marketers fought the cigarette industry's glamorization of cigarette smoking by pointing out the health harm caused by cigarettes. Social marketers are busy helping overweight people to find new ways to reduce their food intake.

The Emergence of the DeGrowth Movement

Nonstop Capitalism pushes consumption far beyond what mankind needs. Powerful advertising persuades people that they need the latest car, clothing, appliances and homes. Many citizens end up feeling stressed and unhappy when they can't do more shopping and buying and accumulating more goods.

William Wordsworth pointed out, in his poem *The World is too Much with Us,* that "Getting and spending, we lay waste our powers." We work so hard to accumulate wealth and leave little time to enjoy our lives.

Nonstop Capitalism is leading to deforestation, overfishing, soil erosion, mass extinction of species, and more fires, extreme storms, and floods.

What Is the Alternative to Nonstop Capitalism?

"Degrowth," namely growing our economy and our population at a slower rate, is one answer. Jason Hickel spelled this out in his thoughtful book *Less is More: How Degrowth Will Save the World.[i]* He spells out how Capitalism's pursuit of endless growth destroys our natural ecological lives and processes.

A Harvard study reports that 51 percent of young Americans (ages 18–39) no longer support American capitalism. Regarding the statement "Capitalism does more harm than good," 69 percent of French agree and 74 percent of Indians agree. A Yale University study in 2018 reported that 70 percent of Americans agreed with the statement that "environmental protection is more important than growth." New Zealand's Prime Minister Jacinda Ardern made headlines in 2019 promising to abandon GDP growth in favor of well-being. The leaders of Scotland and Iceland followed suit. Note that all these leaders are women. And there is young Greta Thunberg speaking to global elites: *"We are at the beginning of a mass extinction and all you can talk about is money and fairy tales of endless economic growth. How dare you!"*

A major consumer research study found that 70 percent of people in middle-and high income countries believe that over-consumption is putting our planet and society at risk, that we should buy less and own less, and that doing so would not compromise our happiness or well-being. Many people are yearning for a better system.

What Actual Steps Can Be Taken?

Persons in advanced economies need to cut down on their consumption. Jason Hickel, in his book *Less is More,* proposed five actions that would help save the planet and improve people's lives. They are:

1. **Cut planned obsolescence.** American Capitalism needs to produce products with short lives so that consumers will need to replace or upgrade them on a regular basis. Some fashion houses design clothes that last only for a few wears or rapidly go out of style. Manufacturers could build appliances that last five times longer with manufacturers guaranteeing to keep them operating. This would greatly reduce material throughput and carbon generation without affecting people's lives.
2. **Cut advertising.** Advertising is the main business tool that drives people to want more than they need. Ads exploit anxieties and make invidious

comparisons that can be solved by products offering higher status, or more social acceptance or glamour. Companies are gathering increased information about each individual consumer so that they could trigger the hot psychological button to generate a purchase.

3. **Shift from ownership to usership.** Most home owned goods stay idle most of the time. The family car, lawn mower, power tools and other possessions are parked in the garage or closets. The idea of *sharing* more idle goods with friends and neighbors is on the rise. Persons owning cars can join Uber and persons with an empty bedroom can join Airbnb. More people are interested in renting goods than owning goods. If 10 neighbors all use the same lawn mower, this saves producing nine lawn mowers and saving a lot of materials and carbon fallout. Members of a community need to do more sharing.
4. **End food waste.** Studies show that 50 percent of food produced each year is destroyed during poor harvests, or on its way to the market or in homes and restaurants. Poor transportation or storage facilities lead to a lot of waste. If much of the waste could be ended, agriculture could meet our food needs with half as much land and create much less carbon. Instead of food waste ending up in landfills, more use should be made of composting the discarded food.
5. **Scale down ecologically destructive industries.** The need is urgent to replace fossil fuel (oil, gas, coal) with renewable sources of energy. A case can also be made that the beef industry generates high levels of methane and requires huge feed and slaughtering areas of land. The country could scale down the arms industry and the private jet industry.

I would add two other polices

6. **Place higher taxes on the rich.** Use the funds to enable poorer families to have a more livable income.
7. **Encourage lower population growth.** Increase women's education and career opportunities so that they will want fewer children.

Questions Still to Be Answered

I confess that there are still questions to be answered in curbing consumption to preserve a healthy planet. Here are key questions and my speculations.

1. In curbing consumption, will the economy be able to produce enough jobs? In any economy transformation, some old jobs are lost and some new jobs are created. We may produce fewer "gas-driven" cars and more electric cars that will last longer and need new job skills and workers. Also the work week needs to be shortened so that people can benefit from having more leisure time.
2. Will people view reduced consumption as a sacrifice or view it as leading to a better lifestyle? This begs the question of whether human consciousness and behavior can be changed. The answer is yes, that people are essentially socialized into new lifestyles as economic conditions change. More people have moved from rural life styles to urban life styles as they moved into urban areas. People will be able to find new pleasures to replace older pleasures. Marketers are always ready to help shape new lifestyles.
3. Does Capitalism need to be replaced by another system? My answer is no. My answer is that Capitalism has to be improved. Look around the world and you will find all types of Capitalism. Let us assume that good Capitalism lies in the number of happy, healthy, and educated people the system produces. Then we would want our Capitalism to move to Nordic Capitalism. The countries of Sweden, Norway, Denmark, Finland and Iceland all have populations of happy, healthy, and highly educated people. Their citizens pay higher taxes and receive in return free health care services, free college education, five week vacations, maternity and paternity paid leaves, and generous childhood benefits. Nordic citizens don't have to be stressed about health and college costs, lack of available housing, and other deprivations.[ii]
4. Will "Less is More" work in the world of poor countries? People in poor countries already live a "Less is More" life by necessity, not by choice. They would prefer to pursue "More is Better." The problem of the world is that too many people have more than they need and even a greater number of people have much less than they need. Much of this article is primarily directed to the richer world in the hope that they may consume less and leave more to the poorer world to consume.
5. If growth is to be slowed down, how quickly should it be slowed down? If consumer spending suddenly dropped by 25 percent, the consequences would be harmful and disastrous. Many jobs would be lost and many

people would not be able to pay their bills. When the Soviet Union disintegrated in 1991, its neighbor Finland went through a depression for four years. Formerly wealthy Finns found themselves going to soup kitchens. They were saved by the strong Finnish social welfare system. Clearly the slower the transition from an endless growth economy to a slower growth economy, the better.

Growth is the unquestioned goal in politics and economics. But this goal will ultimately lead to disaster in a world of diminishing resources. Transitioning to slower growth is the answer. The challenge is to promote wellbeing, equity, and sustainability as guideposts in moving toward more sensible growth. Our aim is to embrace a more sustainable and equitable path of growth. We need to lead leaner, happier, healthier and more satisfying lives.

References

[i] Jason Hinkel, *Less is More. How Degrowth Will Save the World,* London: Penguin-Random House, 2020. ISBN 978–1–786–09121–52020.

[ii] Philip Kotler, "Is America Ready for Nordic Capitalism?" The Sarasota Institute: A 21st Century Think Tank, Sarasota, Florida, December 14, 2020.

Source: June 10, 2023; Degrowth: The Case for Constraining Consumption | by Philip Kotler | Medium

CHAPTER TWENTY FIVE

What Makes the Most Sense for Humanity? High Growth, Low Growth, No Growth or DeGrowth

VIRTUALLY ALL NATIONS OF THE world pin their hopes on growth, economic growth. All nations measure their growth rate by Gross Domestic Product (GDP). If GDP rises, the nation has achieved positive growth. That nation produced more goods and services this year than last year. For several years during China's industrialization, China reported a 10 percent GDP growth rate. More recently, China reported a 5 percent growth rate. India is reporting a 7.2 percent growth rate. Western economies are reporting a 2 percent growth rate. Some nations are reporting a zero growth rate, the sign of a stationary or stagnant economy. Some nations are reporting a negative growth rate. Some nations are actively planning for DeGrowth.

What are the good and bad features of each growth rate?

A High Growth Rate

If asked, most people would favor living in a high growth economy. If income is fairly distributed, every citizen would experience a higher income. If income is not fairly distributed, the rich would get richer and the others might gain at best a small increase in their income. Because income is not fairly distributed, the gain is likely to be small for the poor segment of the population.

China experienced several years of 10 percent GDP growth and the effect was highly beneficial. A great number of Chinese citizens moved out of poverty. The middle class showed good growth and several millionaires and billionaires also emerged.

A growth rate of 10 percent is not likely to continue for long. The higher purchasing power in the public's hands will lead to faster growing expenditures than can be met by the available goods and infrastructure. The result will be inflation. The government will intervene to tame the inflation and the growth rate will start falling to a more normal GDP rate.

A high growth rate will also cause a high rate of carbonization that will lead ultimately to warmer temperatures. Another negative is that a high growth rate will consume energy, minerals and materials to unsustainable levels. The government might decide to tax the rich and transfer more money to the poor and this may slow down growth. The government might impose policies to protect the environment, causing a further slowdown.

A Low Growth Rate

Most countries are stuck with a low GDP growth rate, somewhere between 1 percent and 3 percent. Maybe this low growth rate is due to government interventions to protect the environment from irreparable damage and to protect the poor from inadequate incomes. Most citizens in these countries accept this low growth rate and the fight is mostly over how much to tax the rich and send transfer payments to the poor.

A Zero Growth Rate

The 18th century economist Adam Smith advanced the concept of a stationary economy. He believed that all national economies would eventually reach a stationary state. A stationary economy (sometimes called a steady state economy) occurs when an economy has reached the physical limits of economic growth and reproduces wealth by maintaining capital stocks, replacing worn-out goods, and carefully managing nonrenewable resources. In a stationary economy, the wealth and income of individuals remain unchanged, and the economy does not grow over time.

A stationary economy would do the least damage to the environment and temperatures. Population growth may remain small, many people will know each other, and behavior from day to day is likely to be familiar. Some people may prefer to live in a steady-state economy with its stability and lack of surprises and crises.

A Negative Growth Economy

Many poor nations experience a negative GDP. Production and sales of goods and services fall in relation to the previous year. From year to year, the country gets poorer. The effect is more hunger and hardship. More people die and many will try to leave and enter economies with positive growth rates.

A DeGrowth Economy

A degrowth economy is a special case where a normal low growth economy decides to deliberately plan to achieve a negative growth rate. The public has become super concerned about the planet's health and people's well-being. The public and government worry whether there will be enough energy, materials and food to support life and prevent the earth's temperature from getting too hot. The public is urged to buy less clothes, burn fewer trees for newsprint, conserve water more carefully, avoid luxury goods, and build smaller homes. Advocates call for scaling down destructive sectors such as fossil fuels, mass-produced meat and dairy, fast fashion, advertising, private jets and mansions. There is an attack on the planned obsolescence of products and a call for lengthening the lifespans of manufactured goods and reducing the purchasing power of the rich. By making fewer goods, the nation will slow down the exhaustion of basic materials, minerals, and energy. By pursuing rapid decarbonization and reducing ecological breakdown, social outcomes will improve. Energy and materials are freed up for low- and middle-income countries. The degrowth nation would improve public services such as health care, education, housing, transportation, Internet, renewable energy and nutritious food. The underlying belief is that degrowth can create acceptable prosperity while using less materials and energy.

Conclusion

One needs to think deeper about what happens with different economic growth rates. The world has worshipped high growth but is increasingly realizing that high growth adds some negatives for the planet's health and for what constitutes a good life for earth's citizens.

Source: August 22, 2024. What Makes the Most Sense for Humanity… | by Philip Kotler | Medium

CHAPTER TWENTY SIX

Is America Ready for Nordic Capitalism?

MOST COUNTRIES IN THE WORLD run a Capitalist economy. Yet the form that Capitalism takes in different countries varies greatly. There are many differences between American Capitalism, Swedish Capitalism, Japanese Capitalism, and Chinese Capitalism.

Every Capitalist economy has its own set of problems. One needs to list the problems that keep that country's citizens from being fully productive, happy and healthy. Table 1 lists the major problems besetting American Capitalism.

Table 1. Problems Besetting American Capitalism

- Persistence of poverty.
- Many workers earn less than a livable wage.
- Growing inequality between the working class and the rich.
- A health care system twice as expensive as good systems in other countries.
- A college education means accepting a substantial debt load.
- High and rising food and rent costs facing the working class.
- Racial, ethnic and gender discrimination in businesses and housing.
- More people in prison than in any other country.
- The rich own most of the politicians in both parties.

- The US spends much money on defense and not enough on infrastructure.
- Social assistance programs are insufficient.

Source: For more, see Philip Kotler, Confronting Capitalism: Real Solutions for a Troubled Economic System, New York, New York, AMACOM, 2015.

I hope that you will join me in considering the following six questions:

1. Why do the Major Problems Persist in American Capitalism?
2. What is American Capitalism Really Like?
3. What is Nordic Capitalism and Its Major Benefits?
4. How to Move in American Capitalism into Nordic Capitalism?
5. What Measures Can Be Taken to Reduce Income Inequality?
6. What Conclusions Can We Draw?

Why Do the Major Problems Persist in American Capitalism?

There are at least four reasons why the members of Congress and US Presidents do not take effective actions to mitigate one or more of these problems.

First, workers would be the first to press for solutions of these problems but they are powerless. Following the World War 2, the nation experienced many trade union strikes. The AFL (American Federation of Labor) and CIO (Congress of Industrial Organizations) were strong unions and succeeded in pressuring corporations to give higher wages, needed medical benefits, and better working conditions. Management, instead of seeing these benefits as investments that would increase worker satisfaction and loyalty, saw these benefits as a cost that reduced company's earnings. This led businesses, with the help of wealthy families, to press Congress for new laws to reduce the power of trade unions. Congress passed the Taft-Hartley law in 1947, restricting the activities and power of labor unions. Taft-Hartley amended the 1935 National Labor Relations Act (NLRA), and prohibited unions from engaging in several "unfair labor practices" such as jurisdictional strikes, wildcat strikes, solidarity or political strikes, secondary boycotts, secondary and mass picketing, closed shops, and monetary donations by unions to federal political campaigns. NLRA permitted states to pass right-to-work laws banning union shops. The result: Workers lost their trade union voice in influencing companies and the economy

Second, conservatives have been shouting down progressive measures as Socialism. For years, America had a Socialist Party and a Communist Party, both initially inspired by the 1917 Russian Revolution that replaced Czarist Russia with Communist leadership favoring the rights of workers. Eugene V. Debs led The Socialist party in America and he ran five times for the American Presidency, captivating large crowds, but always lost. Republicans continued to warn Americans against Debs and Socialism. They charged that Socialism would destroy Capitalism, "the engine that produces America's great economic growth". Conservatives warned that there would be fewer businesses, fewer jobs, more unemployment, falling income, less philanthropy, and less long term investment in infrastructure. "Everyone would be poorer." It is reminiscent of Winston Churchill statement: "The inherent vice of Capitalism is the unequal sharing of blessings. The inherent virtue of Socialism is the equal sharing of miseries."

Today, the Trump administration labels every progressive proposal as socialism. Trump charge that the Democrats will "demolish" the American Dream. "Violent anarchists" will take over America. Joe Biden will destroy America and turn it into a **Venezuela on steroids.**

Third, defenders of American Capitalism always describe it as raising the standard of living of all Americans. The expressions include "all boats rise" with Capitalism, and "Everyone has the opportunity to become rich." The rhetoric reads:

- The wealthy create jobs; and wealth will "trickle down" to the workers.
- Do not raise wages; this will kill jobs.
- Do not raise taxes on the wealthy; this will kill jobs.

Moreover, look at all the new products and appliances coming out of capitalism. Life is getting better. Why rock the boat?

However, here is a cartoon of the rising boat.

The persons in the boat fall into two groups: those who are working hard to save the boat from going down and others who are not perturbed at all.

Many critics observe that Capitalism is not broken: it has been highjacked by the superrich. We need a better distribution of the wealth created by Capitalism. Look in Table 2 for information on the great gap between the rich and the poor in American Capitalism.

Table 2. The Distribution of American Income and Wealth

- Capitalism has produced a lot of wealth but it is poorly distributed.
- 13 percent of Americans live below the poverty level.
- 40 percent of Americans are living paycheck to paycheck and many borrow money from a payday firm after getting their check.
- 40 percent of US adults don't have enough cash to meet a $400 emergency expense (US Federal Reserve).
- 29 percent of older Americans have neither a pension nor savings upon retiring (US GAO).
- Many new jobs are gig jobs without social security, health coverage, or pensions.
- Most college graduates are drowning in debt and many are unemployed.
- Not since the Roaring Twenties has income and wealth concentration been so high. Oxfam estimates these conditions in the world today.
- The richest three Americans hold more wealth than the bottom 50 percent of the country.
- In 2018, the world's richest 2,200 billionaires saw a 12 percent increase in wealth, while the world is poorest half saw an 11 percent drop in wealth.
- The American economist Joseph Stiglitz stated that "40 percent of the world's wealth…controlled by 1 percent of the people."
- How rich are the superrich?
- In 10 seconds, Jeff Bezos of Amazon earns more money than the median employee at Amazon makes in an entire year.
- In 2018, Disney CEO Bob Iger received $65.6 million (1,424 times the median Disney employee). Abigail Disney complained that this pay level was "insane." But Bob Iger said that was exceptional. His normal annual pay is only $39 million.
- Here are some fortunes (Forbes, Oct.31, 2018)
- Jeff Bezos $160 billion (before divorce)
- Bill Gates $97 billion

- Warren Buffett $88 billion
- Mark Zuckerberg $61 billion
- Larry Ellison $58 billion
- Larry Page $54 billion
- Charles and David Koch, each $53 billion
- Yet In 2018, the 400 richest families were taxed at a lower rate than the bottom 50 percent of the country.
- Comments of many notables about the excessive income gap.
- President Theodore Roosevelt repeatedly advocated tax policies that would create more equality. He said, "It is important to grapple with the problems connected with the amassing of enormous fortunes swollen beyond all healthy limits."
- President Franklin Delano Roosevelt said of his New Deal in the 1930s that he pledged, "To save capitalism from itself."
- Christine Lagarde, IMF, "Excessive inequality is corrosive to growth; it is corrosive to society. The economics profession and the policy community have downplayed inequality for too long." (2013).

A ***fourth*** factor retarding full action toward progressive policies is that Congress was pressured to pass different relief measures to help those who met misfortune. These measures include Social Security, unemployment insurance, and social assistance organizations. These measures are band-aids that do not really address the source of the problem that keeps workers from getting a better share of the economic pie generated by American Capitalism.

What Is American Capitalism Really Like?

We first need to define Capitalism. Capitalism is an economic system in which:

- The means of production are privately owned and operated for private profit;
- Decisions regarding supply, demand, price, distribution, and investments are made by private actors in the free market; and

- Profit belongs to the owners who invest in the business, and wages are paid to workers employed by the businesses.

This economic system is often embedded in a Mixed Economy where government occasionally assists private enterprise but also imposes regulations.

Socialism describes an economy where the government might run a small number of businesses or industries, such as the railroads, that are necessary for the public good and not for profit.

Communism describes a system where the government runs and owns all businesses and does central planning for the whole economy.

American Capitalism started out as free-wheeling unregulated capitalism. Early Americans started small businesses buying some land and equipment. Some businesses, such as steel, railroads, and consumer goods grew bigger. Laws were passed regulating business scope and rights. Many businesses incorporated. This allowed them to raise money by issuing ownership shares, or debentures, or getting bank loans. Corporations meant that owners were not personally liable for debts or bankruptcy unless there was malfeasance. The aim was to establish fair competition among businesses through antitrust laws and their watchful administration.

The question arose about the purpose of a business. The economist Milton Friedman advanced the view that the purpose of a business is to maximize profits. Furthermore the profits belonged to the shareholders. The business should not get distracted by social problems or causes. Its job is to make profits. The shareholders who gain should be free to dispose of their wealth however they want.

Looking back at Milton Friedman and his counterpart in England, Margaret Thatcher, the ideal society was one of small government with few regulations. This philosophy got the name "neoliberalism." This view of business was taught in business schools, Businesses were run on these principles. When Donald Trump won the Presidency in 2016, he made it clear that he wanted smaller government and fewer regulations.

Yet many businesses are now beginning to share a more expansive view of business and its purpose. From the old view of enriching shareholders who own the business and took the risks (Shareholder Capitalism), the new view is to treat fairly all the stakeholders who make the business successful—customers, employees, suppliers, distributors, and communities—(Stakeholder Capitalism). This is further epitomized by the slogan, "The aim of business is to serve people, profits, and the planet with prosperity."

A growing number of business leaders now care deeply about the nation and its health. They are not from the laissez faire school of Capitalism aiming at maximum short term profits. This group knows that the stakeholders and their love of the business creates profits. Yes, laissez faire capitalism has produced great wealth growth but it does not relieve any national problems. It doesn't end poverty and hunger. If anything, old fashioned capitalism creates growing income and wealth inequality. According to the economist Thomas Piketty, capital will always earn more than labor in a growing economy.

Table 3 summarizes the new thinking in management about the purpose of business.

Table 3. The Evolution of New Ideas about the Purpose of Business

1. Larry Fink, *CEO of Black Rock group*, "Society is demanding that companies, both public and private, serve a social purpose. To prosper over time, every company must not only deliver financial performance but also show how it makes a positive contribution to society" (2018).
2. Stephen Hahn-Griffiths, Reputation Institute: *"It's not enough to just have a high-quality product and deliver results on Wall Street. Social activism, aligning with communities, what you do to make the world a better place—that's the metric."*
3. Professor Klaus Schwab is founder and executive director of the World Economic Forum (WEF). WEF holds its annual meeting in Davos, Switzerland and attracts thousands of eminent business, academic and government leaders and celebrities. WEF collects economic information during the year and traditionally takes a conservative economic position. However, today WEF is pursuing a Great Reset. Klaus Schwab's new book *Covid-10: The Great Reset* (2020) calls for businesses to change many of their past practices, including less frequent air travel and more workers working at home. Many companies are shifting from shareholder capitalism to stakeholder capitalism that they had previously barely

considered. There is greater interest in steering the market toward more equitable outcome shares. Government needs to withdraw fossil-fuel subsidies, and to develop new rules to govern intellectual property, trade, and competition. Governments need to launch large-scale stimulus spending programs. Cities need to commit to "green" urban infrastructure and to environmental, social, and governance (ESG) metrics. Private enterprise and government must do more innovation to improve the common good through better vaccines and health related efforts. The will is forming to build a better society, with the help of more private-sector engagement and more effective government.

4. The Business Roundtable (BRT) is a non-profit association based in Washington, D.C., whose members are CEOs of major US companies. BRT promotes public policies such as NAFTA and No Child Left Behind. BRT opposed Trump's family separation policy. In 2019, BRT redefined its definition of the purpose of a corporation, putting the interests of employees, customers, suppliers and communities on par with shareholders. BRT members include Jamie Dimon of Chase Morgan, Jeff Bezos of Amazon, Tim Cook of Apple, and Mary Barra of General Motors.
5. The American Sustainable Business Council includes business leaders who believe in a living wage, worker dignity, racial justice, well-run workplaces, the circular economy, better climate and energy, and improved infrastructure. The members believe that "jobs are created when consumers have money to spend and destroyed when they don't. Businesses cannot succeed unless consumers have the ability to spend and confidence to spend it."
6. Many leading companies have taken public stands on political issues that have a high level of agreement from voters. This includes Starbucks, Unilever, Levi Strauss, Nike, Body Shop, Patagonia, Ben and Jerry's and many others.
7. Many business leaders and some billionaires want to pay higher income taxes. Bill Gates of Microsoft and Warren Buffett of Berkshire Hathaway have stated this. In addition, Gates and Buffett convinced 204 billionaires to sign the Giving Pledge to give away half of their money to good causes within the next ten years of signing up. The signatories have included Ted Turner, Marc Benioff, Mark Zuckerberg, Michael Bloomberg, Larry Ellison, David Rockefeller, and many others.

8. The Responsible Business Alliance (RBA) is the world's largest industry coalition dedicated to corporate social responsibility in global supply chains. Most companies now acknowledge that they would be advantaged by showing that they care about some public issue, such as water scarcity, overtimbering, overfishing, climate change, racial injustice, income inequality, college student debt, or health care for all. Business must lead the new world order built on climate protection, sustainability, resilience, digital inclusion and equality. Member companies address responsibility in the management of factories, labor, and supply chains.
9. A movement called *Conscious Capitalism,* founded by John Mackey, former CEO of Whole Foods Market and Raj Sisodia, a marketing professor, have a growing membership of individuals and companies who believe that business and capitalism should work for all stakeholders, not just shareholders. Conscious Capitalism holds to four principles to guide a socially responsible and ethical business: 1. Higher purpose beyond money-making. 2. Creating value for all stakeholders. 3. Conscious leadership to focus on value creation. 4. Conscious culture that links stakeholders with each other and with the company's mission, workers and processes.
10. Companies originally thought of corporate social responsibility (CSR) as a polite gesture. Yet in *Corporate Social Responsibility* (2005), Nancy Lee and I described the positive social responsibility activities of 45 leading companies, where each company cared deeply about some social issue. CSR has moved much further since then to ***Brand Activism*** where a company's uses its brand to influence reforms on social, economic and political issues.

What Is Nordic Capitalism and Its Major Benefits?

Here we look at Nordic Capitalism (also called Scandinavian Capitalism). Technically, Scandinavia describes the three countries of Sweden, Denmark, and Norway. If we add Finland and Iceland, the group is Nordic. The five

Nordic countries all practice what has been variously called Economic Democracy, Social Democracy, or Welfare Capitalism.

The Nordic countries enjoy similar economic and social policies as well as cultural practices. The Nordic economic model is a welfare state with collective bargaining and free-market capitalism, strong trade unions and 30 percent employment in the public sector. Prosperous large and small companies operate and export and compete around the world.

People in the Nordic countries enjoy high living standards, high health and happiness, and low income disparity. Table 4 shows the main features and benefit of the Nordic economy.

Table 4. Main Features and Benefits of the Nordic Economy

- Free college tuition
- Free and excellent health care for all citizens
- A much longer worker vacation time
- Maternity and paternity benefits
- Child care and aged parents care
- The Nordic idea is to make a good life for all citizens
- These benefits go with an income tax system whose top rate is 70 percent

Here are some additional characteristics to notice about the Nordic population.

- Nordic countries figure significantly in the 10 happiest countries in 2019 (Finland, Denmark, Norway, Iceland, Netherlands, Switzerland, Sweden, New Zealand, Canada and Austria). The US ranked only 19 in happiness.
- Nordic countries figure significantly in the 10 most health-conscious countries in 2018 (Sweden, Switzerland, Denmark, Norway, Finland, Canada, Australia, Japan, Netherlands, and New Zealand). The United States ranked only 35 in health quality.
- This implies a strong correlation, if not causation between an economy run on Nordic principles and the levels of happiness and health of its people.

How to Move American Capitalism into Nordic Capitalism?

Does America have the interest, will and ability to pursue a form of Capitalism that will improve the livelihood, happiness and wealth of most Americans?

Let's consider whether enough Americans see Nordic capitalism as a promising and better economic system. In 2011, two American social scientists, Michael I. Norton (Harvard Business School) and Dan Ariely (Duke University) published a study. American respondents were asked to:

1. Estimate the current distribution of American wealth, and
2. Construct your ideal level of wealth distribution for the US.

The findings showed that Americans deeply underestimated the current level of wealth inequality. The findings all showed that respondents' ideal wealth distributions were far more equitable than the current wealth distribution in the US.

Then the respondents were asked to vote between three alternative wealth distributions in a country.

a. The current wealth distribution in the US,
b. A completely equal wealth distribution,
c. A wealth distribution equal to the income distribution of Sweden (but Sweden wasn't named).

The result: 92 percent of the Americans preferred Sweden's distribution to the US distribution. And 77 percent preferred complete equality to the US distribution. And 51 percent preferred Sweden to complete equality. The researchers drew the conclusion that the overwhelming majority of Americans thinks that Sweden represents a better social order than America.

Unfortunately, what was omitted from the study is the fact that Nordic citizens get all these benefits at a price. In the US, the highest marginal income tax rate is 37 percent. In Nordic countries, the maximum marginal tax rate is 70 percent, or twice the maximum US tax rate. If the US operated as a Nordic economy, taxes would be higher for most Americans, and especially higher for wealthy Americans.

We need to ask Americans if they would prefer to live with the benefits of Nordic Capitalism and pay a substantially higher income tax rate. The American philosopher Oliver Wendell Holmes, Jr. probably would have said yes. His quote: "I like to pay taxes. With them, I buy civilization."

There is enough evidence that a substantial number of Americans would favor Nordic Capitalism and higher taxes. Senators Bernie Sanders and Elizabeth Warren won big followings, especially among younger Americans, when they ran as Presidential candidates. Bernie Sanders main proposals are shown in Table 5.

Table 5. Main Policies Advocated by Presidential candidate Bernie Sanders

- Medicare for All
- College should be free
- Wages must rise to a living wage
- Unions to give workers a voice
- Free child care and Pre K for all
- Invest more in public education
- Raise tax rates on the rich
- Women's rights and gender equality
- Racial justice

Sander's proposals closely describe Nordic policies. A number of American billionaires and organizations favor a more just Capitalist economy. See Table 6.

Table 6. Developments Favoring a More Just Capitalist System

- *The Giving Pledge.* Bill Gates and Warren Buffett signed up 204 billionaires from 22 countries who have pledged to give away half of their money to philanthropic causes in the next ten years. The pledge does not dictate how the money is to be spent and there is no legal obligation. Their pledges so far total over 500 billion.
- *Patriotic Millionaires.* They are lobbying Congress to raise federal taxes on the rich and to close tax loopholes. They believe that no millionaire should pay at a lower tax rate than middle-class Americans.

- *Some CEOs recently rejected their bonus.* Virginia Rometty, CEO of IBM, turned down a bonus of $8 million based on the company's performance. Barclay's CEO, Antony Jenkins turned down his bonus of $2.8 million for the second year saying "it would not be right." Larry Ellison of Oracle turned down his bonus.

Table 7 lists the names of wealthy dissidents who favor a more progressive Capitalism.

Table 7. Billionaires Favoring a More Progressive Capitalism

- Nick Hanauer, "Beware, Fellow Plutocrats, the Pitchforks are Coming."
- Ray Dalio, founder of hedge fund Bridgwater Associates, says the bottom 60 percent have had no income growth since 1980, while the top ten percent have doubled and the top one percent have tripled.
- Marc Benion, CEO of Salesforce, wants San Francisco to tax its largest companies to raise enough money to double the budget that helps the city's homeless people find housing.
- Abigail Disney, George Soros, and the Pritzkers, favor a moderate wealth tax on the 1 percent.
- *The B Team are* several leading CEOs who want to develop a new tax framework with a set of responsible tax principles. The group includes Paul Polman, Indra Nooyi, Muhammad Yunus, Ratan Tata, and several other high rank executives.
- Bill Gates and Warren Buffett, *The Giving Pledge.*
- The *Patriotic Millionaires* movement.

The case of Bill Gates is interesting. Gates founded Microsoft in 1975 when the top marginal tax rate was 70 percent and the estate tax was even more formidable. That didn't stop Gates for starting Microsoft. Nor would Walt Disney or Richard Branson have stopped expanding their businesses if taxes were higher. Many wealthy people are passionate about their work and causes and profit isn't the only motive. Gates publicly said that he favors paying a higher income tax rate. "That's why I'm for a tax system in which, if you have more money, you pay a higher percentage in taxes. And I think the rich should pay more than they currently do, and that includes Melinda and me." However, he does not favor a wealth tax in addition to a higher income tax rate. "I do think if you tax too much you do risk the capital formation, innovation, US as the desirable place to do innovative companies—I do think you risk that."

A lot of this willingness of superrich people to pay higher taxes is partly due to the rich paying taxes at a lower rate than average Americans. Many prominent persons have spoken about the obscene, glaring and growing gap in income distribution.

- "The defining challenge of our time." Barack Obama
- "An economy of exclusion and inequality." Pope Francis
- "Inequality has gotten worse." Mitt Romney
- "I have often advised managers that a 20-to-1 salary ratio is the limit beyond which they cannot go if they don't want resentment and falling morale to hit their companies," said Peter Drucker.

These well-off people are right to be concerned about growing income inequality. Here are some of the fears:

1. The wealth gap is only getting wider. Low wages lead to inadequate food, clothing and housing, poverty, slums, and homelessness. And the middle class is getting smaller.
2. Some low income people will pursue a life of crime. Many wealthy families live in gated communities with private police forces.
3. The economy leads to gig work which doesn't provide any health insurance or pensions.
4. It is immoral for a country to have so much wealth and so many poor. It can lead to either low productivity or a revolution.

What Measures Can Be Taken to Reduce Income Inequality?

When enough Americans realize the growing income gap, they might put enough pressure on Congress to consider and weigh different proposals for reducing the income gap. Table 8 displays several of the leading proposals.

Table 8. Measures for Reducing Income Inequality

- Raise the minimum wage closer to a living wage
- Make the income tax system more progressive
- Plug the tax loopholes
- Raise the tax on capital gains and carried interest from 23.8 percent to normal tax rate
- Establish a wealth tax on wealth and estates
- Establish a tax on luxury goods
- Establish a tax on financial transactions
- Cap the ratio of top executive pay to median worker pay
- Establish a universal basic income program

Congress should research each proposal and gather the opinions of those who favor and those who object. Some proposals will draw more assent than others. There is much to favor raising the minimum wage, which is not a livable wage at $7.45. Any worker earning this would have to borrow money at high interest rates as soon as receiving the weekly pay check. The worker would stay in debt forever, never accumulating enough to retire on. Fortunately, many states have increased their state minimum wage to $15. The idea is that the worker is "the real job creator." The worker who receives more pay will spend all of it, thereby generating more jobs. Henry Ford illustrated this when he decided to double the pay of his auto workers to $5 and so many more workers ended up buying their first Ford.

Establishing a tax on financial transactions could get quick assent. The stock market is a gambling institution. It is subject to manipulation by large financial interests. Many low and middle income people trade and often lose money in the stock market. A fee on each purchase or sale of stock will discourage wasteful participation and speculation. Senator Bernie Sanders proposed a small excise tax, typically a few hundredths of a percent, on trades of stocks, bonds, derivatives and other securities. A one-basis-point tax on $1,000 worth of stock would cost the stock trader 10 cents. A $100,000 trade would generate a tax of only $10. The nonpartisan Tax Policy Center estimated that a 0.01 percent tax would raise $185 billion over 10 years. That amount could finance an ambitious expansion of prekindergarten programs for 3- and 4-year-klds and restore funding of college assistance for low-income students.

Making the income tax system more progressive will generate a lot of debate. We need to recall that the top income tax rate was as high as 91 percent during WW2. In 1964, the highest tax rate was lowered to 70 percent. President Reagan managed to lower the maximum rate from 70 percent to 50 percent and subsequently down to 38.5 percent. Under President George W. Bush, the maximum tax rate was lowered to 35 percent. During the 2008–2011 fiscal disaster, the top tax rate was raised back to 39.6 percent. The Tax Reform Act of 2019 reduced the maximum tax rate to 37 percent and created a 1.5 trillion dollar deficit. This was "trickle up," redistributing money from the poor to the rich.

New York's mayor Bill de Blasio had a nice homey way of pleading to the rich to pay more: "We will ask the very wealthy to pay a little more in taxes so that we can offer full-day, universal pre-K and after-school programs…Those earning between $500,000 and $1 million…would see their taxes increase by an average of $973 a year. That's less than three bucks a day—about the cost of a small soy latte at your local Starbucks."

Senator Elizabeth Warren favors passing a wealth tax. She called for households to pay an annual 2 percent tax on all assets—net worth—above $50 million, and a 3 percent tax on every dollar of net worth above $1 billion. She recently added possibly raising the billionaire wealth tax rate to 6 percent instead of 3 percent to help pay for education, health and other needed things. One study reported that 74 percent of Americans favored a wealth tax.

Yet there are a great number of Americans who object to many of these proposals. Opponents of a wealth tax say:

- We earned the money honestly and fairly.
- A wealth tax will discourage the rich from investing in risky ventures and hurt our economic growth.
- The superrich have excellent lawyers who will help the rich defer, avoid or minimize the wealth tax or move their wealth abroad.
- A tax on wealth would hurt philanthropy and the support of many museums, universities, and hospitals.
- A wealth tax is unjust and unconstitutional because it confiscates personal property. They will cry out against "redistribution" and "class warfare."
- All this will have to be researched and debated.

From a big picture point of view, moving to a Nordic economy at a faster pace would also benefit from other potential developments:

- Restore strong trade unions.
- Improve public education.
- Educate the working class to act in their own interests. The poor are often the ones who are trying to preserve the little that they have not realizing that they are entitled to much more and need to support progressive causes.
- Gain more social justice for "Black Lives Matter" and other discriminated groups.
- Pay police and firefighters a higher wage and provide more training and best and safest equipment.
- Pass the Universal Basic Income (UBI) so that all people receive a basic payment to meet their expenses.
- Encourage individual states to move faster in adopting progressive measures.
- Ultimately, more people will vote Democratic and this will ultimately increase the support of progressive measures.

What Conclusions Can We Draw?

The essence of capitalism is property rights, economic freedom, regulations, and rule of law.

1. Capitalism takes on many forms: US capitalism, Nordic capitalism, Japanese capitalism, and Chinese capitalism. These vary from "free capitalism," "crony capitalism," and " highly regulated capitalism."
2. Capitalism has been a major contributor to raising the standard of living and innovating new and better products.
3. Capitalism has led to high growth but very unequal income and wealth distribution.

4. The American people would benefit if American Capitalism could move closer to Nordic Capitalism.

The idea is make Capitalism work better for more people.

Source: September 24, 2020; Is America Ready for Nordic Capitalism | by Philip Kotler | Medium

SECTION IV

Business Transformation, Technology, and Sustainable Capitalism

CHAPTER TWENTY SEVEN

Can Artificial Intelligence Improve Marketing Decisions?

Will Artificial Intelligence (AI) Prove to Be a Blessing to Marketing?

I am hearing many conflicting opinions about AI.

There are negative opinions. The neuroscientist Erik Hoel has called it "AI pollution." Others call AI "something like noise." Sequoia Capital says that current AI investments have been running far short of expected returns. Goldman Sachs has echoed the same concerns.

Other skeptics have pointed out some occasional errors in AI output, such as calling Barak Obama a Muslim or that 17th President Andrew Johnson earned thirteen college degrees between 1947 and 2012. Hopefully, these are rare exceptions to the generally correct AI outputs.

Those who are positive about AI's impact on business cite how much more productive AI solutions are compared to "human-only" solutions. AI can speed up the search for solutions to various human diseases. AI can beat the best humans at a game of chess or Go. AI can turn out a preliminary 30 second video story ad in five minutes that might have taken an ad agency a week and many dollars to prepare.

A 2018 McKinsey analysis of more than 400 advanced use cases showed that marketing was the domain where AI would contribute the greatest value. In August 2019, the American Marketing Association reported that AI implementation had jumped 27 percent in the previous year and a half. In 2020 Deloitte reported that AI could help in the following three marketing areas: enhancing existing products and services, creating new products and services, and enhancing relationships with customers.

To move our understanding of AI's potential for marketing, let's distinguish between General AI and Generative AI (such as Chat GPT).

General AI

Companies have told their marketing staff to learn AI and to propose applications that would speed up and/or improve the quality of its decision making. The company needs to identify some important decisions in that business and determine whether a better decision could be made by a *machine solution* or at least by a *person+machine* solution.

Consider a bank that makes lending decisions. Normally, one of the bank's executives specializes in approving lending decisions. This executive has spent years making lending decisions. He has developed a mental framework for making his lending decisions. Most of his past decisions were good but he also made a few bad decisions where the bank lost money. Can the bank build an algorithm that uses this executive's mental framework, but improves it in a way that had the algorithm been used in the past case, the company would have achieved even better results? If this new algorithm is then applied to new lending cases, and the company achieved even better results, tell the bank manager that the bank will use the algorithm and the bank manager should move to making more strategic decisions.

Generative AI

On November 30, 2022, a company called Open AI announced to the public that it had created ChatGPT. ChatGPT is based on building a large language model (LLM) capturing a great deal of the world's past conversations. A copy writer can type in a *prompt*, such as "write a short essay on the planet Mars." In a few minutes, the printer would print some pages presenting a clear description of Mars and its features. Or the prompt may be: "write a love poem about Mars." Or "draw a picture showing Mars laughing at the other planets in the earth's galaxy." Or "create an ad for the sale of 3 pound rocks found on Mars."

The prompt can include the desired length, format, style, level of detail and language. After viewing the output, the marketer may want to submit a more refined prompt to improve the desired output.

Stages in Installing AI in the Company

A company might be enthusiastic about installing AI but needs to know that it will take a long time to become proficient in AI. Why? The company's marketers probably lack training or experience with AI and must go through a cycle of learning. The company needs to hire an AI expert into the department or hire experts on an advisory basis. The marketing department meanwhile must have a good working relationship with the Intelligence Technology (IT) group that will manage and collect the needed data.

One early step would be to prepare a chatbot that can answer a lot of frequently asked consumer questions. The chatbot would operate much like Siri or Alexis in answering questions posed by consumers.

The next step is to identify some routine marketing procedures that can be done faster and better by automation. Any filing work in the department can be done more efficiently with AI with less chance of human error.

Another step is to find an important area of repetitive decision-making and create an algorithm that can make better decisions than humans can make. Over time, the algorithm will be self-learning and improving.

Another early step is to automate high-speed decision making in programmatic ad buying. Still another use of AI is to make individual buying recommendations based on each customer's information. This is called setting up a recommendation engine.

At some point, the company will move from "task automation" to "machine learning (ML)." ML is a subset of AI that allows computers to analyze and interpret data without being explicitly programmed. ML assists humans in solving problems efficiently. The algorithm learns and improves performance and accuracy as more data are fed into the algorithm.

The company can't do ML until it collects a huge amount of quality data on customer buying behavior. The machine will search the data for patterns of behavior and their influencing factors in the hope to gain valuable consumer insights.

What the firm wants is a sales process for managing individual accounts using real-time geolocation data and detailed information on the customer's reading habits, shopping habits, and decision making routines. The marketer needs to know what brands the customer buys, what sizes, with what frequency. The sales system will suggest sending reminders or special offers at the right time and place in a highly personalized way. The system will also suggest when a customer would be ready to move to a higher price item (upselling) or should add another buying category (cross-selling).

AI can be used to write marketing content that can be disseminated in social media posts, email copy, blog posts, and captions. In addition to written content, AI can be used to generate images, audio, and video.

AI can be used to search for new customers. The characteristics of the company's current customers (gender, age, income, etc.) can be used to search for potential clients with similar characteristics. AI can be used to sight the most persuadable clients and to choose the best messages to send to them via chat, phone, email, or video.

Conclusion

Artificial Intelligence (AI) has vast potential in marketing. It leads to collecting valuable data and extracting new insights on buyer behavior. It enables the development of software for data and sales management. It leads to the development of algorithms for better decision making than would have been provided by only relying on human judgment. It leads to the use of GPT to quickly develop messages, images, and virtual ads.

For firms without AI, the time is now to begin the AI journey. AI will ultimately affect the management of all elements of the marketing mix, namely product, price, place, promotion, branding, and marketing research. Some marketers will have to move to new skills and jobs or be replaced. There will be high costs, mistakes and some chaos but it will be worthwhile in terms of the benefits and the increased chance of surviving in this time of radical innovation and rapid change.

For a helpful book with more detail on AI and machine learning (ML) as well as other new developments useful in marketing such as robots, drones, blockchain, the internet of things, and the metaverse, see V. Kumar and Philip Kotler, *Transformative Marketing: Combining New Age Technologies and Human Insights* (Palgrave Executive Essentials), 2024.

Source: August 5, 2024. Can Artificial Intelligence Improve… | by Philip Kotler | Medium

CHAPTER TWENTY EIGHT

The Impact of Superintelligent Robots on Jobs and Society

THERE IS GREAT CONCERN ABOUT how humans will relate to the rapid advances in artificial intelligence (AI) and robots. Humans have already experienced working in highly automated factories run largely by robotic equipment. As robots get smarter, will they take away most jobs? Will the factory in the future consist of one worker and a dog to keep the worker awake?

Kurt Vonnegut, the novelist, presented a dark picture of the future in his book *Player Piano.* He described a society with mass unemployment. All manufacturing jobs were done by factory robots. Most service jobs had been taken over by machines and robots. The only people left with jobs were managers and engineers who are busy designing new robots to replace the few remaining human jobs.

Kurt described how strange he felt standing next to a player piano where the keys played the melody without a pianist. Vonnegut says, "makes you feel kind of creepy, don't it Doctor, watching them keys go up and down?" Vonnegut was wondering what technology will do to human value and meaning. He went on:

"Engineers, think about what technological 'progress' means for humanity. Managers, think about what it is that makes humans 'human' and decide whether or not it is something worth preserving. Make certain that each new technological advancement doesn't strip humanity of its humanness, because once technological progress happens, it can't un-happen."

Here are four questions that concern many persons around the world:

1. Will robots act as our helpmates in our work or will they take away our jobs?
2. In what time sequence will different jobs go to robots?
3. How will retired humans think about themselves when they formerly found rich meaning in their work life? What time-filling activities will they undertake? What can be done to preserve humanity and dignity?
4. Can humans set up controls to prevent superintelligent robots from controlling us or even harming or destroying us?

These questions are very difficult to answer. All one can get is a collection of opinions. I decided that the best way to gather a broad view of opinion is to put these four questions to ChatGPT. Chat CPT covers all the world's talk and opinions. Here are ChatGPT's thoughtful answers about where humanity and technology are headed.

1. Will robots act as our helpmates in our work or will they take away our jobs?

"The rapid advancement of robotics and artificial intelligence (AI) has raised significant concerns about the future of human employment and the broader societal implications of superintelligent machines. As robots become increasingly capable, the prospect of widespread job displacement looms large, with profound consequences for individuals, economies, and the fabric of society. This essay explores the potential impact of superintelligent robots on jobs, the kinds of jobs most likely to be lost, the challenges of supporting a largely jobless population, and the measures that might be taken to preserve human dignity and prevent robotic dominance.

2. In what time sequence will different jobs go to robots?

The Initial Impact on Employment

As robots and AI systems become more sophisticated, they are expected to first displace jobs that are repetitive, routine, and require minimal human creativity or emotional intelligence. These include roles in manufacturing, logistics, and service industries, such as assembly line workers, cashiers, and truck drivers. Robots' ability to perform tasks with precision and efficiency will likely make them the preferred option in these sectors, where cost-cutting and productivity gains are paramount.

Beyond manual labor, white-collar jobs involving data processing, analysis, and decision-making are also at risk. Superintelligent AI could surpass human capabilities in fields like accounting, legal research, and even medical diagnostics, where vast amounts of data must be analyzed quickly and accurately. As robots encroach on these domains, the displacement of human workers could accelerate, leading to widespread unemployment.

3. How will retired humans think about themselves when they formerly found rich meaning in their work life? What time-filling activities will they undertake? What can be done to preserve humanity and dignity?

The Future of a Jobless Society

If robots eventually become capable of performing most jobs, the majority of people may find themselves without traditional employment. This scenario raises critical questions about how to support a jobless population. One potential solution is the implementation of a Universal Basic Income (UBI), where all citizens receive a regular, unconditional sum of money to cover their basic needs. UBI could ensure that people maintain a decent standard of living, even in the absence of work.

However, financial support alone may not be sufficient to address the psychological and social implications of widespread unemployment. Work has long been a source of identity, purpose, and self-worth for many individuals. The absence of traditional jobs could lead to a crisis of meaning, with people struggling to find new ways to contribute to society and feel valued. To mitigate this, it will be crucial to foster a culture that emphasizes creativity, lifelong learning, and community engagement. People might find fulfillment in pursuits like the arts, volunteerism, or personal development, areas where human qualities like empathy and creativity remain irreplaceable.

In a world dominated by superintelligent robots, maintaining a sense of self-worth and humanity will be paramount. Education systems will need to adapt to prepare people for roles that complement, rather than compete with, robots. Emphasizing emotional intelligence, ethical reasoning, and interdisciplinary thinking can help people carve out niches where human intuition and judgment are indispensable.

Moreover, society must safeguard human dignity by ensuring that robots are designed and deployed in ways that enhance human life rather than diminish it. Ethical guidelines and regulations should govern the development and use of AI, with a focus on promoting human welfare and preventing harm. This might include ensuring that robots are programmed with values aligned with human rights and dignity, and that they are transparent in their decision-making processes.

4. Can humans set up controls to prevent superintelligent robots from controlling us or even harming or destroying us?

Preventing Robotic Dominance

The prospect of superintelligent robots gaining control over human affairs or posing a threat to humanity is a legitimate concern. To prevent such outcomes, it is essential to establish robust control mechanisms and governance frameworks. One approach is to embed strict ethical constraints and fail-safes into AI systems, ensuring they cannot act against human interests. For example, AI systems could be designed to require human oversight for critical decisions, particularly those involving national security, justice, and healthcare. In addition, international cooperation will be necessary to develop and enforce regulations that prevent the misuse of AI and robotics. This might involve the creation of global treaties that limit the development of autonomous weapons and ensure that AI technologies are used for peaceful purposes. Public and private sectors must work together to monitor and regulate AI development, with transparency and accountability as guiding principles.

Conclusion

The rise of superintelligent robots presents both unprecedented challenges and opportunities for humanity. While the displacement of jobs is likely, the way society responds will determine whether this transition leads to widespread despair or a new era of human flourishing. By providing economic support, fostering new avenues for personal fulfillment, and implementing robust controls to prevent robotic dominance, humanity can navigate this technological revolution while preserving its dignity, autonomy, and sense of purpose. The future may be uncertain, but with thoughtful planning and ethical foresight, it can be one where humans and robots coexist in a way that benefits all."

Source: August 19, 2024. The Impact of Superintelligent Robots… | by Philip Kotler | Medium

CHAPTER TWENTY NINE

Should Workers Own Stock in Their Companies?

ARE AMERICAN WORKERS FEELING SATISFIED in their jobs? Do they look forward to each working day? Do they feel adequately and fairly paid for their work?

Studies of American workers toward their jobs reveal a disturbing finding: Over half of US workers are unhappy in their jobs.[i]

If they are unhappy, what are the main causes? Some workers find their jobs boring or mind destroying. They see these jobs as dead-ends. Some workers suffer from a bad boss or bad coworkers. The job involves a lot of stress without any breaks. The job presents safety issues. Some women complain of sexual innuendos or harassment. They aren't paid a livable wage. Their health and other benefits are either non-existent or minimal.

If persons are unhappy in their jobs, many will be unhappy in their lives. Their stress may affect their mental or physical health. They might turn to drinking or drugs or sometimes just crying. Some employees will compensate by various pleasures they find after work in sociability, hobbies, and friendships. But a great many, especially who are at a lower income level, will remain unhappy in their lives.

Persons who are unhappy in their jobs still carry out their work but with less thought and effort. They might spend more time chatting with or complaining with other workers, more time in bathroom breaks, show more sick leaves or absences, or quit their jobs more often. These workers are not as productive as they could be if they liked their work and were given some recognition by their company. One study of more than 17,000 US workers in 19 industries found that 71 percent were either "actively looking for new job opportunities" or had the thought "always, often, or sometimes" at work.[ii]

Many companies fail to give recognition or appreciation to their workers. Certain workers are complimented and paid better in an "I-Thou" relationship with management, but most workers are treated in an "I-It" relationship. In the latter case, these workers are just seen as objects, not human beings. This is unfortunate because for many workers, "high touch" recognition is as important as or even more important than their salary. Also, consumers might partly judge a company by how well the company treats its employees.

When these problems are recognized by management, management tries various solutions. Among them:

- Raise workers' pay
- Introduce more work breaks
- Build more of a family or community feeling among workers
- Help workers achieve a better work/life balance
- Offer more employee benefits such as free coffee, snacks, or a napping room
- Provide a paid leave program for workers with family problems
- Prevent discrimination based on age, gender, or sexual orientation
- Train supervisors to be more sensitive to workers and more freely give recognition and encouragement
- Human resources should study the causes of low employee engagement and develop tailored solutions

These actions might help and yield more worker enthusiasm and productivity, and ultimately more profitability. Studies by the Gallup organization shows that companies with better employee engagement have better earnings per share.[iii]

If these measures don't work, the company needs to look for deeper answers.

Analyzing Worker Discontent at a More Basic Level

A deeper understanding of the worker discontent problem can come from looking at the structure of management/labor relations.

1. Companies exist to create value.
2. Value is created with Capital and Labor.
3. Capital gets to keep the profits (or losses).
4. Ordinary Labor only gets a salary and has no other means of support.
5. Yet Labor might be responsible for creating between 40 percent and 70 percent of the profit.
6. Marxian economists hold that labor creates most of the value but most of the profits go to Capital (shareholders). Workers are never able to earn enough to buy shares in their or other companies to become capitalists.

Under these conditions, workers become alienated and will just do enough work to get by and not be fired. There is little they will gain by working harder. They are without any ownership or any voice in where their company is or should be going.

The unhappiness manifests itself in the shrinkage of inventory estimated to be 3–4 percent taken by workers unhappy with their company.

More Fundamental Solutions to Raising Worker Engagement

Recently, executive Pete Stavros of KKR & Company reported that he is on a mission to get more stock of industrial and manufacturing companies into the hands of their workers. He is promoting the benefits of awarding stock to factory workers and other hourly wage earners. Pete is launching a non-profit called the Center for Shared Ownership and pledging $10 million to support it. The organization will provide companies with resources to help them adopt employee-ownership programs, funding academic research and potentially pushing for new government incentives. He believes that giving ownership to lower-level employees better aligns their interests with those of management and shareholders, makes them more engaged and creates a stronger culture.[iv]

Let's discuss four different plans for lifting worker engagement and happiness on the job.

1. Create an Employee Savings Plan or Employee Profit Sharing Plan
2. Create an ESOP (Employee Stock Ownership Plan)
3. Create the Company as a Cooperative
4. Accept a Workers Union with Co-determination

Create an Employee Savings Plan or an Employee Profit Sharing Plan

Let's start with the company creating an Employee Savings Plan (ESP). The employer allows employees to set aside a portion of their pre-tax wages for retirement savings or other long-term goals such as paying for college tuition or purchasing a home. Many employers match their employees' contributions up to a certain dollar amount, or by a certain percentage. The most popular ESP in the US is the 401(k) retirement plan. Under this plan, employees are able to save up to $19,500 a year for retirement, sometimes with additional contributions made by an employer match.

Alternatively, an employer can offer an Employee Profit-sharing Plan. This is a retirement plan that gives employees a share in the profits of a company. An employee receives a percentage of a company's profits based on its quarterly or annual earnings. The company decides how much of its profits to share with employees. The company alone makes the contributions. Employees cannot make them too. This plan, also known as a deferred profit-sharing plan (DPSP), grants to each employee a share of the profits according to the employee's share of total employee earnings. In some bad years, the company might make zero contributions. The company can establish an employee profit sharing plan even if its employees also have an employee savings plan. This is a great way for a business to give its employees a sense of ownership in the company. By employees holding stock in the company, this gives employees the same interest as stockholders in making the company successful.

Many companies would like their employees to hold stock in their company even if the company did not offer either an employee savings plan or employee profit plan. An employee is always free to buy shares of stock in the company in the open market. Some companies can offer their employees a plan to buy stock at a discount from the stock's quoted price in the stock market. The company might make this offer occasionally to its employees.

Company Creates an ESOP (Employee Stock Option Plan)

Here we deal with a company that wants to be or become a partial or fully employee owned company. The employer sets up an ESOP trust fund that will belong to the employees. The employer either contributes cash or shares of stock to the trust fund or gets the trust fund to borrow money to be paid back over time. Note that setting up the trust fund does not involve the employees making any contributions. This differs from companies that set up employee savings plans or employee profit sharing plans.

The trust begins allocating shares to the retirement accounts of employees. Shares are distributed to employees according to their relative pay or some other formula to result in an equitable distribution. When employees leave the company, they cash out. They benefit from having received a significant retirement amount. The ESOP results in the company continuing as an employee-owned enterprise and going concern. The original owner can stay or cash out.

About two-thirds of ESOPs are used to provide a market for the shares of a departing owner of a profitable, closely held company. Most of the remainder are used either as a supplemental employee benefit plan or as a means to borrow money in a tax-favored manner. Less than 10 percent of plans are in public companies.

A 2000 Rutgers study found that ESOP companies grow 2.3 percent to 2.4 percent faster after setting up their ESOP than they would have achieved without it. Companies that combine employee ownership with employee workplace participation programs show even more substantial gains in performance. A 1986 NCEO study found that employee ownership firms that practice participative management grow 8 percent to 11 percent per year faster with their ownership plans than they would have without them.[v]

Notable majority employee-owned companies include Publix Super Markets (200,000 employees), Amsted Industries (18,000 employees), W.L. Gore and Associates (maker of Gore-Tex, 10,720 employees), and Davey Tree Expert (10,500 employees). All these companies exhibit successful results. As an example, Publix is an employee owned company with 5 percent turnover, ranks 39th in happy employees, and the CEO earns eight times the lowest paid employee.

Companies with ESOPs and other broad-based employee ownership plans account for well over half of Fortune Magazine's "100 Best Companies to Work for in America" list year after year. Being in an ESOP is associated with higher household net wealth, higher net income from wages, higher retirement savings, and longer job tenure.

Create a Cooperative

Members of the public can create co-operative organizations where worker ownership and rights are paramount over the rights of capital. A cooperative, or co-op, is an organization owned and controlled by the people who use the products or services the business produces. Cooperatives operate for the benefit of members, rather than to earn profits for investors. The profits earned are normally reinvested or part might be distributed to members. The aim of cooperatives is to provide members goods and services at reasonable rates.

There are different types of cooperatives. *Producer cooperatives* process their members' products and service and market them and share the proceeds. An example would be agricultural cooperatives. A *multi-stakeholder cooperative* has members who share a common interest such as providing home care services. A *worker cooperative* provides their members with work and the coop is owned by the members. A *consumer cooperative* provides their members with goods and services for their personal use, such as a food cooperative or a housing cooperative.

Cooperatives are found in many nations of the world, including the US, Canada, Spain, India, and other countries. One of the best examples of a cooperative is Migros of Switzerland, organized originally in Zurich in 1925. Today Migros includes supermarket food stores, restaurants, gasoline stations, language schools, and a bank and an insurance company. It employs more than 100,000 persons. Here is a summary of some characteristics of Migros and its "responsible" philosophy:

- Does not sell any alcoholic beverages nor any tobacco;
- Does not pay any dividend;
- If the earnings before interest and taxes (EBIT) reaches 5 percent of the market value of the company, the supermarkets have to lower their prices;
- Organized as a cooperative (federation of regional cooperatives), with more than two million shareholders;
- Every adult living in Switzerland can become a member (receive a share for free) and vote at the general assembly;
- Uses 0.5 percent of its revenue to social and cultural projects.

Accept a Workers Union with Co-Determination

Companies are typically set up by entrepreneurs with the purpose of making a profit for the company's owners and shareholders. Companies proceed to hire workers and give them salaries plus some benefits. Hired workers have no official role to play in the company's business strategy. Management, appointed by the owner and shareholders, sets up all the company systems and terms. Workers are expected to accept these systems and terms or leave the company.

Even workers who spend their entire life in one company typically do not participate in the profits that result from labor and capital. Capital keeps all the profit. Unless there is a profit sharing employee plan, workers simply earn a salary.

Worker unions were started in companies to address grievances and to press for higher pay and benefits. These unions were always met with strong company resistance, with company efforts to break them up or beat them down with the help of the police. Over time, each country had to pass laws regulating on how unions could be formed and voted on and how unions and management could conduct business together. Unions were limited in their use of their main weapon, worker strikes, by further legislation.

Union organizers understandably face difficult challenges in trying to bring a worker union into an ongoing business. Intense campaigns erupt for and against accepting a union. Laws are passed to establish fair results. From management's point of view, unions threaten to raise labor costs (salary and benefits). Management sees unions as interfering with the rights of Capital to maximize shareholder return. Management doesn't see any reason why workers should participate in company business strategy.

Workers, however, have a great interest in management decisions beyond worker pay and benefits. Is the company planning to move the factory to another location or overseas? Is the company's operations polluting the air and water and hurting the quality of community life? Do workers agree with the chemicals that the workers use to produce the products? Is the company paying equal pay to men and women doing the same work? Is the company using the right promotion standards for selecting employees for promotion?

Germany provides a good example of how companies can shape an acceptable relationship between worker unions and management. Germany passed the Co-Determination Act in 1976 to require at least one third of company board seats to be assigned to employee union representatives in the planning, steering and organizational decisions of German companies. The number of employee board members is not to exceed one half. The idea is to avoid or reduce conflict between labor and management. In giving workers a voice in company decisions, German unions agreed not to agitate for a socialist state.

These employee representatives on the board participate in making high-level strategic decisions, including how to invest profits and whom to hire for senior management positions. Workers also elect representatives to works councils that deal with day-to-day issues such as overtime pay, major layoffs and monitoring and evaluation.

Has co-determination been good for German companies? Some research shows that co-determination has a positive effect, especially through work councils, and some research shows no effect. Co-determination didn't seem to lead to more corporate growth and profits, nor did it seem to undermine growth either. US Senator Elizabeth Warren found the idea of co-determination to be interesting. She proposed legislation to reserve 40 percent of board seats of US companies with revenues over $1bn for workers' representatives.

Recent Developments Affecting the World of Work

The life and well-being of workers are greatly affected by many trends occurring in the world and in the workplace. Consider the following:

1. Covid-19 has had a major impact on work and workers. Covid led to a great number of deaths, many businesses closing down, workers losing their jobs, and companies allowing many remaining workers to work at home. Vaccines were first allocated to senior citizens, health care workers, workers in food production and service, and workers in essential industries. Businesses had to construct new pay arrangements and benefit plans.
2. Companies experienced mounting civic pressure to increase the diversity of its workforce while preventing any discrimination by sex, age, or lifestyle variables.
3. Companies had to increase the flexibility of work schedules and deadlines to accommodate workers who had to meet various family needs.
4. Companies faced growing pressure to reduce the gender pay gap and the racial pay gap.
5. Companies had to establish better rules and regulations bearing on sexual discrimination or harassment.
6. Companies are under greater pressure to be careful on how much automation and digitalization to allow that will hurt the number of jobs.

As the world makes progress toward reducing Covid, will business return to the old normal? What will the workplace look like? Here are some likely outcomes that depart from the old normal:

- Companies will allow more jobs to be done at home. Companies will try to evaluate the relative effectiveness of both office and remote work. The fact that home workers won't lose time in a twice a day commute to the office each working day needs to be taken into account. On the other hand, the divided workforce might impact negatively on innovation, mentoring, the initiation of new projects, and the company's culture. Even those who work at home might be asked to work at the company one or two days a week. If so, home-based employees should have a desk or be able to book a desk on days when they will go to the office.

- There will be a reduction in the amount of needed office space and a decline in the earnings of owners of office real estate properties. Companies need to maintain a significant co-located workplace and use digital innovations to improve employee and customer engagement and safety.
- Companies that have good experience with employees working at home are at liberty to hire more persons outside the local area, persons who have talent or could add more diversity to the company's workforce.
- Companies that resorted to selling their goods to online buyers who would pick them up or rely on the company delivering these goods would be wise to maintain these systems because of the likelihood of future viruses or pandemics.
- Workers will dress more casually in the office because of the freedom they had while working at home.
- Companies will learn more of the value of running a happy and satisfied workforce, even if this means involving some worker representatives to participate in company business strategy.
- More companies will expand their benefit package for employees, including nod pads, free snack food and coffee, and ping pong tables for recreation.

Conclusions

We started with the question of what percentage of US workers are unhappy in their jobs. The answer is close to 50 percent. These workers are probably less productive, have their minds on other things, fail to think creatively about their job and company growth, and may deal poorly with other employees and even customers.

A company is advised to identify the unengaged or disengaged employees and find out the main forces at work. Employee disengagement can be due to bad bosses or supervision, low pay, low opportunity, bad working conditions and a number of other factors. The company must try to remedy each of these depressing causes. Overall, everything starts from the top. If management is casual about its workers, slow to acknowledge or appreciate its employees' work, these ill effects will continue to occur. So much of this is correctible.

The more basic problem is that US companies are set up to maximize profits. The profits are produced by labor and capital. Labor only receives wages, wages that are often insufficient to cover middle class living needs. Capital, represented by the shareholders, receive all the profits.

Would more workers be engaged if they owned some shares in the companies in which they work? Wouldn't they see more purpose in helping the company grow and be profitable? This thinking leads alert companies to offer employee savings plans and even better, employee profit sharing plans. Privately held companies can be reformed into ESOPs to capture more employee interest. More new companies can be organized as cooperatives. More companies could accept a worker union with co-determination participation.

Employee experience in the workplace has been impacted in recent times by many factors, including the Covid pandemic, civic pressure to diversify the workforce and to prevent racial or gender discrimination, the rise of digitalization, automation and artificial intelligence, among others. Covid itself has led to more home-based employees, more extensive use of digital systems to carry on co-located work, and more company flexibility allowing employees to handle family problems.

The diminution of Covid is unlikely to just restore the old normal. Many practices created in response to Covid are likely to continue in what will be the new normal.

Some Final Questions

Most of this discussion applied to employees working in large shareholding public corporations. The aim was to engage employees to be shareholders too. The assumption was that employees who are also shareholders would be more engaged in helping the company grow and make profits. This begs the question whether shareholding employees actually have enough shares to care. Or whether initial employee enthusiasm is sustained over time. Or the question of whether employees will be depressed as the value of their shares go down in bad times.

Our discussion does not cover employees working in other types of companies. There are a huge number of family owned businesses without stock shares. Family owned companies have to figure out their own solutions to engage and enthuse their employees. Going further, there are many workers who have one or more gig jobs and company loyalty and engagement is hardly likely to take place. We have less hope in these cases to turn employees into partial capitalists. Here unionization is the more promising answer.

References

[i] Jack Kelly, "More Than Half of U.S. Workers Are Unhappy in Their Jobs: Here's Why and What Needs to be Done Now," Forbes, October 25, 2019. The findings were reported in a comprehensive study of 6,600 workers conducted jointly by the Lumina Foundation, the Bill & Melinda Gates Foundation, Omiya Network, and Gallup.

[ii] The 2017 Mind the Workplace report, released by the nonprofit group Mental Health America (MHA) and The Favas Foundation.

[iii] *Companies with an average of 9.3 engaged employees for every actively disengaged employee in 2010–2011 experienced 147% higher EPS compared with their competition in 2011–2012.* https://www.gallup.com/workplace/236927/employee-engagement-drives-growth.aspx: https://employeeengagement.com/gallup-employee-engagement-a-leading-indicator-of-financial-performance/

[iv] Miriam Gottfried, "KKR Executive Sees Progress in Push for Employee Stock Ownership," Wall St. Journal, February 19, 2001

[v] www.lb7.uscourts.gov/documents/14-31811.pdf

Source: March 9, 2021; Should Workers Own Stock in Their Companies? | by Philip Kotler | Medium

CHAPTER THIRTY

Welcome to the Age of Demarketing!

MOST OF THE COMMERCIAL WORLD spends its time trying to increase the demand for products and services. But we also need a science of "Demarketing" to help decrease the demand for certain products and services. It would be applied to decrease the demand for "vice" products such as hard drugs, cigarettes, and fatty foods. It would also be used to reduce the use of scarce resources, such as water, clean air, certain fish, and certain minerals. California doesn't have enough water and in Beijing, 9,000 citizens are in hospitals with respiratory sickness because of the lack of clean air. For some things, the task is not marketing but demarketing.

In 1971, Sidney Levy and I published an article in the Harvard Business Review entitled "Demarketing, Yes, Demarketing." We argued that shortages can be as much of a problem as surpluses. We defined demarketing as ". . . that aspect of marketing that deals with discouraging customers in general or a certain class of customers in particular on a temporary or permanent basis."

Today many people are concerned about the planet's "carrying capacity" to provide the resources on the scale needed to support the world's growing population and the needs of this and the next generation.

The "ecological footprint" concept says that we would need the equivalent of six to eight more earths of resources if all people in the world want to achieve the level of US living standard under the current rate of resource consumption. Furthermore one generation can exploit the existing resources—oil, water, air, timber, fish—so intensely that the next generation is doomed to accept a lower standard of living. As the earth's resources diminish, we may have to move from the Age of Marketing to the Age of Demarketing.

How does this bear on business decision making? Companies that embrace sustainability need to make some basic changes in their production and marketing strategies and practices. Paul Polman, CEO of Unilever "Our ambitions are to double our business, but to do that while reducing our environmental impact and footprint… It has to be done via more responsible consumption…"

If every company sets the goal of doubling its business, then if they succeed, sustainability will be impossible to achieve. If the less developed countries would by some miracle achieve middle-class living standards, the pollution, road and air traffic, and energy power outages would smother our quality of life. Something between a zero growth goal and a modest growth goal would make more sense.

Sustainability-driven companies need to introduce clear criteria to direct their new product development programs, invest more in reuse and recycling, and convince their stakeholders—employees, channels, suppliers, and investors—to fight waste and accept some limits to growth.

Companies will have to change their compensation package to encourage their managers to set a better balance between the goals of growth and sustainability. The CEO needs to earn a payout based on achieving the planned growth rate while reducing environmental costs by a planned percent.

Enter Demarketing

Companies need to build in demarketing thinking into their demand management strategy. Demarketing is another name for *demand reduction.* Four situations call for demand reduction.

1. *Managing an existing shortage.* The Middle East is short of water and must ration it to competing users. Frequent energy blackouts in various countries require campaigns to discourage unnecessary or wasteful energy consumption.
2. *Avoiding potential shortages.* Overfishing must be curtailed in order to maintain the fish supply. Timber cutting must be matched by active replanting.
3. *Minimizing harm to individuals.* Efforts are needed to reduce cigarette smoking and hard drug use and eating foods too high in sugar, salt, and fat.
4. *Minimizing harm to nature or unique resources.* Discouraging many people from visiting Yellowstone National Park or other over-attended tourist areas.

What are the tools of demarketing? Let's examine Russia's effort to discourage its citizens from overdrinking vodka and other alcoholic beverages. Vodka dependency results in fights, marriage breakups, injuries and deaths. The 4Ps serve as an initial marketing framework to be used by the Russian government and NGOs to reduce vodka consumption:

- Product. The government would order lower production of vodka. It might also limit consumers to buying only one quart a week.
- Price. The government would substantially increase the price of vodka.
- Place. The government would limit the number of distribution outlets that sell vodka and make them difficult or inconvenient to visit.
- Promotion. The government would run advertising and news campaigns on the harm done to individuals and families by excessive vodka consumption.

There is a caution, however, when trying to reduce demand for a desired object. ***First,*** the demarketing campaign might make the product or service more desirable: banning a book or movie often has this effect. ***Second,*** it can create a criminal class that will prosper during the induced scarcity, as happened in the prohibition era in the US when liquor was banned. ***Third,*** human rights advocates will complain about the government's interference with what they consider citizens' rights.

Demarketing efforts have been applied in a wide range of situations: to persuade legislators to limit the number of licenses for hunting and fishing, to discourage the number of visitors to overcrowded national parks, to persuade hotel guests to request fewer towels, to persuade homeowners to use less air conditioning and electricity, to persuade car buyers to purchase more fuel-efficient cars.

Demarketing poses difficult choices between individual freedom and the public good. Without demarketing, we experience the Tragedy of the Commons where everyone uses too much of a public good. With demarketing, we experience a limit on our individual freedom. Demarketing works best when there is high citizen consensus that the consumption of some good or service should be reduced.

Source: January 30, 2021; Welcome to the Age of Demarketing! | by Philip Kotler | Medium

CHAPTER THIRTY ONE

Does Marketing Contribute to or Harm American Life?

When I am introduced to someone, I am described as a marketing scholar. My host will add "Professor Kotler is considered the father of Modern Marketing." Some people are impressed and they bring up their favorite marketing story. Others are unimpressed and some carry real concerns about marketing's impact on American life.

I am always ready to admit that some marketing practices are disturbing, if not definitely harmful. I can also easily find negative things to say about financial practices, production practices, and even human relations practices.

I feel that the time is ripe to gather and confront the most criticized marketing practices. One way to put together a list is to ask ChatGPT the following prompt: "List the most criticized marketing practices that have come up in public discussion." After all, Chat GPT has access to all the world's conversations and can do a better job than I can do to find, say, the twelve major criticisms of marketing practice. So I went ahead and put the following prompt to ChatGPT. "List the twelve major criticisms of marketing."

Here are the twelve major criticisms often leveled at modern marketing:

1. **Intrusiveness:** Modern marketing, particularly digital marketing, is often seen as invasive. Pop-up ads, targeted ads based on browsing history, and unsolicited emails or messages can disrupt user experience and create a sense of privacy invasion.
2. **Overemphasis on Data:** The reliance on data analytics in marketing can lead to a reduction in creativity. Marketers may focus too heavily on metrics, optimizing for short-term gains rather than fostering long-term brand loyalty or creating truly innovative campaigns.
3. **Manipulation and Deception:** Some marketing tactics are criticized for being manipulative, using psychological tricks or misleading information to persuade consumers. This can erode trust in brands and contribute to consumer cynicism.
4. **Exploitation of Consumer Vulnerabilities:** Modern marketing often targets vulnerable populations, such as children, elderly, or individuals with certain addictions, exploiting their weaknesses to drive sales.
5. **Environmental Impact:** The focus on consumerism in marketing promotes overconsumption, leading to environmental degradation. Fast fashion and planned obsolescence are examples where marketing drives unsustainable practices.
6. **Creation of Unrealistic Expectations:** Marketing often sets unrealistic standards for beauty, success, and happiness, contributing to societal issues like low self-esteem, anxiety, and depression.
7. **Increased Consumerism:** Modern marketing fuels a culture of materialism and overconsumption, encouraging people to buy more than they need and equating personal worth with possessions.
8. **Lack of Authenticity:** With the rise of influencer marketing and paid endorsements, consumers are increasingly skeptical of the authenticity of brand messages. This can lead to a disconnect between brands and their audiences.
9. **Cultural Homogenization:** Global marketing campaigns often promote a homogenized culture, undermining local traditions, values, and identities in favor of global consumerism.
10. **Short-term Focus:** Many modern marketing strategies prioritize short-term sales boosts over long-term brand building, leading to a lack of sustainable growth and brand loyalty.

11. **Ethical Concerns with Targeting:** The use of big data in marketing raises ethical questions, particularly around targeting specific demographics based on sensitive information like health status, race, or income level.
12. **Dependency on Algorithms:** As platforms like Google and Facebook increasingly dictate what content is seen through their algorithms, marketers are forced to cater to these systems, often at the expense of genuine creativity and human connection.

These criticisms highlight the complex and often contentious role that modern marketing plays in society, balancing business objectives with ethical considerations.

However, are all these twelve criticisms of marketing valid? Is there a way to justify each criticism? I decided to ask ChatGPT how it would answer or refute each criticism? Here is my prompt:

"I am submitting a list of twelve well-known criticisms of modern marketing below. Please provide the best answers or refutations to each criticism as they might come from professional marketers."

1. Intrusiveness:

Response: Marketers strive to balance relevance with user experience. Advanced targeting allows ads to be more relevant, reducing the overall volume of irrelevant content. Consumers can often opt out or adjust preferences, giving them control over their ad experiences. Additionally, many free services are funded by advertising, making it a necessary part of the digital ecosystem.

2. Overemphasis on Data:

Response: Data-driven marketing enhances creativity by providing insights into what resonates with audiences. It allows for more informed decisions, leading to campaigns that are both innovative and effective. Far from stifling creativity, data can inspire new ways to connect with consumers.

3. Manipulation and Deception:

Response: Ethical marketing practices are essential, and most reputable marketers prioritize honesty and transparency. Regulations like the FTC guidelines in the US help ensure that deceptive practices are minimized. Marketers understand that trust is crucial for long-term success, and misleading consumers is counterproductive.

4. Exploitation of Consumer Vulnerabilities:
Response: Responsible marketers recognize the importance of ethical considerations and aim to protect vulnerable populations. Many companies adhere to strict guidelines to avoid targeting vulnerable groups inappropriately. Marketing can also play a positive role in educating and empowering consumers.

5. Environmental Impact:
Response: The marketing industry is increasingly focused on sustainability, with many brands adopting eco-friendly practices and promoting sustainable products. Marketing can drive positive change by encouraging consumers to make environmentally conscious choices and supporting brands that prioritize sustainability.

6. Creation of Unrealistic Expectations:
Response: The shift toward more authentic and inclusive marketing is addressing this issue. Many brands now celebrate diversity and promote realistic standards of beauty and success. The industry is evolving to reflect a broader range of experiences and perspectives, which can help mitigate the negative impact of unrealistic expectations.

7. Increased Consumerism:
Response: Marketing is about meeting consumer needs and wants. It reflects consumer demand rather than creating it. Moreover, many modern marketing campaigns focus on experiences, values, and purpose-driven messages rather than mere material acquisition. This shift encourages more thoughtful consumption.

8. Lack of Authenticity:
Response: Authenticity is increasingly valued in modern marketing, with consumers gravitating toward brands that are genuine and transparent. Brands

are now more focused on building real connections with their audiences, often through storytelling, transparency, and social responsibility.

9. Cultural Homogenization:
Response: While global campaigns may have a broad reach, they can also be tailored to local markets to respect and celebrate cultural differences. Many brands invest in understanding local cultures and create region-specific content that resonates with diverse audiences, preserving cultural uniqueness.

10. Short-term Focus:
Response: While short-term metrics are important, many brands also invest in long-term brand building. Integrated marketing strategies balance immediate sales goals with brand equity growth, ensuring sustainable success. The best marketers know that brand loyalty and long-term relationships are key to enduring success.

11. Ethical Concerns with Targeting:
Response: Marketers increasingly prioritize ethical data practices, with many adopting privacy-first approaches. Transparency and consumer consent are becoming standard practices, ensuring that data is used responsibly and respectfully. Ethical targeting aims to enhance relevance without compromising privacy or fairness.

12. Dependency on Algorithms:
Response: Algorithms are tools that help deliver content that is more relevant to users, enhancing their experience. However, marketers are aware of the need for human creativity and intuition, balancing algorithmic insights with creative thinking to craft compelling campaigns that resonate on a deeper level.

The above responses highlight how the marketing industry is evolving to address these criticisms while continuing to drive business success.

Every marketing organization would benefit from reviewing where it stands on each criticism and what it can do to reduce that criticism. We must acknowledge that many marketing organizations won't change their practices at all, especially if those practices continue to produce good results. My hope, however, is that many companies will change one or more practices that clearly harm consumers or the society in some ways. To some extent, we will need to rely on the "good practice" marketing companies continue to outperform the "bad practice" marketing companies. If all else fails, I would predict that government and consumer groups will find it necessary to propose new regulations and laws to reduce the frequency of bad marketing practices.

So how do we answer the question in the title, namely "Does Marketing Contribute to or Harm American Life?" This debate is likely to continue forever. My answer is twofold. Marketing has been a major force in bringing about more goods and services that have increased prosperity and made the life of most Americans better. However, Marketing has also brought some harm to American lives and expectations by damaging the environment and presenting a superficial picture of what constitutes true happiness and well-being.

Source: August 13, 2024. Does Marketing Contribute to or Harm… | by Philip Kotler | Medium

CHAPTER THIRTY TWO

Does Marketing Need Curtailment for the Sake of Sustainability?

MARKETING, A SUBJECT THAT I dearly love, needs to be reformulated in terms of its purpose and constraints. Otherwise, marketing will continue to work at cross-purposes with the growing societal need for achieving sustainability.

Marketing's normal purpose is to help companies increase their sales. Coca Cola marketers work to convince customers to buy and consume more Coca Cola. Boeing marketers work to convince airlines to buy and fly more airplanes. These "growth marketers" will be judged and rewarded on how much sales growth they achieve.

The problem is that producing and selling more Coca Cola or more Boeing airplanes will generate more greenhouse gases that will warm up the earth and create climatic crises in the form of more floods, droughts, forest fires and other disasters.

We can't order these companies or their marketers to curtail their planned economic growth. This would strike at the heart of Capitalism. Companies everywhere in the world are driven to compete and to win, not to slow down for the public good.

Are there some ways to achieve a reasonable slowdown in economic growth for the sake of saving the planet?

The ultimate solution must come from changes in the normal behavior of consumers, businesses and governments. Here are the needed changes:

- **Consumers** must increasingly acknowledge their role in helping create climate disasters. Could they replace Coca Cola by drinking fresh tap water coming out of their faucet? Could they make a home drink as tasty as Coca Cola by mixing a powder with water, thereby removing the need for factories producing the drink, bottling it, and shipping bottles all over the world.
- **Businesses** need to rethink the way they conduct their business. Could a business executive who might ordinarily fly to all of his accounts to meet and entertain them instead conduct his business by phone or zoom? Can we hope that new technologies will emerge to help businesses meet their needs in a more zero-greenhouse gas emissions way?
- **Governments** need to pass laws and develop taxes that induce more decarbonized behavior on the part of consumers and businesses. As an example, governments could pass a law banning the use of plastic as a packaging material. In addition, government could subsidize R&D to find an efficient and safe material to replace plastic.

Although these three key institutions could do more to limit harmful greenhouse gas growth, they are likely to continue their normal behaviors unless (1) they develop a new mindset and (2) encounter skillful organized opposition.

A Revised Citizen Mindset

Businesses have done their best to push a consumer mindset on to citizens. Our television programs are interrupted every 15 minutes with 30-second commercial pitches to buy something. Our telephone rings several times a day with a robo-call to buy something. Our magazines carry flashy full page ads of beautiful models telling how some skin care product won them a handsome husband. No wonder citizens see themselves as mainly consumers.

Businesses needed citizens to see themselves primarily as consumers. With the growth of mass production, business needed citizens to see themselves as mass consumers. Marketers operated on the premise that "human wants are infinite." Marketers primarily operated on human material wants. People would be motivated to accumulate material branded objects that reflected their status and power. A person owning a Cadillac would get much more attention than if he owned a Chevy. And even the Cadillac owner aspires to own a Mercedes. Persons establish their standing in the world by what they consumed. We can say that much of human behavior could be characterized as "consumer warfare." The economist Thorstein Veblen captured much of this behavior in his writings on "conspicuous consumption."[i]

How do we change the chokehold that consumerism has on contemporary American culture? Homer Warren and Linette Stratford make the case that Consumer Consciousness needs to be replaced by Producer Consciousness.[ii] Instead of a citizen staying in the passive state of a consumer waiting for new tempting goods to come into their purview, persons need to operate as active producers of the kind of life they want and to take the steps to create it.

There are many examples of citizens acting as producers. Consider the woman who decides to become a vegetarian or a vegan. Consider the young man who decides that he doesn't need a car and that a bicycle will suffice. Consider the retired executive who decides to become active in the Sierra Club. People who face the question of "Who am I" often make fresh decisions.

Many citizens are changing as a result of the terrible coronavirus pandemic. This pandemic put citizens through a long period of deprivation and anxiety. I predict that the pandemic will usher in new consumer attitudes and behaviors that might even change the type of today's Capitalism. Citizens will reexamine what they consume, how much they consume, and how all this is influenced by class issues and inequality. Citizens need to reexamine contemporary Capitalism and emerge with a new, more equitable form of Capitalism.

The Growing Number of Anti-Consumerists

There are signs today of a growing anti-consumerist movement. We can distinguish at least five types of anti-consumerists.

First, a number of consumers are becoming *life simplifiers,* persons who want to eat less and buy less. They are reacting to the clutter of "stuff." They want to downsize their possessions, many of which lie around unused and unnecessary. Some life-simplifiers are less interested in owning goods such as cars or even homes; they prefer renting to buying and owning.

Second, there is an increase in the number of *degrowth activists* who feel that too much time and effort are going into consuming. This feeling is captured in William Wordworth's poem,

> *"The world is too much with us…*
> *Getting and spending, we lay waste our powers:*
> *Little we see in Nature that is ours;*
> *We have given our hearts away, a sordid boon!"*

Degrowth activists worry that consumption will outpace the carrying capacity of the earth. In 1970, the world population was 3.7 billion. By 2011, the world population grew to 7.0 billion. Today (2020) the world population stands at 7.7 billion. The U.N. expects the world population to grow to 9.8 billion by 2050. The nightmare would be that the earth cannot feed so many people. The amount of arable land is limited and the top soil is getting poorer. Several parts of our oceans are dead zones with no living marine life. Degrowth activists call for conservation and reducing our material needs. They worry about the people in the emerging poor nations aspiring to achieve the same standard of living found in advanced countries, something that is not possible. They see greedy producers doing their best to create "false and unsustainable needs."

Third, another group consists of *climate activists* who worry about the harm and risk that high-volume buying consumers are doing to our planet through generating so much carbon footprints that pollute our air and water. Climate activists carry a strong respect for nature and science and have genuine concerns about the future of our planet.

Fourth, there are *sane food choosers* who have turned into vegetarians and vegans. They are upset with how we kill animals to get our food. Everyone could eat well and nutritiously on a plant, vegetable and fruit diet. Livestock managers fatten up their cows and chickens to grow fast, and then kill them to sell animal parts in the pursuit of profits. Meanwhile cows are a major emitter of methane that heats our earth and leads to higher temperatures, faster glacial melting, and flooding of cities. To produce one kilogram of beef, requires between 15,000 and 20,000 liters of water as well as so much roughage to feed the animals.

Fifth, we hear about *conservation activists* who plead not to destroy existing goods but to reuse, repair, redecorate them or give them to needy people. Conservationists want companies to develop better and fewer goods that last longer. They criticize a company such as Zara that every two weeks produces a new set of women's clothing styles that would only be available for two weeks. Conservationists oppose any acts of planned obsolescence. They are hostile to the luxury goods industry. Many are environmentalists and anti-globalists.[iii]

Many persons are taking steps on their own to limit their consumption.

Organized Opposition to Consumerism and Endless Growth

There are a number of groups advocating a slowdown in growth to avoid a natural calamity. Continuous growth is going to cause us to run out of certain non-renewable resources and do terrible damage to our environment and the planet. In 1972, Donella H. Meadows, Dennis L. Meadows, and Jergen Randers published a famous study called *The Limits to Growth.**[iv]***. It was commissioned by the Club of Rome and compiled by an international team of experts. It used a computer model called World3, based on system dynamics, to analyze 12 scenarios of different possible patterns of growth and environmental outcomes of world development over the two centuries 1900–2100. The scenarios used different rates of population growth and different natural resource requirements to show the possibility of not only running out of certain non-renewable resources and land and food shortages, but also severe environmental damage from air and water pollution and climate change.

The computer showed many "overshoots" of the carrying capacity of the earth to support the level of consumption and the planet's sustainability. They showed that the earth could not supply the resources needed by humanity and absorb the dangerous carbon footprint emissions.

The *Limits to Growth* has been updated.[v] Each time the findings grow more dire about the carrying capacity of the earth to sustain the consumption growth taking place without doing great harm to the planet and to people's expectations. Here is a small sample of environmental concerns cited:

- "Sea level has risen 10–20 cm since 1900. Most non-polar glaciers are retreating, and the extent and thickness of Arctic sea ice is decreasing in summer."
- "In 2002, the Food and Agriculture Organization of the UN estimated that 75 percent of the world's oceanic fisheries were fished at or beyond capacity. The North Atlantic cod fishery, fished sustainably for hundreds of years, has collapsed, and the cod species may have been pushed to biological extinction."
- "The first global assessment of soil loss, based on studies of hundreds of experts, found that 38 percent, or nearly 1.4 billion acres, of currently used agricultural land has been degraded."

Citizens would face a growing scarcity of water, dwindling oil supplies, deforestation, overfishing, global climate change, species extinction, pollution, urban congestion, and intensifying competition for remaining resources. It seems that the public prefers to keep its head in the sand than to favor taking actions to prevent a human and planetary crisis from occurring.

In response to Limits to Growth are thousands of nonprofit organizations pressing for conservation and restraint. Among them are Environmental Defense Fund, Friends of the Earth, Greenpeace, Sierra Club, The Nature Conservancy, The Wildlife Society, Worldwatch Institute, and many others. In addition are government organizations such as United States Department of the Interior, Environmental Protection Agency, Fish and Wildlife Service, National Park Service and others. Hopefully, such organizations will grow in power and influence.

The Future: Two Types of Marketers

Earlier we said that marketing's conventional task is to sell all the products of the society. This will be the largest group of marketers and they can be called "growth marketers." We see the rise of another group of marketers who will compete with the growth marketers. This group can be called the "sustainability marketers." Their job is to use social marketing tools and demarketing tools to constrain economic growth. They will try to change the mindset of citizens to seeing themselves as producers and not consumers. They will try to influence companies to aim for zero emission of greenhouse gases. They will try to influence governments to pass laws and new taxes to drive more friendly earth policies.

Ironically, the marketing world will consists of two groups of marketers using the same tools of marketing to compete with each other. The growth marketers will face the sustainability marketers in the battle for growth vs. sustainability. Furthermore, every major company will have to hire at least one sustainability marketer to face and deal with the company's growth marketers.

References

[i] See Thorstein Veblen, *The Theory of the Leisure Class.* 1899.

[ii] Homer Warren and Linette Stratford, *Producer Consciousness,* 2016 (self-published).

[iii] The anti-consumerism movement has produced a growing literature. One major critic is Naomi Klein with her books *No Logo, This Changes Everything, and The Shock Doctrine.* Also see the documentary film *The Corporation by* Mark Achbar and Jennifer Abbott.

[iv] Donella H. Meadows, Dennis L. Meadows, and Jørgen Randers, and William W. Behrens III, *The Limits to Growth,* op.cit.

[v] The *Limits to Growth: The 30-Year Update* (published in 2004) reports the worsening of the environment since the influential book's original publication in 1972.

Source: July 31, 2021; Does Marketing Need Curtailment for the Sake of Sustainability? | by Philip Kotler | Medium

CHAPTER THIRTY THREE

Marketing Needs 6Ps for Strategic Marketing

FOR DECADES, MARKETERS THRIVED ON the use of 4Ps—Product, Price, Place, Promotion—to conduct their Tactical Marketing Planning.

Now we have to ask whether the 4P marketing mix is a sufficient starting framework for strategic marketing planning. Or is an expanding 6P marketing mix a better way to conduct Strategic Marketing Planning?

A Brief History of the 4Ps Paradigm

In 1960, Professor Jerry McCarthy published *Basic Marketing* in which he introduced the 4P marketing framework. Jerry had studied marketing under Professor Richard Clewett at Northwestern University. Clewett taught students that marketing consists of making decisions on product, price, promotion and distribution. Clewett held that the heart of marketing laid in distribution, the setting up of channels of distribution. Jerry decided to replace "distribution" with "place" so that marketers could use the more convenient toolset of the 4Ps. Marketers were especially competent in "place" marketing.

I chose to use the 4P framework in writing my marketing textbooks. I went further and applied the 4P framework not only to commercial organizations but to all organizations—such as colleges, museums, government agencies, etc. All organizations seek marketing results. I called this "broadening marketing."

More recently, I recognized the need to add a few more marketing tools to the 4Ps. Marketers needed to add Service and Brand to their Product thinking. What good is a product if it doesn't include good service? What good is the product if it doesn't exhibit a strong brand? Then I added one more tool to Price, namely Incentives. Altogether, I added 3 more marketing tools. Unfortunately these three new tools did not begin with the letter P.

The Need for a New 6P Framework for Strategic Marketing

Peter Drucker, the father of modern management, said that every business must ask this question: What is the purpose of my business? The easy answer to this question is to say "profits." Is that really the only reason to start a business? Is "selling more stuff" the essence of purpose? Does "profits" sound like a lifting purpose for the company's employees? Are employees happy that their job is to produce profit for the company's stakeholders?

I began to think about a Strategic Marketing Planning process that would be founded on a sequence of 6Ps.

Purpose → People → Partners → Peace → Planet → Prosperity

The six P's lifts marketing out of its narrow commercial lane and places it in a broader human, social, and planetary context. In an age of climate anxiety, social fragmentation, inflation, AI, and hyper-competition, marketing must serve a higher order of purpose.

Let's look at each of the 6Ps in turn.

1. Purpose

Every organization, brand, or person needs to have a purpose. This is more than a mission statement framed in a boardroom. Purpose answers *why we exist* beyond profit. Brands with a strong purpose, brands such as Nike, Unilever, Walmart, Amazon and others will grow. Purpose is not just a decorative slogan but a strategic engine. Purpose aligns and motivates employees, attracts customers who share values, and gives the organization a moral north star. A strong purpose will help organizations meet Gen Z's demand for authenticity. If the "why" of a business is weak, the rest of the marketing plan is just transactional.

2. People

A market is a set of people. Marketers aim to create value for a defined set of buyers. Marketers try to provide an acceptable solution that satisfies a well-defined customer need or want.

In the process, the marketer must also satisfy the needs of employees. Imagine a hotel trying to satisfy its guests. That hotel should also try to satisfy the hotel's employees. The hotel's guests will be affected by the quality of the restaurant's staff, the room cleaning service, and other groups of employees. The hotel's success will depend on how well the hotel trains and motivates its employees. In such fields as hotels, banks, colleges, and hospitals, all employees must live the role of brand ambassadors.

3. Partnerships

Every organization must form partnerships with **human groups** to accomplish its purpose. Partnerships usually include suppliers, distributors, universities, NGOs, and technology platforms.

Successful partnerships begin with a **win–win mindset.** With it, partnerships become engines of innovation, market access, and even social impact.

4. Peace

People are productive when they work in a peaceful atmosphere. Peace operates at multiple levels:

1. **Peace within the organization**—a culture without toxic politics, fear, or instability.

2. **Peace in the marketplace and society**—businesses thrive in stable, peaceful environments.
3. **Peace of mind for customers**—the ultimate goal of marketing is not just to sell, but to reduce anxiety, friction, confusion, and risks for the customers.

Organizations need to create trust, reassurance, and long-term relationships. A peaceful world is good for business—and businesses have a role in creating that peace through ethical communication, fair treatment, and social responsibility.

5. Planet

Businesses often fail to account for *the environmental externalities* of their value creation process. This means that pollution, carbon, waste, and resource depletion are treated as "someone else's problem."

Organizations must design for sustainability—responsible sourcing, circularity, reduced packaging, greener logistics. Consumers must become mindful of *what* they consume and *how* they consume it. Marketing must stop glorifying endless consumption and start educating, nudging, and offering sustainable alternatives.

Market planning that ignores the planet will lose relevance, regulation will catch up, and younger consumers will move away. A healthy Planet is now part of the value proposition.

6. Prosperity

Real prosperity is only possible **after** the first five Ps are in place. If the organization has a clear purpose, cares for its people, builds genuine partnerships, contributes to peace, and protects the planet, then the prosperity that comes is healthier, more distributed, and more resilient.

In such a system, shareholders remain important—but not *the most* important, and not the only voice. Employees, customers, communities, the environment and the planet all become stakeholders. Prosperity becomes a collective outcome, not an individual extraction.

Why This 6Ps Framework Matters Now

This new 6Ps model represents an effort to humanize marketing. Where the original 4Ps marketing mix helped marketers *do* tactical marketing, the 6Ps help organizations do strategic marketing where the aim is to be responsible, relevant, and fit to serving the future. The 6P approach moves marketing…

- **From tactics to philosophy**—It moves marketing from tools to values.
- **From selling to serving**—It reframes the marketer as a steward of people relationships and the environment.
- **From short term to long term**—It aligns with sustainability, ESG, and stakeholder capitalism.

This framework is not just for Western multinationals. It is for developing markets, family businesses, public sector institutions, education providers—any entity that wants to grow without harming people or the planet.

Message to marketers: **Do well, but do good first.**

Thanks also goes to Denzil Indrajith Perera of Sri Lanka for our discussion of the 6Ps.

Source: November 10, 2025; https://4pkotler.medium.com/marketing-needs-6ps-for-strategic-marketing-b63afee8ce91

CHAPTER THIRTY FOUR

Doubts about Economic and Political Systems Are Worth Examining

I HAVE ALWAYS BEEN INTERESTED in people who have a clear mind about their beliefs. Such a person might believe that Capitalism is the best economic system or that democracy is the best political system or that Christianity is the best religious system.

Now I am wondering whether such believers have **an open mind or a closed mind.** I am beginning to believe that these people have closed minds. They will tend to be dogmatic and not be open to doubts or contrary beliefs.

I then began to realize that I had a set of beliefs that I blindly accepted and never deeply examined.

I published *Confronting Capitalism* in 2015 with the assumption that Capitalism is the best economic system although I added that it needs many improvements.

In 2016, I published *Democracy in Decline* and I assumed that democracy is the best political system although it also needs many improvements.

Lately I have begun to have deeper doubts about these two systems and their performances. Capitalism and Democracy came into existence in the 1700s. They both merit deep rethinking.

Is Capitalism the Best Economic System?

In most countries, businesses are owned and operated by private individuals seeking to earn a profit. These businesses hire workers and assemble the equipment and resources they need. The legal system respects the contracts that are freely made between buyers and sellers. Each business owner decides how to use and distribute the profits.

Early capitalism performed as a nation of shopkeepers. Consumers bought their supplies from locally owned shops. Consumers knew the shopkeepers.

Over time, many businesses have grown into huge oligopolies. General Electric became a leader in the aircraft engine business, the health care system, and the consumer appliances business. Each GE business carefully watched its competitors and often bought up their emerging competitors. Anti-trust was lax in regulating the growth of these companies. Some huge companies and banks were too big to break up and cut down in size. Furthermore, these companies managed to operate without unions. Labor wasn't allowed to have a voice in company strategy or in working conditions.

The result is that capitalism provided workers with an eight-hour job and often low pay while profits provided high pay to the firm's managers and investors. Workers get two weeks of paid vacation time a year. If the company encounters a recession, many workers are laid off. The working class has little hope for job and pays improvement. They are without power to improve their conditions. Many workers are likely to be unmotivated and unhappy in their work lives and this may show up in poor company performance.

Big company capitalism is a system designed to grow the wealth of the owners and managerial class. The system creates multimillionaires and billionaires while many workers toil with inadequate pay and little hope of a better livelihood.

Is There a Better System for Capitalism?

Can businesses be designed to generate more loyalty, involvement and enthusiasm for the working class? The answer is yes. How about designing more businesses in the form of Worker-owned or Consumer-owned Cooperatives?

Here are some well-known European cooperatives.

1. **Mondragon Worker-owned Corporation (Spain).** Employs 80,000 workers who are owners of the cooperative. Operates in industry, finance, retail and education. Includes a university and its own bank.
2. **Coop Group (Switzerland).** 95,000 workers with 2 million consumer owners. Operates retail chains, wholesale, production.
3. **The Co-operative Group (UK).** 60,000 workers. A consumer cooperative with some worker participation. Operates in retail, funerals, legal services, and insurance. Democratic governance and ethical supply chains.
4. **Fagor Electrodomésticos (Spain)**—part of Mondragon. Operates in appliances.
5. **La Nef (France).** Cooperative bank with customers as members. Transparent lending focused on social and environmental impact.
6. **REWE Group (Germany).** 380,000 workers. Retail cooperative owned by independent retailers. Supermarkets.

These cooperatives show the following strengths:

1. **Resilience:** Cooperatives are **more resilient in economic crises,** often due to long-term thinking and stakeholder commitment.
2. **Lower Turnover:** Worker-owned firms tend to have **lower employee turnover,** increasing organizational knowledge and performance.
3. **Productivity:** Many cooperatives report **high productivity** because workers have a direct stake in outcomes.
4. **Ethical Governance:** Cooperative are more likely to uphold social and environmental goals due to democratic structure.

These cooperatives also face certain challenges:

1. **Capital Constraints:** Raising capital can be harder due to limited access to equity markets.
2. **Slower Decision-Making:** Consensus-oriented structures can sometimes slow strategic moves.

3. **Scale and Expansion:** Scaling internationally can be more complex due to democratic governance and profit-sharing expectations.

Are Cooperatives Competent Competitors?

- **Competence** varies by sector and management. Mondragon and REWE have shown that cooperatives can compete with or outperform private firms in manufacturing, retail, and finance.
- However, **not all cooperatives succeed**—Fagor's collapse shows that market pressures and mismanagement affect cooperatives just as they do traditional firms. Their success often hinges not on the ownership model alone, but on **good governance, innovation, and adaptability**—just like any other business.
- My conclusion is that cooperatives as a business model are likely to provide better work lives and performance than privately held for-profit firms. Admittedly coops may not perform well in industries and firms where there is high risk and volatility and where workers' job security is low.

Is Democracy the Best Political System?

I always felt that democracy is the best political system. Policies should be determined by a voting public expressing their individual ideas of what they want from their government. Majority opinion should determine winning policies but minority interests and rights should be respected as well.

Democracy makes good sense as a political system in small communities. A small local community could invite all interested citizens to show up for voting on a set of important issues. Citizens know each other and are highly invested in their community.

However, today's major cities consist of people who don't know each other. Issues arise and proposed solutions can take the form of referendums. Comments come from different interested parties seeking to sway voter opinions. The political atmosphere is filled with an increasing amount of disinformation (e.g., lies) and misinformation (passing on uninformed opinion). To make things worse, only 50 percent of eligible voters turn out to vote.

Most countries have replaced a **democratic voting system** with a **representative voting system.** Members of the public don't vote on each issue but vote on who they want to represent their overall interests. Democracy has been replaced with a Republic. Voters have to trust their elected representatives to carry out their interests. Here we face a number of challenges.

1. During the election of the public's representatives, less than 50 percent of voters may vote. They are often mainly people with active and personal interests, not necessarily popular interests. Even if 100 percent of the eligible voters show up, many will have been overly brainwashed by the media they get their news from. Most voters are poorly informed about local events, let alone about domestic and international events. The average American may know nothing about where South Korea is located or how South Korea influences their lives. The ignorance of many American voters is extreme.
2. The elected representatives often don't hear much from average voters after being elected. Representatives hear mostly from lobbyists who press for special interests. Representatives are also greatly influenced by important donors who helped them get elected. Representatives will do their best to refrain from voting against their best donors' interests.
3. Representatives will represent so many people who they never met. They may call for public meetings or send out opinion surveys and get poor attendance or response. They may hear mostly from highly opinionated individuals or groups who don't represent average opinion in the group they represent.
4. The main hope is that elected representatives will want to win in the next election. This leads representatives to deliver what they think the majority of voters want. The representative's past voting record is the best way for voters to know what to expect from their representative.

Is there a better political system than relying on voting for representatives? We have to assume that representatives will vote along political party lines. We just saw how Republican members of Congress didn't think for themselves and very few Republicans had the courage to vote against a very bad omnibus budget bill.

The political system that would best serve the public interest would need to include ***expert opinions*** to influence the voters. Consider the following cases:

- Should the Department of Health allow its appointed leader, Robert Kennedy, to discourage normal vaccinations or Covid shots based on his private opinion or should his department invite the opinion of medical experts on these issues and make decisions based on what the majority of experts agree is best for the country?
- Should the Department of Defense allow its appointed leader, Pete Hegseth, to make military decisions or should experts in the Pentagon have major influence in military decision making utilizing their years of experience?

Where can expertise come from to influence decision making in a representative-run government? Expertise can come from former US Presidents, long-term civil servants, well-respected journalists, and well-regarded associations of experts. Hopefully, each representative will admit how little they know about each issue and be ready to engage known unbiased experts for their opinion about what position will best advance the Common Good.

Conclusion

Most people want to live in a country that operates with Capitalism as the economic system and Democracy as the political system. The faults and the glaring misery of living under other systems, such as Dictatorship, Fascism, Communism, and Socialism are well-documented. At the same time, it would pay for more voters to recognize the imperfections of Capitalism and Democracy. In both books of mine, I point out the major deficiencies of Capitalism and Democracy as well as the best possible reforms.

Capitalism is a system that produces a few winners with fantastic wealth and many workers who rarely advance in their income and well-being. The

Nordic countries of Sweden, Norway, Denmark, Finland and Iceland manage to give their citizens a better version of Capitalism that incorporates more wealth sharing, longer vacations, more maternal and old age benefits, and more business social responsibility. The Nordic countries provide evidence that better forms of Capitalism exist.

Democracy is a system that elects representatives who presumably will represent their voters' interests but who in practice are guided by lobbyists and rich donors. The growth of party politics leads more representatives to stop thinking about what is good for their public than what is good for their political party. Democracy's performance is improved to the extent that the public and their representatives allow experts (who are able to see the long-term consequences of decisions) to participate in the decision-making process.

Source: July 13, 2025; Doubts About Economic and Political Systems Are Worth Examining | by Philip Kotler | Jul, 2025 | Medium

CHAPTER THIRTY FIVE

How Companies Need to Think About the Future. The Case of Unilever

UNILEVER IS AN ANGLO-DUTCH COMPANY founded by William Lever in 1870. Lever defined the mission of Lever Brothers "to make cleanliness commonplace and lessen the load for women." In trying to make life easier for women, Lever could be seen as an early feminist.

Today Unilever is 151 years old. Like any long surviving company, Unilever showed that it could ride through both good and bad times.

I have followed Unilever's recent history during the brilliant leadership of CEO Paul Polman (2009–2019). Paul became CEO in 2009 with the aim of bringing Unilever into the 21st century. He was far ahead of other CEOs in his thinking about "What is the purpose of a company." He didn't think that the purpose of Unilever should be to maximize annual profits for the shareholders. That was the purpose of most CEOs, who literally and enthusiastically adopted University of Chicago Professor Milton Friedman's position. Polman was aware that many groups are impacted, favorably or unfavorably, by a company's activities. He was also troubled by the looming social problems of poverty, hunger, social unrest, crime, and climate change, all of which affect directly or indirectly the success of companies.

Rather than ignore these problems and pursue short run profit maximization, Polman wanted to look ahead and develop a long run program for building a sustainable and profitable Unilever. During his Unilever leadership, he contributed many ideas.

The company should serve and fairly reward all the major stakeholders of Unilever, not just the shareholders. Unilever uses a seven-stakeholder model ordered according to the importance of each stakeholder group: *Consumers, Customers, Business partners (mainly employees), Suppliers, Agencies, Communities, the Planet,* and *Shareholders.* By paying attention to the first six groups, Polman believes that the seventh group, shareholders, will be rewarded even more than if Unilever only paid attention to maximizing the payoff to the shareholders.

Polman believed in the critical importance of every company pursuing sustainability as well as profits. The climate change problem was real. The planet was destined to get warmer and suffer from a growing number of floods, hurricanes, typhoons, and major fires unless the use of fossil fuels and carbonization could be limited. Companies must set sustainability goals as well as profit goals. As a result, Polman implemented an ambitious Sustainable Living Plan which aimed to double the company's growth, halve its environmental impact and triple its social impact. The plan succeeded, with Unilever's annual sales rising from $38 billion to more than $60 billion during his management. Unilever became a beacon for other CEOs who needed evidence that there was no tradeoff between sustainability and financial performance. He showed that a company could deliver better financial outcomes through a multi stakeholder responsible model.

Polman's financial achievement was remarkable because Unilever is a publicly traded company with shareholders eager for a good return. On Polman's first day as CEO, he announced he would no longer be issuing quarterly share guidance and reports, to break free of the tyranny of short-termism. Over his tenure, Unilever delivered a total shareholder return of 290 percent.

Polman spoke on the importance of attracting people who are purpose-driven and attracted to the mission of the company. He wanted to recruit talented and purpose-driving people. He knew that young people want to work for companies that are conducting themselves to high social and environmental standards. He wanted Unilever to be a magnet for the best. Unilever became a consumer company of choice for young people leaving colleges in 52 or 54 countries. The company believes that 75 percent of the people that came in, came in because of the Unilever Sustainable Living plan. Attracting the best people certainly gives Unilever a competitive advantage.

Polman believed that every Unilever brand needed to define its *purpose* and its *value proposition*. Polman asked each brand team to develop and pursue a thoughtful purpose for their brand that goes beyond just selling it. He wanted brand management to do good deeds, not just set good goals. Polman also wanted Unilever brand managers to pay close attention to *product and packaging issues*. Packaging, especially plastic packaging, is becoming a major issue.

Here are the purposes of some of Unilever's top brands. (1) Lifebuoy. Lifebuoy is a soap whose aim is cleanliness and hygiene. One of its larger goals is to save the lives of kids under the age of five who often get sick from polluted water, food, or air. Its immediate purpose is to get children to wash their hands regularly. (2) Dove. Dove helps women give good personal care to their skin. The brand has done a lot to help all Unilever women customers to feel beautiful. The Campaign for Real Beauty aims to help young girls raise their self-esteem. Their broad mission is people and planet-positive beauty. (3) Domestos. Domestos is a toilet cleaner that fights for decent sanitation for all. Domestos campaigns for cleaner toilets around the world. (4) Ben & Jerry's. Ben and Jerry's has a reputation for making excellent ice cream. They built an unassailable reputation fighting for climate change, LGBTQI rights, and racial justice. They also give away a percentage of their profits to needy communities.

A company that cares about environmental and social issues will inevitably get involved in political issues such as inequality and racial justice. Companies need to take a stand. The company should avoid party politics but be ready to side with favorable public policies. Why is it important for a company to take a stand on societal and environmental issues? ***First,*** brands that do this outgrow other brands. There is a gigantic body of evidence that profits come more from value creation than from margin improvement. ***Second,*** a company can find ways to take out much cost through sustainable sourcing. There's an initial cost, but over time, cost savings occur and these drive growth. ***Third,*** investing in sustainability reduces the risk of being left behind. ***Fourth,*** there is no healthy Unilever on an unhealthy planet. Unilever sales are often lower because of extraordinary typhoons in Southeast Asia and the Philippines, fires in Australia or the West Coast. Unilever's CMOs need to learn how to integrate purpose and sustainability into brand propositions. Ultimately, Unilever is making a business case, not just supporting a moral imperative.

Each of Unilever's divisions, and not only each Unilever brand, needs to be crystal clear on their contribution to sustainability. Unilever calls its foods division its Future Foods which develop foods on a more sustainable and plant-based food system. And Unilever's home care business runs a platform called Clean Futures, which states that "we will replace 100 percent of the chemicals in our cleaning business that are sourced from fossil fuels, with carbon that comes from renewable or recycled sources." Each division is absolutely crystal clear on their contribution to sustainability.

Marketing needs to play a critical role as a business partner, not a functional leader. Good marketers are curious about the world around them, genuinely interested in people. Marketing requires a combination of left and right brain skills, a ruthless focus on consumers and not the competition. Too many marketers get distracted in war gaming and keeping up with the competition. Marketers today have to be massive systems thinkers. Several things are happening in the world that marketers need to follow. (1) The economic power shift east and south. It's not going to be about Western Europe and North America. The East is where the action is. (2) The bio economy. Marketers must understand renewable bio resources, epigenetics, microbiomes, and longer lifespans. It's going to really change how people behave and think. (3) Technology, including AI, robotics, nanotech, connected world, all of that's changing marketing.

In the future, fewer companies will be standalone companies. Companies will be networks of value exchange. Rigid hierarchies will fall apart. Companies will consist of agile teams, working on specific problems and then moving on.

There will not be standalone R&D Labs. They will be replaced by collaborative networks of invention. Our employee's will not all come to a fixed office. It will be hybrid working.

Today Unilever's new CEO, Alan Jope, even runs a global town hall. Every Tuesday, at lunchtime, 7,000 or more employees will listen. He gives a 5–10 minute talk and then he features someone like Unilever's chief medical officer. The next 40 minutes brings something like 400 questions and they are listened to and some are voted on.

Source: March 31, 2021; How Companies Need to Think about the Future. The Case of Unilever. | by Philip Kotler | Medium

SECTION V

Leadership, Politics, Democratic Reform

CHAPTER THIRTY SIX

How to Handle a Corrupt and Egotistical National Leader

DONALD TRUMP IS PRESSURING THE National Football League to name its new stadium for the Washington Commanders as the Trump Stadium. Does this matter to you or me?

Yes. It matters to me because I don't want to be reminded every time, I go to that Stadium how much harm Trump has done to America.

It matters to you because no institution remains safe from a would-be dictator who wants to put his name everywhere. Wherever you find a dictator, you will find his picture on every wall.

So far, US President Donald Trump has thrust his name in several places:

- He suggested that the new White House ballroom be named "The President Donald J. Trump Ballroom."
- He proposed renaming the John F. Kennedy Center for the Performing Arts the Donald J. Trump Center for the Performing Arts. He also proposed parts of the Opera House be named the "First Lady Melania Trump Opera House."
- A stretch of road in Palm Beach County was unanimously approved to be ceremonially renamed "President Donald J. Trump Boulevard."
- Back in 2005, Trump launched the Trump University to teach real estate. The New York State Education Department ordered it to stop calling itself

a university, causing it to be renamed Trump Entrepreneur Initiative. It ceased operations entirely amid mounting complaints and legal scrutiny.

- Trump pressured the Nobel Prize people to award him the Peace Prize.
- Trump's people hope that his face could be added at Mount Rushmore next to George Washington, Thomas Jefferson, Abraham Lincoln and Theodore Roosevelt.
- Trump has suggested changing well-known names to other names that he preferred.
- Trump tried to rename the body of water known as the "Gulf of Mexico" to "Gulf of America."
- Trump signed orders to rename the mountain Denali (Alaska) back to "Mount McKinley."

What Might the Democrats Do When They Get Back Their Power

There is little question that half of all Americans despise or dislike Donald Trump. Many regard Trump as the worst of all American presidents. Many want to reduce the use of Trump's name.

One step is to restore the original names that Trump had replaced with his name. For example, Democrats would replace the Trump Center name with its original name, the Kennedy Center.

A more serious move would be to develop a permanent list of all the terrible things that Trump did as President. This list would be presented to every newly elected American president at inauguration time as a warning about "misleadership." The list would be highlighted in educational programs discussing Presidential abuses.

I asked ChatGPT to prepare a list of the 15 worst Trump actions, policies, and behaviors according to historians, legal scholars, economists, national-security experts, and ethics watchdogs.

Trump's Fifteen Major Abuses of Presidential Power

1. Attempting to Overturn the 2020 Election
   Efforts included pressuring state officials, encouraging fake electors, and leaning on the Department of Justice to declare the election corrupt.

2. Inciting the January 6 Capitol Attack
   His rhetoric and actions leading up to the attack are viewed by critics as undermining the peaceful transfer of power—the foundation of American democracy.
3. Withholding Military Aid to Ukraine (Impeachment #1)
   He withheld congressionally approved security assistance while pressuring Ukraine to investigate a political rival, prompting impeachment for abuse of power.
4. Attempting to Obstruct Federal Investigations (Impeachment #2 & Mueller Report)
   Repeated attempts to interfere with the Mueller investigation—ordering the firing of the Special Counsel, pressuring witnesses, etc.
5. Systematic Attacks on US Democratic Institutions
   Relentless delegitimization of the judiciary, intelligence agencies, free press, and elections themselves undermined public trust in core institutions.
6. Mishandling the Covid-19 pandemic
   Downplaying the virus, contradicting scientists, promoting unproven treatments, and delaying coordinated federal response contributed to excess mortality.
7. Separating Migrant Children from Parents ("Zero-Tolerance" Policy)
   Thousands of children were forcibly separated from their families at the border; many were never reunited promptly due to chaotic record-keeping.
8. Dismantling Environmental Protections
   Rolling back more than 100 environmental rules harmed climate-mitigation efforts, air and water quality, and public health safeguards.
9. Using the Presidency for Personal Gain
   Profiting from Trump-owned properties (hotel payments, foreign delegations, Secret Service expenditures) raised unprecedented conflicts-of-interest concerns.
10. Weakening US Alliances (NATO, South Korea, Japan)
    Threatening NATO withdrawal, publicly siding with adversaries over US intelligence agencies, and alienating allies weakened American global credibility.

11. Embracing Authoritarian Leaders
Open admiration for Vladimir Putin, Kim Jong-un, and other autocrats contradicted long-standing US commitments to democracy and human rights.
12. Massive Tax Cuts Heavily Favoring the Wealthy
The 2017 tax law added trillions to the national debt and disproportionately benefited corporations and high-income individuals.
13. Undermining Science and Public Agencies
Weakening the CDC, sidelining career experts, and interfering in climate science and environmental reports damaged long-term scientific capacity.
14. Demonizing Immigrants and Minorities
Rhetoric portraying immigrants as criminals, attacks on Muslim Americans, and the travel ban have been widely criticized for fueling polarization and prejudice.
15. Mishandling Classified Documents After Leaving Office
Retaining top-secret materials, obstructing efforts to retrieve them, and keeping them in unsecured locations created serious national-security risks.

Conclusion

This is a FACT: Donald Trump is the only US president to ever be IMPEACHED twice, INDICTED four times, and CONVICTED of a crime.

In the future, the name "Donald Trump" will refer to a person and a period when an evil corrupt man came to power in the US and polluted everything. He unilaterally decided to destroy the East End of the White House, shift around the locations of pictures of Past Presidents in the White House, and load the White House with gold and silver objects to suggest the power of Kings. His ambition was to be admired and feared.

Hopefully Donald Trump will be remembered more as a tyrant similar to the Roman Emperor Nero had the audacity to play his fiddle while Rome burned.

Source: November 15, 2025; How to Handle a Corrupt and Egotistical National Leader | by Philip Kotler | Nov, 2025 | Medium

CHAPTER THIRTY SEVEN

What's Wrong with "Make America Great Again"

DONALD TRUMP HAS BEEN RUNNING on the MAGA theme "Make America Great Again." He has attracted millions of Americans to this theme. Members of the MAGA party can be spotted at his rallies wearing their MAGA hats, applauding wildly to his random remarks, and sharing his hates to "Lock Them Up" with his audience.

Members of MAGA look like ordinary Americans. Most of them are white men and women and many are middle age. They all have grievances about their incomes, jobs and lifestyle in current America. MAGA people think that there are too many Black people, too many gay people, and too many immigrants in current America. The irony is that we always had Black people but they were forced to live in separate facilities from white people and you didn't have to sit in the same restaurant with them. We always had gay people but they were forced to conceal their gayness or lose their jobs or friendships. We always valued immigrants as long as they came to us as White Europeans.

MAGA people are racists. They only like other white people. They imagine a time when American families led a happier life. If they were from the Deep South, they might want the return of segregation. If they were from the North, they might imagine the 1950s, where America had won World War 2 and was the acknowledged leader of the world. Jobs were plentiful and the ideal was the well-dressed, well-behaved Organization Man. Wasn't this the period when America was at its greatest? The middle class was able to own a home, have regular meals, buy a car and travel together on yearly vacations. There was no connection or concern with Black people, gay people, or non-European immigrants.

We lost the 1950s to the 1960s when there were student rebellions, dangerous drugs, and new alternative lifestyles. There were now civil rights activists, Black Panthers, women libbers, hippies and anarchists. Added to these were new technologies designed to enhance life such as television, computers, software, smart phones, high-speed wireless, TV streaming, the Internet, drones and robots. Most people not only appreciated these new technologies but realized that life in the 1950s was relatively nostalgic absent these technologies. Wanting America to return to the 1950s without these new tools was unimaginable.

MAGA is a movement lacking a vision of what would Make America Great Again. Every MAGA member is left to imagine a past when he or she was happier. Maybe it was a period of lower taxes, or cheaper goods, or more smiling neighbors. It is clear that Donald Trump prefers not to define the ingredients that would Make America Great Again. The only ingredient is that Trump is President of the US Trump claims that he will adopt policies that will increase the happiness and well-being of ordinary Americans.

But according to Trump, he has publicly stated that he would remove 13 million illegals and move them back to their country of origin. There are Trump haters who will have to be jailed. Trump will have to fire many members of the civil service and from academia who are liberals and who aim to pollute Trump's vision of a good society.

So, with the Presidential election about to take place, we ask how many of you expect that a Trump victory will lead to happier times? If you are a MAGA person, do you believe that the years following 2024 with a Trump victory will bring more peace and prosperity to your life and to fellow Americans? Or would it be better to let Kamala Harris and Tim Walz continue their promise to Make America Great. Let's drop the world "Again." Kamala and Harris favor building a society of Opportunities that will increase the Common Good and lead to Common Prosperity. Wouldn't those be the goals of a Great Society?

Source: October 3, 2024; What's Wrong with "Make America Great Again" | by Philip Kotler | Medium

CHAPTER THIRTY EIGHT

Decarcerating: Strategies for Reducing the Prison Population

THE US HAS THE LARGEST prison population in the world per 100,000 inhabitants! I would argue that too many persons are imprisoned and steps should be taken to release many of them to lead a more normal life. The movement to reduce the prison population in a humane way is called decarceration, as opposed to incarceration.

Most nations keep statistics on the number of persons making up their *correctional population*. The correctional population consists of two groups. One group is the number of adults supervised in the community on probation or parole. The other group is the number of adults under the jurisdiction of state or federal prisons or in the custody of local jails.

The total adult (18 or older) correctional population in the US in 2019 was 6,343,300, of which 4,357,700 were under correctional supervision (3,492,400 under probation and 878,900 under parole). The incarcerated population consisted of 2,086,000 (with 1,215,800 in prison and 734,500 in local jails).

World Prison Population

A shocking number of persons are in prison around the world. According to World Prison Population, there are more than 11.5 million prisoners worldwide (2021).

The size of the prison population varies greatly in different countries. Table 1 shows the number of prisoners in some major countries.

Top 10 Countries with the Most People in Prison

- United States—2,068,800
- China—1,690,000
- Brazil—811,707
- India—478,600
- Russia—471,490
- Thailand—309,282
- Turkey—291,198
- Indonesia—266,259
- Mexico—220,866
- Iran—189,000

Since countries differ greatly in size, prison populations need to be ranked by the *incarceration rate* per 100,000 national population in different nations.

Countries Ranked by the Incarceration Rate per 100,000 People in That Country

1. United States—629
2. Brazil—381
3. Russia—326
4. Mexico—169
5. Canada—104
6. China—119
7. Japan—37
8. India—35

Note the following:

1. The US stands with the highest incarceration rate (629), almost double the next largest incarceration rate of Brazil (381).
2. The US's two neighbors, Mexico (169) and Canada (104), have drastically lower incarceration rates.
3. The largest countries in Asia have relatively low incarceration rates, China (119), Japan (37) and India (35).

What Are the Characteristics of US Prisoners?

Let's look at the composition of incarcerated persons in the US.

- At midyear 2021, about 49 percent of local jail inmates were white, 35 percent were Black, and 14 percent were Hispanic. Other groups (Native Americans, Alaska Natives, Asians, accounted for only 2 percent of the total jail population in 2022).
- The system of mass incarceration particularly targets Black people, who are 13 percent of the US population but are 38 percent of the people in jails and prisons (2022). Black prisoners faced more punishment than white ones, leading to loss of privileges, longer stays in solitary confinement and, ultimately, more time behind bars.
- Males account for 90 percent of the prisoners; female account for 10 percent. Women have become the fastest-growing segment of the incarcerated population. (May 17, 2021).
- Prisoner ages ran from teenagers to over 65. Over 75 percent of prisoners were between ages 26 and 46.
- Drug offenses of 31.7 percent broke down into Methamphetamine (26.2 percent), marijuana (25.2 percent), powder cocaine (20.6 percent), heroin (10.0 percent), crack cocaine (9.7 percent), other (7.6 percent) as of 2014.
- The main offenses are drugs (31.7 percent), immigration (29.3 percent), firearms (10.5 percent), fraud (10.0 percent), non-fraud white collar (3.7 percent), child pornography (2.5 percent), larceny (1.9 percent), and other (10.4 percent). These percentages applied to the year 2014.

How Did the US Reach Such a High Imprisonment Rate?

The US imprisoned population was relatively low until the 1970s. In 1971, President Richard Nixon declared drug abuse to be "public enemy number one" and began "the War on Drugs." Drug arrests picked up with increased funding from the Drug Enforcement Administration. In 1981, President Ronald Reagan greatly expanded the drug war and favored criminal punishment over treatment. The US Congress passed the Anti-Drug Abuse Act in 1986 along with "mandatory minimum" prison sentences for different drug offenses. Because many African Americans were involved in crack, it led to a great increase in Black prisoners.

At the same time, crime was increasing and the media gave it front page coverage.

The US prison population increased from 200,000 incarcerated in 1973 to its peak of 2,400,000 in 2009. Fortunately, it went down to 2,086,000 in 2019. The main contributors to this large prison population were the war on drugs, longer sentences, media-driven campaigns about rising crime, and the "get tough on crime" response.

Processes in Managing Crime and Criminals

The existence of prisoners requires understanding the main processes that fill and re-fill our prisons. We distinguish six processes that take place:

1. Crime
2. Arrests
3. Sentencing
4. Incarceration
5. Release
6. Recidivism

1. Crime

Every society experiences some degree of crime ranging from minor crimes (lying, stealing, blackmailing) to major crimes (physical harm and murder).

Most societies develop a culture defining good behavior and bad behavior. Children grow up being taught the difference. The culture uses stories and testaments to illustrate good behavior and also defines the punishments that will follow bad behavior.

The society's very existence depends on most people practicing good behavior. When bad behavior is on the rise, the society uses police and its laws to arrest and imprison offenders until the bad behavior lessens.

The society operates on some assumption about the nature and behavior of mankind. The society's dominant religion might assume that mankind is bad and sinful, that people are driven by greed and self-interest. Bad behaviors come from individuals strivings to gain money, status, or power. Bad behavior must be prevented or contained by force and punishment.

Some bad behavior comes from impulse or passion at the moment. Other bad behavior come from calculated efforts to improve one's condition legally or illegally.

Most societies exhibit class differences, with some people living a rich and full life and others living deeply deprived lives of poverty and hunger. Those living a deprived life are aware and ashamed of their condition. They will be tempted to take advantage of every opportunity to improve their life. They might steal or threaten others. They might join gangs to increase their share of power.

This suggests that great inequality in access to resources is likely to increase crime coming from the poorer classes. This also suggests that efforts to create a fairer distribution of resources would help reduce the amount of crime.

2. Arrests

Societies develop mechanisms to prevent or arrest persons committing "bad behavior." The society defines what is legal and the likely punishments that would follow different types of bad behavior. The society develops a police force that has the power to arrest persons committing bad behavior. The society also develops a court system, judges, prisons and parole boards to handle those arrested. Many persons will be held in a pre-trial stage of arrest waiting for a busy court to become available. Those waiting for a trial either post bail or wait in jail.

3. Sentencing

Societies create a judicial system to establish the innocence or guilt of a person charged with an offense. For persons found guilty, the court and jury are to render sentences within a range of severity proportionate to the gravity of offenses, the harms done to crime victims, and the blameworthiness of offenders.

Where persons admit guilt, the judge will follow the sentencing rules that are spelled out for this crime. Sometimes the rules are indeterminate allowing the judge a lot of discretion. The judge might give consideration to possible merits that the offender might have. On the other hand, some judges may take an intense dislike of the offender and set a maximum sentence. When the amount of indeterminacy gets excessive, pressure arises to make sentences more determinant, leaving the judges with less discretion.

The judge might decide on granting probation to the offender who pleads guilty with strict conditions governing his/her whereabouts while under probation. Eventually that person might appear before a parole committee that might further reduce or remove the conditions.

In the great majority of cases, the offender will be incarcerated. The judge decides or recommends which jail or prison the offender goes to.

4. Incarceration

The real question is how offenders are treated during incarceration. Some prisons are set up to treat the offenders with *retribution and punishment.* The prison hires tough guards who use their power to punish prisoners and these prisons offer few benefits of education or health. Other prisons are set up to treat prisoners with *rehabilitation and education.* The prison takes a humane view of prisoners and wants to give them every opportunity to study and prepare for a better life and job after leaving prison. Many prisons offer both treatments by running separate areas of the prison for hardened criminals and another area for first offenders or light offenders.

A strong case can be made for treating prisoners more humanely. They are more likely to rehabilitate and reintegrate into society. There is likely to be less recidivism. There is likely to be less violence of prisoners toward each other and toward prison staff. By providing education, healthcare, and other basic needs, prisoners are likely to develop a sense of self-worth and confidence, making it easier to find jobs and housing upon release. Countries such as Norway, Sweden, Finland and Germany prioritize rehabilitation over punishment and provide education, healthcare, and other basic needs and experience much less recidivism.

5. Release

Prisoners are released when their sentence is over. Some may be released earlier on probation or parole on the grounds of good behavior. Those who are released when their sentence is over may be released with no restrictive conditions; others may be released with specific corrective supervision.

The real question is: where do prisoners go when they are released? The lucky ones return to their family or friends. Others might become homeless or rejoin gangs. As job applicants, ex-convicts will be questioned about whether they have a criminal record. If yes, most employees won't offer a job. Fortunately, there are some kinds of businesses when individual firms are ready to accept persons with a criminal record. Examples include restaurants, beauty shops, small factories and construction companies. Even here, former prisoners normally are paid less than their peers with similar educational backgrounds. The John Howard Association helps prisoners get more justice while in prison and out of prison.

6. Recidivism

Unfortunately, many released offenders may not have families or friends and they return to gangs or behaviors similar to their criminal past. Recidivism rates in the US are some of the highest in the world. Almost 44 percent of criminals released returning to prison within their first year out. More than eight out of every 10 youth offenders are arrested again within five years of release 2022. Native Americans and Alaska Natives face the highest levels of recidivism at 79 percent but are 1 percent of the total prison population. Black prisoners have the second-highest recidivism rate, at 74 percent over five years, and are about 40 percent of total prisoners. To handle offenders who recidivate several times, California passed the "three strikes law" in 1994 that imposed a 25 year life sentence on multiple recidivists.

Why is the recidivism rate so high in the US? Causes include social interactions during incarceration, depression, lack of employment and economic opportunity, and a failure to reduce the prisoner's criminal tendencies during imprisonment.

What Can Be Done to Decarcerate, i.e., to Reduce the Number of Persons in Prisons?

My reason to comment on the "crime-arrest-sentencing-incarcerate-release-recidivism" cycle is to identify areas where better practice can reduce the number of persons in prison.

1. We need more policies to reduce the conditions that lead to more crime. We need to improve the educational system so more people find satisfying jobs and compensation. We need to reduce the amount of poverty and penury that drives people into crime.
2. Police need to be better trained in when to arrest and how to treat the assumed offenders in jailing them.
3. Judges must be given clearer guidelines on just sentencing.
4. Offenders must receive better treatment in prison on a humane rehabilitation model.
5. Offenders need to be helped upon release to return to normal life and job opportunities.
6. Offenders who return to crime frequently need longer sentences.

All these better practices will lead to a reduction in the number of persons going to jail or returning to jail.

Why Is It So Important to Reduce the Prison Population?

First, many persons were convicted for drug possession with long sentences and there is a new attitude favoring reducing their sentences or releasing them. ***Second,*** US prisons are terribly overcrowded which makes the prison experience more exhausting, hardening, and health-injuring. ***Third,*** many prison budgets are being cut for food and health services, making prison conditions more severe. ***Fourth,*** over 8 percent of prisons are privately owned and engage lobbyists to advocate longer sentences to keep these prisons profitable.

All said, there is a growing US movement favoring decarcerating. Unfortunately, the Republican Party favors more toughness on crime and criminals. The Democratic Party hesitates to favor less toughness because it might lose a lot of votes. The political result is to postpone progress in reducing the size of the prison population.

Source: June 10, 2023. Decarcerating: Strategies for Reducing… | by Philip Kotler | Medium

CHAPTER THIRTY NINE

How Should Government Regulate Questionable Products and Services?

AMONG THE MILLIONS OF PRODUCTS and services produced each year, some are frequently questioned about their healthfulness, safety or morality. Take a look at the map showing the degree to which different states are involved in such questionable products as alcohol, tobacco products, casinos, racing, and video gaming/pari-mutual (Source: "Mapping Sin Tax Revenues Across America [MAP]," June 7, 2016, by Valuewalk Staff).

We will mention these and other products and services and ask whether they should be regulated or even prohibited. If they are to be regulated, what are the main tools that society can use to regulate these questionable products and services?

Four Types of Questionable Products and Services

We can distinguish four types of questionable products and services:

- Addictive products harmful to health: cigarettes, alcohol, hard drugs (called vice products),

- Products or ingredients whose excessive use leads to obesity and other health problems (sugar, salt and fat),
- Products raising issues of safety: automobiles, motorcycles, guns, ladders,
- Services offensive to morality: gambling, prostitution, pornography.

Before examining these classes of products, we need to acknowledge that some people see any regulation as anathema to the concept of a free market. Each product or service has users who are making a free choice to buy and use that product. Most users know of the product's potential harmfulness and are either unable to resist or comfortable with the consequences of using it. On these grounds, libertarians could object to any product regulation or banning. They prefer free choice. We will keep this issue of free choice versus regulation in mind as we review these products and services.

Addictive Products Harmful to Health: Cigarettes, Alcohol, Hard Drugs

This class of products—"alcohol, cigarettes, hard drugs"—has been loosely called "sin" or "vice" products. These are viewed by most people as "unhealthy products and services" deserving some level of social control. The government—whether in a city, state, or nation—might be encouraged to ban, tax, or "scandalize" them to reduce their consumption. The issue is if, when and how should governments undertake to reduce the consumption of these "sin" products and services.

We know that regulating "sin" products poses a contentious challenge. Just read the tragic results of the US Congress ratifying the Eighteen Amendment in January 16, 1919 to prohibit the manufacturing, transportation and sale of intoxicating liquors. Alcohol went underground. It was available in speakeasies, private clubs, brothels, and thousands of other locations. Many citizens showed their contempt for the law by imbibing alcohol whenever they could do so safely. City police would often break in and arrest sponsors and participants, but many more underground venues would sprout up to take their place. The worst thing was that liquor production and distribution fell into the hands of criminals. Bootlegging of alcohol became ever more lucrative. Criminals made so much money that they could bribe politicians and mayors to carry out their "wishes." Prohibition finally ended 13 years later with the ratification of the Twenty-first Amendment that repealed the 1920 Eighteenth Amendment on December 5, 1933.

Consider the endless effort to put an end to cigarettes and smoking. Tobacco companies for decades glamorized smoking and challenged the claims that smoking was harmful. When the evidence of cigarette's harmful effects to the heart and lungs became irrefutable, tobacco companies had to retreat and state on the cigarette package that smoking could be harmful to one's health. Anti-cigarette groups successful applied a number of tools to reduce smoking, including creating anti-smoking cures, passing higher taxes on cigarettes, circulating photos of dying smokers, and prohibiting indoor smoking in offices and public places. Efforts were made to legally sue tobacco companies to pay for the health injury that various smokers experienced and use the money to intensify anti-smoking efforts.

Hard drugs—marijuana, heroin, cocaine, and others—are extremely addictive and harmful to one's health. These drugs have been the most resistant to social control. Powerful gangs in Mexico and other locations monopolize these drugs, ship them to locations of high consumption such as the US, make enormous profits, and use these profits to bribe officials. These gangs do their best of launder the money so that it comes out as new legitimate-looking businesses. In the meantime, federal and state officials are arresting suppliers and heavy users of these drugs, filling up our prisons and requiring the building of additional prisons. This anti-drug policy has been a failure and a tragedy in many ways. This realization has lately led to a softening of anti-drug enforcement, much came about with marijuana becoming recognized as a helpful medical drug in a number of cases. Some states—California, Colorado among them—allow businesses to be formed to provide cannabis either medically or even for more general use.

Products or Ingredients Whose Excessive Use Leads to Obesity and other Health Problems: Sugar, Salt and Fat

In the United States, most products sell without regulation. However, in the case of food and drinks, we need some regulation. Food safety and quality is governed by approximately thirty federal laws and regulations administered by fifteen federal agencies. The Food and Drug Administration (FDA) and the US Department of Agriculture (USDA) share primary responsibility for overseeing the safety of our food supply.

More recently, a class of familiar and common products has drawn increasing attention as being harmful to our health if used in excess. There are foods that use too much sugar, salt and fat that clearly contribute to the growing obesity problem in the US and in many other parts of the world. Obesity can lead to a number of illnesses, including heart disease, stroke, high blood pressure, diabetes, some cancers, gallbladder disease and gallstones, osteoarthritis, gout, and breathing problems. Some of the firms may try to deny that these problems exist but the evidence is strong that the heavy consumption of sodas, candy, ice cream and a number of other food products can be harmful to long term health.

Berkeley, California ran a successful campaign in 2014, calling it a fight against "big soda." Their proposal won over 76 percent approval. Today the anti-sugar movement is spreading across the country. Some battles will be lost—that was the case in El Monte and Richmond, California. One reason is that the beverage industry spends millions of dollars on lobbyists to defeat these taxes.

Probably the most recent well-publicized episode of regulation was carried on by New York City's Mayor Michael Bloomberg. He initially pushed through a sales tax on large size (over 16 fluid ounces) soda bottles. In 2016, New York City passed a new sugar tax that affected every sugary drink. Bloomberg wanted companies that produced drinks like Coca-Cola, Gatorade and tonic water to work hard to reduce the amount of sugar in their recipes.

Those who opposed this tax argued that the tax fell heavily on the poor who were the heavy users of soft drinks, especially large size ones. The critics argued that the tax didn't really limit consumption and only made the poor poorer. The beverage industry has claimed that many jobs of bottlers, truck drivers, and ad people might be lost if many people shift to drinking water or "safer" beverages. We can discount this because safe beverages also require bottlers, truck drivers, and ad people.

As early as June 2010, Washington state legislators decided that candy, gum, and soda had to pay taxes. But the taxes typically have been small and not effective in driving down America's thirst for sugary drinks. Higher taxes might be necessary to effectively discourage high consumption. In 2015, the US House Ways and Means Committee proposed a provision that would tax soda and candy. This measure was not passed, however.

"Obesity" taxes are more prevalent in Europe. The Danish government has taxed candy for nearly 90 years! And Denmark was the first country in the world to pass a law banning trans fats, with Austria and Switzerland following closely after.

Romania considered passing a "fat tax", expanding beyond sodas and candies and trans fats to hit "junk food" more broadly. The "fat tax" revenue would be used to fund investments for improving healthy behavior and the healthcare system.

Today Hungary is probably the most active European country trying to reduce the consumption of foods with high fat, salt and sugar content. Hungary imposed special taxes because of the country's 18.8 percent obesity rate, which is more than 3.3 percentage points higher than the European Union average of 15.5 percent. Adult obesity In Germany is 13.6 percent and as low in Romania as 7.9 percent.

Hungary's obesity is no surprise when you consider their pastry. Hungary's best known treat after goulash is the *dobostorta* cake, a five-layer vanilla and chocolate buttercream dessert with a caramel-glazed top layer. Hungarian food uses cooking ingredients such as pork and goose fat and pieces of pure lard.

The Hungarian government argues that foods high in fat, sugar and salt need to be taxed to discourage their consumption and to provide money to pay for increased medical and hospital costs. The "fat tax" includes soft drinks with added sugar, energy drinks with added sugar and caffeine, pre-packaged sweetened products, salty snacks, high salt content condiments, soup mixes, gravy mixes and bases. The "fat" tax is to fall on those who live unhealthy lives.

The real point of "demarketing" is to raise people's consciousness that what they eat or drink shapes their lives and health. We can't leave it to one-sided messaging that "glamorizes" these sugared or artificially sweetened drinks. We can use "demarketing" to stigmatize or "deglamorize" drinking these beverages.

Products Harmful to Safety: Automobiles, Motorcycles, Guns, Ladders

Regulation has also been applied to manufacturers and users of "equipment products" that need to be used carefully to avoid injury. From the earliest days of automobiles, cities and states passed legislation to insure that cars were made safely. Car speed was limited, tires had to be made of good quality, and the various mechanical parts of the car had to pass certain tests. Attention was also directed to regulating who could get a driver's license. One's license can be cancelled for reckless driving, drunk driving, poor vision, or old age. Most members of the public readily accept and want these regulations.

As motorcycles became prominent, legislators addressed the question of the noisiness of motorcycles and whether motorcycle owners had to wear a helmet. States and cities have differed greatly in their regulations. Motorcycle owners have often challenged the helmet law and believed that they should have free choice. Critics however point to the large number of motorcycle accidents and the high public cost of repairing those who are injured.

The big regulatory issue today centers on the rights of gun owners. The National Rifle Association (NRA) would want everyone to have one or more guns of any kind to be carried in any place, including restaurants, schools, churches, movie theatres, among other venues. The fact that students in 18 different schools in the US have lost their lives in recent years due to mentally ill shooters has once again driven public demands for regulation. The initiatives include prohibiting the sale of guns to persons under 21 years of age, testing the mental fitness of any gun buyer, limiting or preventing the purchase semi-automatic assault guns (such as AR-15s), and restricting or preventing carrying a gun in certain in certain spaces or places. An extreme position would be to prohibit the ownership of guns by private individuals. This is the case in some American cities and in some European countries. The problem is that the Second Amendment to the United States Constitution protects the right of the people "to keep and bear arms." Yet In 1991, former Chief Justice Warren Burger said that the idea that the Second Amendment recognizes an individual right to gun ownership was "a fraud" on the public. The arguments for and against gun ownership are likely to go on for a very long time before any legislation settles the issues.

Many other types of equipment are regulated. There is extensive regulation of equipment in factories that can cut or maim workers. Even the familiar ladder carries a large number of regulations by OSHA (Occupational Safety and Health Administration) regarding size and construction of step ladders and extension ladders.

Services Offensive to Morality: Gambling, Prostitution, Pornography

A growing share of our national output comes in the form of services rather than products. Just think of workers involved in retailing, restaurants, beauty services, air and ship travel, and other service occupations. Three particular services have received moral condemnation over the years. They are gambling, prostitution, and pornography.

Gambling. A large number of people are addicted to gambling, even though they know that the odds of winning are stacked against them. Gamblers include grandmas who sit all day putting coins into "one-arm bandits" hoping for a jackpot. Other gamblers play poker, blackjack, dice games and many others for money. They populate casinos in Las Vegas, Atlantic City, and an increasing number of other American cities. Gamblers with more money are likely to travel abroad to casinos in Macau (China), Monte Carlo (Monaco), Paris and other locations. Some of them are willing to stick around a casino until 4am along with other addicts. They think their lives are more interesting than those of rational, boring people whose lives revolve around their work, children and pets.

Given that gamblers enjoy gambling, what is the moral case against gambling? If wealthy persons lose a lot of money in gambling, they still have a lot of money left. But if average income family persons spend a lot of money gambling, they risk having less money left to feed their families. Ironically, they are gambling in the hope for a jackpot to escape their low income. But most of them just lose money, many turn to drink, and wreck their marriages. The moral opprobrium arises from the harm they do to their families.

Some cities have laws against gambling or prohibit casinos, horse racing or dog racing from entering their city. Yet casinos are appearing in more cities using the argument that they can donate a percentage of their earnings to fund the school system or some other important causes. Ultimately, we can hope that fewer people get caught up in gambling and that therapists find more effective cures to help gamblers give up their addiction.

Prostitution. Every nation faces the problem of prostitution and how to regulate it. At one extreme, prostitution can be outlawed and prostitutes and their clients can be jailed. Or they can be fined and given a warning of jail if caught again. Or the city can leave it alone as something they cannot control. Or the city can limit prostitution to one location out of sight and regulate it by requiring prostitutes to register and have frequent checkups to prevent sexual diseases from spreading.

The moral opprobrium is based on the notion that prostitutes are only making their bodies available out of desperation. They sell their service for money either because they cannot find any work or any work that pays as much as they can earn through prostitution. The belief is that these women do not want to be prostitutes, they don't enjoy selling their sex, and they are clearly being exploited. Prostitution is an example of a service activity that begs for some kind of regulation.

Pornography. The publication and distribution of pornographic writing and nude pictures has a long history that goes way back to ancient times. The arrival of the movie industry in the 1900s gave it a further platform. Theatres showing pornographic films was outlawed for a long time. The arrival of Playboy magazine in 1953 gave pornography a more public face and degree of acceptability. Some respectable major companies were even placing their ads in Playboy magazine because it had a five million circulation. Then pornography heated up with the debut of Penthouse magazine in 1965 and heated up further with the debut of Hustler magazine in 1974 that was clearly pornographic.

With the advent of DVDs and the Internet, pornographers rushed to make films and develop TV networks featuring pornographic films. Now teen agers and others could gain easy access to view heterosexual, gay and other forms of sex. The fear is that this viewing familiarity will excite more people to seek sex or engage in sexual acts. The idea of romantic love, of loving someone for themselves and not making it conditional on sexual favors, dissipates in the presence of such pornographic experiences.

Should the nation try to reduce pornography by confiscating all film, setting high fines or jail sentences on pornographers, or remove all pornography from the Internet if this is possible? Today the sexual act takes place in many movies and network TV shows. Even if it could be banned or curtailed, pornography will continue to appear in books and magazine articles. Do we want to repeat the time when books like Lady Chatterley's Lover by D.H. Lawrence was banned? Or should we just ignore pornography?

Policy Options in Regulating Questionable Products and Services

We described many questionable products and services that governments might target for demarketing and deconsumption.

We need to ask the following three questions:

1. Should government engage in discouraging the consumption of certain products and services?
2. What are the most effective tools for reducing the consumption of questionable products and services?
3. How successful is government control efforts likely to be?

Should Government Engage in Discouraging the Consumption of Questionable Products?

The case for demarketing questionable products and services is that they harm the user and very often others around the user. The prohibition of liquor beverages in 1920 aimed to reduce the growing problem of drunkenness. A drunk was in danger of hurting himself or herself and hurting others by driving while drunk or beating their spouse. The problem of eating unhealthy food is that it produces more illnesses and shortens the lives of their consumers. This not only hurts the individual but hurts his or her family and will raise medical and hospital costs.

However, those against government regulation of questionable products see regulation as deeply interfering with personal freedom of choice. They would want people to freely eat what they like and be responsible for the consequences. They argue that when a person wants some food or drink item, if they don't get it, they can become very depressed or troubled. They may go underground to get the products that are banned. This can raise the prices of banned products and lead to increased criminal activity.

There are critics don't want the government to act as a "nanny." Yet the same critics say that it is okay for companies to aim their advertisements at children and build children's interest in eating sugary products. Why can't government try to regulate these commercial messages? The critics worry that the government will expand their regulations to cover more and more consumption activities. Government may tell us not to eat steaks because this can injure a person's heart or because cattle are a big factor in polluting our atmosphere? Will the government discourage attendance at football games to reduce the number of head concussions? This "slippery slope" argument is often raised.

Generally, every regulation proposal has to be discussed on its merits. Some level of social control will occur when there is high citizen consensus favoring control and high social cost of damage when the control is missing. Normally the government will pay attention to the percentage of local citizens favoring or opposing social control. In 2013, a Harris Interactive/Health Day poll showed that twice as many people were against government taxes on sugar drinks and candy. Two-thirds agreed with the statement, "It should not be the role of government to influence what we eat and drink to make healthier choices." This type of finding will help those who oppose regulation. An opposite finding would help those who favor regulation.

What Are the Most Effective Tools for Reducing the Consumption of Questionable Products and Services?

Four major tools are available to discourage the consumption of questionable products and services.

1. Banning. Banning involve passing a law that makes the production and distribution of a product or service illegal. We have seen this applied to alcoholic beverages in the "prohibition era" and to hard drugs in the

"criminalizing era." What is clear is that banning doesn't work when the product is very pleasurable or addictive or both. Users will do almost anything to get the product. Many will be fined or jailed. The product will go "underground." There is a danger that banning will glamorize the "forbidden fruit." In the past, when a book such as Henry Miller's *Tropic of Cancer* was banned, it had the effect of increasing the public's interest in reading the book.

2. Taxing. Many government agencies chose to levy a tax on a questionable product. For example, Hungarians pay an extra 25 percent tax on certain questionable foods and drinks. The new tax hits low-income groups the hardest because they consume more of those foods and drinks. If Hungarian consumers decide to shift away from the taxed food and drink, they may end up eating less or eating at a higher cost level. The tax creates a new revenue source for the government. If the government sets the tax too low, it would not reduce consumption by very much. If they set the tax too high, consumption can decline substantially and the tax revenue will be lost. Most government try to set a tax at a level that it will continue to generate revenue, even if it doesn't reduce consumption by very much.
3. Raising the channel cost of getting the product. The government may take steps to limit the physical availability of the product. The Swedish government runs the liquor stores and limits the number of stores so that consumers may have to go far to get liquor. The government also limits the buyer to purchasing only one bottle of liquor each week. In the United States, Mayor Michael Bloomberg wanted to require stores selling cigarettes to hide the cigarettes behind a door making them less visible and making the consumer wait a little longer for the product.
4. Anti-product campaigns. Governments might require special packaging of questionable products. Cigarette companies may have to include a health warning on the packaging and even show a picture of a person suffering from some disease resulting from heavy smoking. Government or nonprofit groups can hire an advertising agency to develop a social marketing campaign that describes all the ill-health effects of smoking. Canada sponsored an active demarketing campaign against hard drugs using the motto "Say no!" Social marketers can develop several campaigns for different users, test them, and continue to show the more successful campaigns.

How Successful Are Government Control Efforts Likely to Be?

We have seen that each of the four regulatory methods have their limitations. The stronger the consumption habit and the consumer insistence of continuing with the consumption, the lower the likely success rate will be.

A nation, state or city should recognize that consumption habits are formed early and therefore good consumption guidance should begin early. Sweden and Canada are two countries that work hard to encourage parents to raise their children early on healthy eating and drinking habits. Parents raise their children to enjoy vegetables and fruit as an important part of their diet. Parents are made aware of the obesity danger of their kids consuming too much sugar, salt, and fat. Parents have actively discouraged the consumption of alcohol, hard drugs and cigarette smoking. A nation that succeeds in raising the children in the right way will have little need for campaigns against questionable products.

Source: February 9, 2021; How Should Government Regulate Questionable Products and Services? | by Philip Kotler | Medium

CHAPTER FORTY

Be Glad You Are Woke

FOR A LONG TIME, WE classified people politically as being radical, liberal, conservative or far right. The competing ideas of each group are fairly clear to citizens.

Today we have a new political language in classifying people. You are either woke, anti-woke, or a mix (sometimes woke, sometimes anti-woke).

What Is "Woke"?

The term "woke" first arose with Black Americans in their search for places to safely eat or find hospitality. The United States was deeply segregated and Black people "had to know their place." Most restaurants and many hotels were for "whites only." A Black person would be safe if he was "woke," that he knew where he can't eat or stay. He is "awakened."

In today's usage, woke describes people who want to improve racial equality, women's rights, gay rights, and other *social justice* causes. Woke people vary between those who are "woke" mainly in their mindset and those who are actively undertaking woke actions. The latter group are the real woke activists. They wouldn't let certain statements go unchallenged, such as bad jokes about an ethnic group, an unfair stereotype, an injustice against someone.

Celebrities such as Stanley Tucci, Aaron Paul, and Aly Raisman said they would take responsibility and action for the following incidents:

They said this in the wake of police brutality and the killing of George Floyd in May 2020. They circulated the "I take responsibility" campaign on social media, in the press, and in the blogosphere.

All said, woke people see themselves as fighters for social justice and energized by progressive ideas.

The "Woke/Anti-Woke" Culture War

The word "woke" has become a fighting term in today's culture wars. Ron DeSantis, Florida's governor, boasts about being "anti-woke." DeSantis aims to eliminate "wokeness" in Florida. In seeing too many college professors as "woke," he helped change New College from being a well-respected intellectual school into more of an ordinary college with an athletic emphasis. DeSantis presses for banning books that talk about racial injustice, abortion rights, gay rights or other social issues. There are already over 600 banned books. DeSantis doesn't want people to say "gay" or professors to teach "Rosa Parks." He said "I recognize that the woke mind virus represents a war on the truth, so we will wage a war on the woke… We will fight the woke in education; we will fight the woke in corporations, we will fight the woke in the halls of Congress!"

To fight "woke indoctrination," DeSantis signed his "Stop Woke Act," setting limits on what can be taught about race in schools and workplace training. He has also banned DEI (diversity, equity, and inclusion) initiatives at Florida public colleges, claiming that "DEI is better viewed as standing for discrimination, exclusion, and indoctrination." When asked by a reporter to define woke, he exclaimed: "It's a form of cultural Marxism. It's about putting merit and achievement behind identity politics, and it's basically a war on the truth." DeSantis sees woke is the new "Communism" or "Socialism," or the new "Clinton" or "Obama."

Most people don't seem to define woke in that way. In a *USA Today* poll (March 2023), 56 percent of Americans, including most Independents and a third of Republicans, believe the term means "to be informed, educated on, and aware of social injustices." Only 39 percent think it means "to be overly politically correct and police others' words." Furthermore, 56 percent of workers support DEI and 60 percent of Americans won't work for a company that doesn't speak out against racial injustice.

Yet the War on Woke threatens to strip LGBTQ Americans of their hard-won human rights. The ACLU (American Civil Liberties Union) has tracked nearly 500 anti-LGBTQ bills across the country that restrict gender-affirming medical care, ban instruction about sexual orientation or gender identity in primary schools.

Let's switch to Elon Musk. In a recent interview, he was asked why he is "anti-woke." He said he doesn't like people who take it as their mission to change other people's attitudes and behavior. In buying Twitter (he renamed it X), he aimed to enlarge the opportunity for free speech and the right of people to say what they believe. Musk recently created an alternative ChatGPT model that he called Grok, designed to be "anti-woke" in that its answers to prompting questions will be freer of woke influence.

Organizations such as the Heritage Foundation and the Federalist Society are busy raising money to fight "woke mindedness" before the 2024 election. These organizations believe that "woke" thinking is bad for business, bad for religion, and bad for government.

The Complaints of Anti-Woke Critics

Attacks on "wokeness" is a growing theme in Republican politics. While many Republicans admit that American society still carries layers of oppression, inequality, racism, homophobia and sexism, Republicans don't like the "heavy handed" way woke people try to dismantle these oppressions.

The best insight came from the *Guardian* newspaper that described "Anti-woke as a way to rebrand bigotry." It attempts to make bigotry look respectable. Anti-woke can be seen as an attack on affirmative action, multiculturalism and diversity, equity and inclusion. Those is power want to maintain their control over historically excluded groups.

Anti-woke groups counter by arguing that woke actions infringe on free speech, remove a focus on merit and excellence in hiring, and expose school age children to inappropriate materials. Anti-woke critics find other faults in Woke-ism. They see celebrities using "woke" to gain more attention, visibility and fans. They characterize wokes as "snowflakes," soft-headed in their thinking and actions. They accuse wokes of not wanting to dig deeper into the complexity of social problems. Wokes simply want to mouth popular indictments on social issues. Wokes are white people who "got it wrong while trying to 'do right.'" Woke persons are self-serving, insincere, and manipulative. All of this is repeated to give more ideological coherence to the anti-woke movement.

Right-wing agitators warn that some progressive states and cities inject "social justice" ideology into many classes including math and science. They charge that company programs of "diversity, equity and inclusion" now promote more polarization and bitterness, rather than understanding. They warn that reducing police presence would increase crime. Clearly woke excess can end up driving more voters to turn right.

Liberals and progressives need to control these excesses to avoid strengthening right-wing anti-woke backlash.

Is Wokeness Good for Companies?

Many companies have adopted a wokeness mindset. They want Black Americans to have equal opportunities. They favor diversity and want to hire Black Americans and others from marginal groups. They approve of gay and trans Americans. "Woke" becomes a badge of honor for brands that helps differentiate them from other competitors.

There are two reasons why companies go "woke." ***First,*** the company perceives that its customers and prospects are people who favor wokeness. ***Second,*** the company wants to hire millennials (born between 1981 and 1996) and Gen Z (born between 1996 and 2012) employees who want to work for companies that have "good values." It is no longer enough for a company to make excellent products and services while ignoring social problems. Nike in 2018 chose to sponsor the Black American athlete Colin Kaepernick who had been expelled from professional football for showing his solidarity with the #BlackLivesMatter (BLM) movement.

Companies are keenly aware of the growing interest of the public in social justice. Here are some findings:

- Approximately 80 percent of Americans favor laws that would protect LGBTQ+ people against discrimination in jobs and housing.
- Over 90 percent of Americans believe that either major or minor police reform is needed.
- Sixty-two percent of Americans believe safe abortions should be legal.

Yet companies need to be careful. Their wokeness must not be "window-dressing" only. Their wokeness must be sincere and authentic. Even then, anti-woke groups might attack companies that espouse racial equity and gayness. They might call for boycotting woke companies or at least not buying their brands. Recently *Target, Bud Light* and some other companies were singled out for being woke and their sales fell. No company wants to be a victim of "cancel culture" (the mass withdrawal of support from public figures, celebrities, brands or companies who have done things that are not socially accepted). As a result, some woke companies slowly reduced mentioning their causes.

Cultural wars are generally not good for business. Disney's CEO Robert Iger has had to fight Governor DeSantis and spend huge amounts defending his company and not give up on hard-fought-rights for Americans.

Companies don't want government to dictate how to run their business or what customers and employees they can welcome. Companies need to be clear about their values with their customers and employees. Some companies are anti-woke because they largely cater to anti-woke customers. Companies need to review their values, their customers and their political campaign contributions. They must each consider whether being woke or anti-woke will affect their business in the long run.

Is Wokeness Good for Religion (Christianity)?

One would think that religion (especially Christianity) would embrace wokeness as being consistent with values of equality, kindness, and helping others. Yet Owen Strachan of Grace Bible Theological Seminary takes aim at wokeness. He sees wokeness as shaming white people for their "whiteness." They are shammed into either being silent or compliant. In his *Christianity and Wokeness,* Strachan explains why wokeness is inconsistent with the biblical Christianity and could cause irreparable harm. He says that the Gospel of

Jesus Christ, not wokeness, is the answer to the challenges. Tommy Nelson, senior pastor of Denton Bible Church in Texas, said this about Strachan's book: "The best thing I have ever read on wokeness. We have a Marxist disease that is plaguing our country. Men and women must speak up, and Owen Strachan has done so clearly and concisely. His book will be required reading for my church."

My view is that Strachan is extreme in his view that woke people are enemies of Christian religion. I would expect the views of other Christians, including religious Jews and Muslims, would look more kindly on woke people and woke causes.

Is Wokeness Good for the Government?

Americans are apprehensive about the 2024 election, inflation, political division, and the nation's future. Many Republican politicians would describe America's problem differently: It's wokeness. Mike Pence attacked "woke capitalism" as a nefarious scheme through which "the woke left is poised to conquer America." The "War on Woke" is taking form in several policy areas including DEI (Diversity, Equity, and Inclusion), ESG (Environmental, Social, and Corporate Governance), legislation banning teaching of American history about slavery, and anti-LGBTQ legislation. The *Chronicle for Higher Education* lists 37 anti-DEI bills that have been introduced in 21 states. Four have become law.

Supreme Court decisions for or against diversity and affirmative action can affect the pool of highly qualified future workers and business leaders. There might be a large wave of reverse discrimination suits and litigation.

ESG aims to create sustainable investing is another attack target. In 2023, Republican states introduced 99 anti-ESG bills. Seven have already become law. DeSantis in Florida signed a law barring state officials and pension funds from promoting ESG goals.

Republicans have also pointed out a "woke military." They have attacked DEI programs in the Armed Forces. According to Senator Ted Cruz, the "woke cancer" perpetuated by "Dem politicians and the woke media" is creating a "woke, emasculated military" and "turning them into pansies."

Under previous President George W. Bush, Republicans had pivoted away from endless culture warmongering. Bush ran as a "compassionate conservative." But the War on Woke has lit a vicious streak in the Republicans party. They are happy to rail against Disney and Bud Light for promoting LGBTQ inclusion. Cruz was happy when Target removed its Pride displays for fear of right-wing violence. He hoped that it would "make a real impression on [other] executives...we want to stop corporate America from going woke."

The Growing Difference Between the Two Political Parties' Views of Governing a Nation

American government is run on a two-party system. The Democrats are liberal, the Republicans are conservative. In the past, they would work out their differences state-by-state in a contentious but fairly consenting way.

How different the two parties are today! The Republican Party is anti-woke. When they take over a state, they introduce harsh social regulations. They stigmatize LGBTQ persons, they abolish women's right to an abortion, they ban books, they won't allow college professors to teach certain ideas, they make it harder for citizens to vote, they gerrymander districts to reduce minority representation.

When Democrats win in a state, they are busy working for the Common Good. They are woke and support women's rights, the rights of LGBTQ citizens, workers' rights to organize a union, they increase voting rights, raise wages to at least a $15 minimum, and expand tax credits for low-income families.

The two parties have a deeply different theory about the purpose of government. Every nation needs to examine what it is contributing to improving the lives of its people. All citizens need opportunities if they are to earn a livelihood and realize their potential. A good government will try to mitigate social injustices to increase the Common Good and the well-being of its citizens. Wokeness is an intrinsic feature of a *humane nation.* Anti-wokeness is an effort to preserve bigotry. Be glad, reader, you are woke!

Source: January 5, 2024; Be Glad You Are Woke. Be Glad You Are Woke! | by Philip Kotler | Medium